★ ★ ★ ★ ★ ★ ★ ★ ★ ★ ★ ★ ★ ★ ★

HAIL TO THE CANDIDATE

HAIL
— TO THE —
CANDIDATE
PRESIDENTIAL CAMPAIGNS
FROM BANNERS TO BROADCASTS

KEITH MELDER

Smithsonian Institution Press ★ Washington & London

Acquisitions editor: Mark Hirsch
Editor and caption writer: Lorraine Atherton
Book and cover designer: Richard Hendel
Picture researcher: Heidi M. Lumberg
Production manager: Kenneth Sabol
Typesetter: Graphic Composition, Inc.

Printed in the United States of America
97 96 95 94 93 92   5 4 3 2 1

Library of Congress Cataloging-in-Publication Data
Melder, Keith E.
   Hail to the candidate : presidential campaigns from banners to broadcasts / Keith E. Melder.
      p.   cm.
   Includes bibliographical references and index.
   ISBN 1-56098-177-6. —ISBN 1-56098-178-4 (pbk.)
   1. Presidents—United States—Election—History.   2. United States—Politics and government.   3. Campaign paraphernalia—United States.   4. Political collectibles—United States.   I. Title.
E176.1.M455   1992
324.973—dc20   91-5179
                                                      CIP

British Library Cataloging-in-Publication data available

For permission to reproduce any of the illustrations, please correspond directly with the owners of the works, as shown by page number in the Reference Notes and Illustration Sources section at the back of the book. The Smithsonian Institution Press does not retain reproduction rights for these illustrations individually or maintain a file of addresses for photo sources.

Cover art is from the collection of the Division of Political History, National Museum of American History, Smithsonian Institution.

CONTENTS

FOREWORD

There was a time when Americans enjoyed governing themselves. They didn't complain about self-government. They celebrated politics, and themselves in it and because of it. This book recalls that time.

Within living memory we had a presidential candidate (Al Smith, in 1928) who rejoiced in the process of getting elected and even more so in what could be done for the country after being elected. It was a glorious thing to join in the democratic process and to use government, the people's corporation, to make life better than it would have been if you and your friends had stayed home pouting. Neither Al Smith nor his constituents thought it ridiculous for him to call himself a Happy Warrior (he lost, it is true). Forty years later, as recently as 1968, sane persons were still to be found who could talk of the politics of joy. To be joyous about politics you must believe in the democratic process. You must, to put it simply, think it wonderful to be able to do the people's will.

A corollary to this heartening idea is that the outcome of politics, of turning to the people to decide large issues, is likely to produce better results than, say, turning only to a junta of military officers, to a fasces of corporate executives, to a syndicalist assembly of union officials, to the latifundistas of big farmers, to the apparatchiks of a socialist state, to the proletariat or the aristocracy. The opposite view, that we would be better off leaving things to any of those subgroups, expresses itself in the stance of those who hate democratic politics. They say it is silly to love politics, that only a fool would be happy in politics, that politics is dirty. The message is that we are unworthy to govern ourselves. When that message is repeated over and over again, we begin to believe it. We begin to think it fatuous to enjoy going after the votes of people like us.

It is quite possible that, softened up to believe this hideous heresy, we are entering the Age of Rancor. Such an age would follow an age of disenchantment and precede an age of despair. Then, unless the process were reversed, the Age of Despair would decline into something much worse. That would be the Age of Manipulative Cynicism, when democracy would be relinquished, as it has been in other times and places from Athens to Weimar Germany. Once we decide we hate politics – democratic politics – we are on the way to deciding that we would like a prince or a führer, a high priest, an emperor, or an ayatollah a lot better, because he (and *he* it would be) would assign those tasks, and we could get back to the TV.

Television is not responsible for the decline of participatory democracy described in this book. As the authors demonstrate, politics had become a spectator sport before television. I will not rehearse their powerful analysis of the reasons for that sad regression away from the high hopes of the founders of our nation. My subject in these introductory remarks is not the slow weakening of our public pulse but the consequences of its continued weakening. The fault lies not in television, a marvelous medium devised by blameless engineers. They did what engineers do, not what politicians do. They invented means, not ends, methods, not intentions. The fault, as Cassius told Brutus, lies not in the stars, not even the stars of stage, screen, radio, or television. It is not they who beguile us away from politics, keeping us tranquilized, inert, and irresponsible. The fault is our own. It's we who have become indolent and, worse, acquiescent, accepting the heresy that deciding between candidates is as simple as deciding between brands of deodorant. We know what that says about us, yet we go on rewarding the people who treat us as stupid. No wonder we hate politics. We are learning to hate ourselves for accepting what we have made of politics.

Government is, of course, the consequence of politics. We hate politics with the same fervor that we hate government. The one has contaminated the other. Democrats and Republicans alike tell us that the mechanism created by the founding fathers to do the people's will is the enemy of the people. And who, we might ask, are the people's friends? Entertainers? Corporate bureaucrats or labor union bureaucrats? Television pundits? Television evangelists? If we don't believe in the people's politics and in the people's governments, what are our political beliefs? Perhaps we don't believe in anything. Bitterly, we acquiesce in whatever comes along to beguile us until bedtime.

This book helps us understand our own time by permitting us to contrast it with periods in which Americans loved politics. Especially do the authors recall for us the exuberant, reforming, hopeful, ebullient 1830s, 1840s, and 1850s. (Ralph Becker, the collector of political Americana who made this book possible, would have been at home in that time. He has lived nobly, however, in our own.) I am well aware that that was also the period of Indian removal, of Manifest Destiny, of the justification of slavery by intellectuals of the Old South while their loathsome institution was practiced in the lower Mississippi Valley in ways that disgusted all but the most callous. It was also the period in which the factory system was displacing that class of independent American artisans who made up the urban backbone of Jacksonian America. Their displacement and the reformist passions unleashed by it far antedated the displacement of the middle class of lawyers, teachers, and preachers who responded by giving us a second burst of reformist zeal in the Progressive Era. But the historical example of the nation joyously and consciously dealing with its problems through democratic politics should give us hope. As readers of this book can observe, those citizens took to the streets, abandoned their recumbency, cheered and marched and exercised their rights, and accomplished a great deal. They did not leave the world as they found it. Nor did they let their sins committed against neighbors go without plenty of public criticism. All the unhappy story of their attitudes toward weaker neighbors was attended by a remarkable amount of self-criticism, leading to later correction.

My point is that they got from where they started – morally, economically, and, indeed, in the physical conditions of life – to something in nearly all cases better, and they did so amid a din of commentary. That commentary was radically unlike that of our own era. It did not have a weary tone. It was full of expectation that they could and would do better. Americans paid attention to their politics, not as a grinding and distasteful necessity but as an occasion for improving their lives and feeling better about themselves. Peculiarly, almost astonishingly for us of the mean 1980s and dispirited 1990s, they were very much interested in improving the lives of others as well. The world was neither pretty nor easy, but they believed in themselves and in their politics as a way of conducting their common undertakings.

That had been true of Americans during the revolution of 1776 and during Thomas Jefferson's self-proclaimed revolution of 1800. It was true of the Age of Reform, from the 1820s through the 1840s, when the nation began to protect women and children at work, moved toward the abolition of slavery (an institution largely unchallenged for several thousand years), and hotly debated what might be a responsible stance toward the earlier occupants of the territory into which the United States was expanding. It was true when the Civil War, fought for limited objectives (the prevention of secession and the violent expansion of slavery), became a war for the abolition of slavery. How many wars have carried in their aftermath not the repression and looting of the losers but a broadening of opportunity, a constitutional assertion of human rights, and a series of endeavors toward an honest recognition that a humane victory required further expenses? Yes, indeed, the Freedmen's Bureau was "phased out," as the current expression goes. Yes, indeed, what was, in effect, a corporate junta took over as the nation became cynical in the aftermath of the death of Abraham Lincoln, who believed in politics as many of his successors did not. But the reforming, hopeful spirit survived into the Populist Crusade and the Progressive Era. When the nation went to sleep again in the 1920s, when privatism prevailed over the public interest once again, there were people who picked themselves up after the defeat of Al Smith and let us believe again that we could govern ourselves proudly. We did not become a fascist state, though many of the arguments made against politics today were made in the 1930s to take us in that direction.

We are, I believe, in a time much like that of the exhausted and cynical 1870s, like the 1920s. I believe that we are ready for another surge of public spirit, another reaffirmation of belief in popular government. I believe that politics will be fun again, because its purposes will be serious again. As an old Minnesota Republican, I am looking forward to the appearance of another Happy Warrior in another period of the Politics of Joy.

Roger Kennedy
Director, National Museum of American History
Smithsonian Institution

★   ★   ★   ★   ★   ★   ★   ★   ★

ACKNOWLEDGMENTS

Most of the photographs that appear in this book illustrate objects from presidential campaign collections in the Division of Political History, National Museum of American History, Smithsonian Institution. These materials have largely been preserved through the generosity of private donors who chose to give their valuable collections to the American people, in custody of the Smithsonian Institution. Foremost is Ralph E. Becker, donor of the Ralph E. Becker Collection of Political Americana represented in illustrations throughout this book. Other significant donors of objects depicted in the book include Paul Beckwith, Russell C. Chase, George L. and Mary E. Compton, Michael V. DiSalle, Rachel M. Goetz, Dr. Harry and Mrs. Sara Lepman, E. A. Rogers, the Stack brothers, and the Unexcelled Fireworks Company. All of these are acknowledged here with gratitude.

During the past seven years, the project to complete an interpretive study of the presidential campaign collections in the Division of Political History has taken many turns and evolved in several different directions. The initial plan changed extensively over the years. During the research and writing stages of the project, many individuals contributed.

Ralph E. Becker's wonderful collection inspired and provided much of the raw material for the present study. Initially Mr. Becker persuaded Roger G. Kennedy, Director of the National Museum of American History, that the project should be undertaken. Mr. Becker aided the project with a generous donation for research expenses and served as an advisor and intellectual guide throughout the study's development, helping to formulate its design.

In early years of the work, 1985–1986, Dr. Jerry K. Frye, research associate, served as principal project investigator. Dr. Frye's scholarship in the field of communications was applied to the study's research efforts. His investigations and early chapter drafts helped clarify conceptual approaches, identify issues, and elicit factual data that informed the entire study. Although the final published text is very different from the early chapters that he prepared, Dr. Frye's contributions were important. They are acknowledged here with gratitude.

Numerous people in the National Museum of American History supported and participated in the work. Roger G. Kennedy has sustained the project from its beginning. Richard Nicastro helped administratively. Successive chairmen of the Department of Social and Cultural History—Gary Kulik, Tom Crouch, and Spencer Crew—gave continuing encouragement and helped solve problems. Edith P. Mayo (author of chapter 7) and William L. Bird, Jr. (author of chapter 8) gave advice and counsel throughout, and produced thoughtful chapters under pressure. Other members of the Division of Political History staff—Kate Henderson, Marilyn Higgins, Harry R. Rubenstein, Cynthia Williams, Sandra Williams—helped in various ways. Lonnie G. Bunch III and Margaret B. Klapthor provided special emotional and intellectual support.

Other Smithsonian Institution staff members who contributed to the project include Rhoda Ratner and James Roan of the National Museum of American History branch of the Smithsonian Institution Libraries. Amy Pastan of the Smithsonian Institution Press gave critical advice concerning publication of the study. Mark Hirsch, acquisitions editor for American studies at the Smithsonian Institution Press, has been a consistent supporter of the project. He devoted extraordinary talent, time, and energy in bringing the text into final form and seeing the publication to completion. Selene M. Leiva and Frances Spiegel provided timely assistance in organizing transparencies and other art.

Grateful acknowledgment is made to the Office of Printing and Photographic Services, Smithsonian Institution, and for new Smithsonian photography to Eric Long.

Many volunteers and interns gave long hours to different phases of the project. The following list includes volunteers who helped: Elizabeth Branch, Kathleen Dejardin, Robert Fratis, Jim McDonald, Susan O'Brian, Mary Thaler, and Margaret Wilson. Throughout the study's duration, student interns contributed: Michael Bartos, Christina Browning, Dennis Bui, David Burrell, Elizabeth J. Cochrane, Fred Deleyiannis, Alan D. Eisler, David Frazee, Terry Douglas Goldsworthy, Todd Hartline, David Heydasch, Nguyen Hong Hoang, Sarah Kendall, Dianne Kemp, James Malero, Robert McSweeny, Kevin Sheets, Brent Sterling, Leah Sullivan.

Useful help came from Bruce Felknor and C. Langhorne Washburn. Melinda Y. Frye offered continuous support, generous advice, and good cheer when the going got rough.

Early versions and parts of several chapters appeared in *Campaigns & Elections: The Journal of Political Action*: "A History of Partisan Press," Spring 1985, pp. 60–64; "The Birth of Modern Campaigning," Summer 1985, pp. 48–53; "The First Media Campaign," Fall 1985, pp. 62–68; "Creating Candidate Imagery, Part I: The Man on Horseback," Winter 1986, pp. 6–11; "Origins of the Personal Campaign," May–June 1986, pp. 46–50. They are incorporated here with permission of the publishers of *Campaigns & Elections*.

NOTE ON SOURCES AND CREDITS

References to sources and illustration credits are located at the back of the book. Note numbers are not used. References to individual items are identified by page number and an identifying phrase or quotation from the text or illustration caption.

PROLOGUE

BY RALPH E. BECKER

I have been asked several times: "How did you acquire such a large collection of political Americana? Why did you give it away?" To begin with, by looking high and low for more than fifty years, I was fortunate to gather the largest collection of political Americana in the United States. To preserve that collection for posterity, I donated it to the Smithsonian and other public institutions.

I became a collector as a teenager. Collecting political items paralleled my interest in law, politics, and government. In high school I was employed in one of the oldest law offices in Westchester County, New York. My boss and later my partner, Benjamin I. Taylor, often took me to Albany, for court appearances or for political reasons, as he was also a public official. In Albany I met John Scopes, a bookseller and antiquarian. It was from Scopes that I purchased ferrotypes, ribbons, and shell badges, as well as legal prints and books. In the late twenties, I became one of the founders of the Young Republican movement and began to collect badges, ribbons, buttons, and souvenirs at Young Republican conventions and later at regular Republican county, state, and national conventions. I soon found this hobby fascinating, inspiring, and educational, and it engulfed me for many years. Someone once said that collecting is a disease as well as an art. I can certainly give credence to that theory.

There has never been a single store or supermarket where one could find shelves of political artifacts of all categories and vintages. My collecting sources in the early days included dealers, auctions, antique shops, book stores, and exhibitions; dealers and collectors advertised political items in national and regional publications. At first I collected anything and everything without regard to specific categories. Later I went into classifications and specifics. At the Republican conventions I would obtain posters, badges, banners, bunting – things that were difficult to get once the convention was over, because cleaning crews considered them trash and swept the floor clean. For large items, transport and storage could be a problem. At one convention, my wife, my son Bill (who was working as a page), and I filled an entire station wagon with banners, posters, fans, and other material. At the New Hampshire primaries, which bore little resemblance to the recent primaries, I would ask congressmen, senators, and their staff members to collect for me all the political materials used in the primary. Such materials became rare after the election because, once the campaign headquarters closed, everything in the storefront offices was discarded. Often the offices were empty by the following day. My friends in the Democratic party, including members of Congress and their staffs, would collect many convention items for me. Eventually I made formal arrangements with the national chairmen of both parties to send campaign materials directly to the Smithsonian.

I concentrated on the presidential campaigns. Later I sought out presidential families and descendants, obtaining material from them. If the items were nonpolitical they went to a relevant division of the Smithsonian and became part of the presidential collections. They include clothing, equipment for hobbies such as sports and fishing, and gifts from foreign countries. The scope of my collection also includes cabinet members, congressmen, and governors who ran as favorite-son candidates. I did not, however, exclude important Americana at lower political levels, because officeholders could become nationally important at a later date. So my interest has been broad, encompassing the spectrum of American political history.

Another question I hear frequently is "What is political Americana?" From my point of view, it covers every aspect of publicizing the image of a candidate for political office, from running in primaries to nominations, elections, inaugurations, and memorials. In many cases if the candidate was a victor, political items will span his tenure in office. The losers are important too because they were leaders of their respective parties and often ran again later. Political collectibles came in various sizes, shapes, and materials, including metal, pewter, glass, china, porcelain, lusterware, and leather, at all sorts of prices. There was no yardstick or guideline. It was a willing buyer's market. Some items now have multiple values as antiques or commemoratives or cultural survivals. What I classify as political objects were also of prime interest to other types of collectors – those who specialized in glass, ceramics, manuscripts, autographs, numismatics, and textiles.

A vast array of items come under the heading of political Americana. A representative cross-section of campaign and presidential items I acquired would include metal buttons from the time of George Washington, later types of buttons made of celluloid and plastic, ferrotypes, shell badges, ribbons, lapel devices (including mechanical devices), jugates, badges, banners, flags, posters, and bandannas. All types of novelties and gadgets represent candidates, issues, slogans, and political parties: jewelry, torches, lanterns, log cabins, floats, canes, hats, pennants, ballots, watch fobs, tobacco devices including pipes and lighters, razors, beer trays bearing images of the candidates, campaign and presidential sheet music, photographs, postcards, pens and pencils, license plates, and bumper stickers. There are items to appeal to all classes of the population – young people, wives, mothers, and families – even those who could not vote. Whiskey decanters, flasks, soap, and perfume bottles sometimes depicted candidates, and they too made their way into the collection. I was always searching for, and often found, one-of-a-kind items, considered American folk art. Paper ephemera, pamphlets, newspapers, magazines, and lithographs come within the scope of my collection. Nathaniel Currier in the 1840s (later Currier and Ives) produced beautiful lithographs originally in watercolor. Later political engravings were produced in mass quantities under the name "Grand National Banner." A firm in Hartford, Connecticut, Kellogg and Hanmer, produced posters in color, which were added to the collection. Advertisements in newspapers and magazines are also legitimate items of political Americana. Ads distributed by stores and manufacturers are hard to find, but my collection contains a substantial number of them. Cartoons, of course, are an integral part of the collection because they have played a key role in American politics. In due course I accumulated an extensive library of biographies and autobiographies, books written as campaign literature, pamphlets, and special campaign newspapers written about presidential candidates. Some books were written by prominent authors, such as Nathaniel Hawthorne's *Franklin Pierce*. Political textiles are special favorites of mine, utilizing silk, linen, burlap, cotton, velvet, and oilcloth. An interesting silk broadside commemorates Thomas Jefferson's death on July 4, 1826. It copies the last letter he wrote, declining an invitation to attend the celebration of the fiftieth anniversary of the Declaration of Independence. Political Americana includes all these items plus many other kinds.

One of the earliest historical political objects in my collection is the John Hanson pitcher. Hanson was a patriot of Maryland and became in 1781 the first president of the United States in Congress Assembled. This porcelain pitcher bears the legend "J. Hanson and Trade for ever."

Its acquisition (from a Washington auctioneer) was important, first because it represented an individual and second because of the slogan – trade and tariff protection were issues of the early republic and have been burning issues ever since. And it appears to be one of a kind.

Many people helped me expand the collection. One of my sources for acquisitions was Charles "Chuck" Johnson, a personal friend and career government official. Charles McSorley, who has the largest collection of paper ballots in the country, was another good source. Tom Warnecke of Long Island also helped me acquire artifacts. Tom was known as a picker, a person who has a list of requests to hunt down for dealers or collectors. He worked exclusively for me for several years, scouring the farms and countrysides of New England, New York, Pennsylvania, and New Jersey in his truck and bringing back all kinds of interesting, unusual, and rare political material.

Once Tom brought two large boxes to my office in Washington. After I examined them and paid him, I left them in my office, one on the couch and one on the floor. I had begun donating to the Smithsonian, so I called Herb Collins on the staff to have the items picked up as usual. The following day, when I phoned about the boxes, I found they had never arrived. It dawned on me that perhaps the cleaning staff at the office had mistaken them for trash. I spent a sleepless night imagining the Lincoln item, a Garfield lamp, an 1840 brush, a Garfield herbal tea – more than fifteen items in all – tossed in the incinerator. When I had a chance to question the cleaning woman, she admitted discarding the material, all except the brush; she had saved it because it looked ideal for scrubbing her back. It turned out to be an 1840 campaign hairbrush with a picture of William Henry Harrison painted on it.

Another story concerns a hand-painted portrait banner associated with the inauguration of Thomas Jefferson. The banner, emblazoned with the slogan "T. Jefferson President of the United States of America, John Adams is no more," was found rolled up and lying along a railroad track by a thirteen-year-old boy near Pittsfield, Massachusetts. Authorities speculate that the banner may have fallen from the mail car of a passing train. The boy took the piece to school, where it aroused so much interest that the family gained an impression of its historical value. The boy's mother tried to sell the banner to the pioneer collector J. Doyle DeWitt. She wanted a scholarship for her son, but DeWitt turned her down. Subsequently, she tried various means of advertising the banner for sale. She even appeared on a television variety show asking for an audience response to the mysterious banner, but no one responded to her plea. A few years later I told Congressman Joe Martin, former Speaker of the House from Massachusetts, the story of the banner and how I wanted to obtain it for the Smithsonian. He communicated with the attorney general of Massachusetts, who contacted the boy's mother. Fortunately she still had the banner. We worked out a deal whereby a guardian would be appointed by the court, the banner would be appraised, and I would acquire it for the appraised price. Then I presented the banner to the Smithsonian. It is one of the most important historical items in the entire Smithsonian collection.

My wife, Ann, was a partner with me for many years in all my interests. She found many special items in a variety of ways. She would sometimes come across political Americana in antique shops on her trips. We collected a surprisingly large number on our travels to antique stores and at house, estate, tag, and farm sales.

While I was busy with my profession as a lawyer, my civic and cultural activities increased, diminishing the time I could spend adding to my collection. I simply didn't have the time to maintain what I had already collected in a proper environment. I therefore selected the Smithsonian as the main institution to conserve the collection for posterity. The idea of donating to the Smithsonian emerged in 1956, when my wife and I were trying to authenticate a few of our items. We spoke with Margaret Klapthor, a curator who had done a remarkable job with the First Ladies' collection, making the First Ladies' Hall a magnet of the Smithsonian's permanent exhibition area. During our meeting she was able to authenticate the items in question and asked me, "Did you ever think of giving your collection to the Smithsonian?" I said no, but Ann jumped at the suggestion. All the boxes and barrels I had accumulated over the years had never been catalogued or indexed. Klapthor, as well as Leonard Carmichael, secretary of the Smithsonian, and Jim Bradley, deputy secretary, were elated that I would consider donating my collection.

There were several good reasons to make this gift. The overriding reason was so that the collection would be kept permanently and exhibited in a national institution in the nation's capital. It was never my intention to dispose of the collection commercially but to preserve it somehow for generations to come. At the ceremony of the accession of my grant, I made remarks that Senator Clinton Anderson repeated for inclusion in the *Congressional Record* of March 24, 1961: "It is my fond hope that the Smithsonian will make my collection available to not only the casual visitor, but to the school children of America and the serious student of political history and science. I trust that by observance and study of my collection, many Americans will be brought to a fuller appreciation of our political heritage and a greater understanding of man's noble experiments in government – American democracy."

The second reason for my donation was that it had become difficult for me personally to conserve the paper, textile, glass, and other fragile items. Since the Smithsonian had that expertise, it was an ideal home for the collection, permitting exhibition, preservation, and conservation. In turn, the collection could fill a gap at the Smithsonian in the area of political Americana. The donation assured that my collection would be housed with many other items associated with the presidents and their families in a proper setting.

I am even happier about the donation now than I was when I first made the gift in 1961. My remarks made in 1975, when I was honored with the James Smithson Benefactor Medal, still hold true today. I feel the Smithsonian has given me the gift, not the reverse, "in making me feel that the collection I have put together over the past fifty years and the small efforts I have made on behalf of this institution will live on for all to enjoy and benefit from."

Hurrah for the Campaign!

"Tippecanoe and Tyler Too!" Shouting and singing, Americans echoed this Whig party political slogan across the United States during the summer of 1840, engaging in an extravagant display of political drama and enthusiasm. Never before had an American presidential campaign been so wildly celebrated. During the contest hundreds of local and regional Whig rallies glorified William Henry Harrison for president and John Tyler for vice president. In frequent high-spirited parades and gatherings, the party faithful celebrated their candidates and Whig symbols of the contest: the log cabin and hard cider, General Harrison's favorite beverage.

In his reminiscences, A. B. Norton described a typical party festival in Ohio: "The people were here! The hardy and industrious yeomanry of the Buckeye soil . . . with appropriate badges and banners, with log cabins, Fort Meigs, and balls rolling, with bands of music . . . reverberating wildly through our highland hills and valleys for many a mile." A partisan wrote of Whig rallies in the Middle West: "There is a constant gathering of the people by the thousands for the purpose of warming each other up for the fight." Another enthusiast urged "friends of Harrison and Tyler" to organize. "We must work! . . . Complete your State, County and Town organization. . . . Form a Tippecanoe Club or whatever you choose to call it in every Town, Village and neighborhood." Far out on the Illinois prairies, a young Whig named Abraham Lincoln threw himself into the contest with energy and determination. Preparing instructions to Whig partisans throughout the state, Lincoln urged county committee members to organize so "that every Whig can be brought to the polls" to defeat the Democrats, those "corrupt powers that now control our beloved country."

The Tippecanoe contest of 1840 represented a grand era in American political culture. "Hurrah" campaigns such as this one were typical of political festivals during the middle and later years of the nineteenth century. They produced a variety of lively devices and vivid images designed to interest, entertain, and influence voters. Characterized by outpourings of popular enjoyment and widespread participation, political celebrations drummed up unprecedented electoral enthusiasm. Across the country in 1840, 80 percent of eligible voters turned out at the polls. National turnouts in subsequent nineteenth-century presidential elections ranged between 69 percent and 83 percent of those eligible. Not until the twentieth century did turnouts decline below 60 percent of the electorate.

Presidential campaigns and elections are the most intense and widely celebrated occasions of American politics, representing a quadrennial patriotic ritual for the whole nation. Called by one observer "the longest folk festival in the world," the presidential race engages the interest of leaders and ordinary citizens alike. Each campaign is "an expedition full of adventure, camaraderie, desperation, gallantry, foolishness, redundancy and splendid new irrelevancies at every turn," as Charles McDowell describes it. Among all their participants, campaigns give rise to innumerable warm and bitter recollections. In the press and other mass media they generate millions of words and images. Their most tangible remains, though, are electioneering devices – images and artifacts of political Americana.

During the nineteenth century American politics was transformed from the concern of a minority of the people into a massive expression of popular excitement. This book shows how presidential elections grew from relatively sedate contests among leaders to explosive, hurrah-style celebrations of democracy. The new style appeared in the second quarter of the nineteenth century and persisted until the century's end. A key factor in its vitality was public participation. From the late 1820s on, people were not content to stand on the sidelines as spectators. Men, plain and privileged, many women, even whole families, joined in the spectacle, in fireworks, nighttime parades, and other political demonstrations. Engagement, not observation, was the rule.

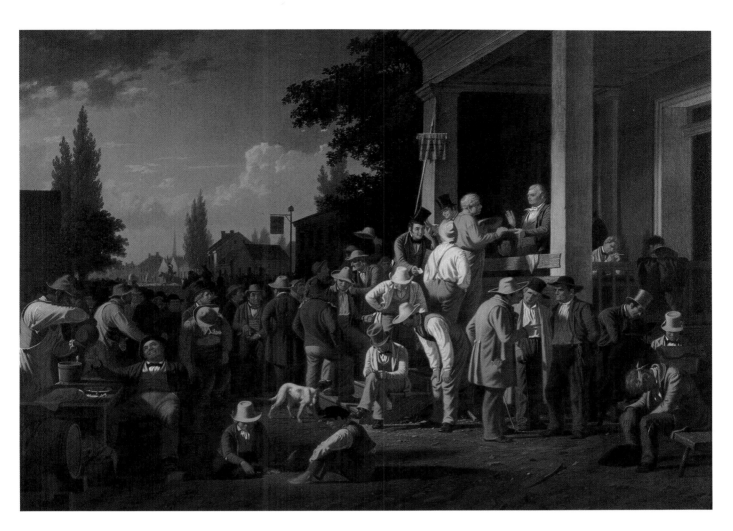

The County Election, 1852 *(George Caleb Bingham, oil on canvas). In a western town of the mid-nineteenth century, men drink election-day liquor and endure a campaigner's last-minute pitch while standing in line to vote. The banner on the pillar reads, "The will of the people, the supreme law."*

Wide-Awake sheet music, 1860. *Local marching clubs published special sheet music for their bands. This quick-step cover from Albany, New York, pictures a Wide-Awake marcher in typical uniform, carrying a lantern and protected by an oilcloth cape. Composed by Max Mayo, the music was dedicated to Capt. J. Owen Moore of Company A Central Club and performed by Schreiber's Albany Cornet Band. It was sold through Tweddle Hall Music Store.*

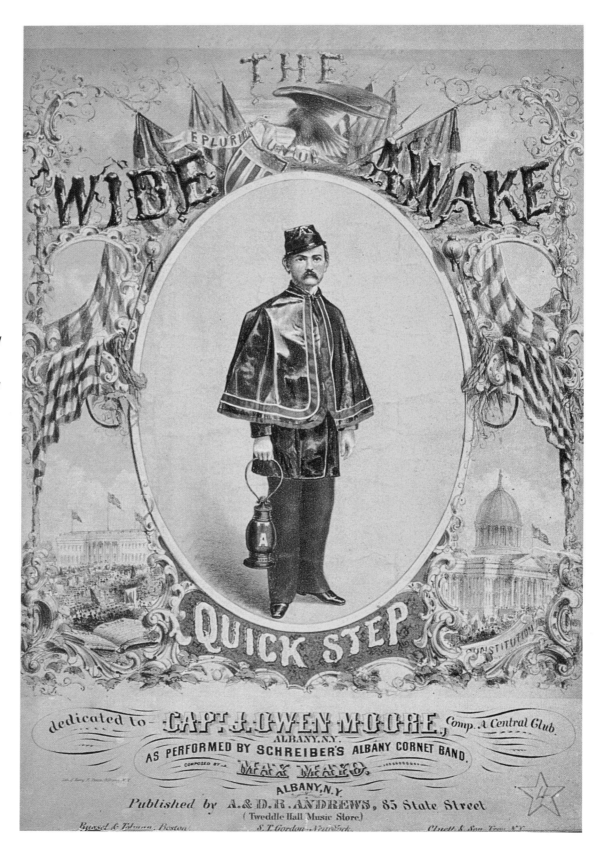

Jackson snuff box, 1828. *Andrew Jackson and Napoleon were contemporaries, and early in his military career Jackson cultivated an image similar to the French general's. Its appearance on this commonplace object reflects the power of the cult of the military hero.*

Teddy Roosevelt novelty, 1912. *This grinning cat recalls both the Cheshire cat of Lewis Carroll and Roosevelt's image as a jovial, charismatic candidate. During the election campaign of 1912, when Roosevelt ran as a Progressive, the toothy grin would have unmistakably identified the owner of this metal pin (2.5 in. long) as a Teddy supporter.*

Lincoln-Johnson poster, 1864. *In his second presidential campaign, Lincoln ran on a Union (rather than Republican) ticket with Democrat Andrew Johnson to position himself as the protector of the Union rather than the leader of a single faction. Posters like this (approx. 14 x 20 in.) would have been displayed in shop windows and other public places.*

By the end of that century, however, the enthusiastic displays had begun to decline. Twentieth-century electioneering became more restrained, less festive and joyful. Above all, the traditions of participation diminished. Campaigning fell under the control of professional organizers who borrowed the techniques of business management in conducting struggles for public office. New voting regulations limited balloting to registered voters, and voter turnouts fell. New techniques of mass communication replaced rallies and parades, campaign symbols and political artifacts. Radio and television were the media of choice instead of banners and novelties. In the twentieth century, as campaigns became less colorful and electioneering devices less popular, politics took on a passive spectator interest instead of a lively participatory character.

This book examines the multiplicity and magnitude of those changes in political expression. Chapter 1 provides an overview of the diverse languages and imagery of campaign techniques and devices, showing how different approaches have been used to appeal to voters. Chapters 2,

Party convention pamphlet, 1950s. *When television cameras invaded political convention halls, parties felt the need to impose some discipline on their usually raucous gatherings. This pamphlet instructed delegates on how to behave for the TV audience.*

Coolidge stogie, c. 1924. *An image of Calvin Coolidge, a rather dour New Englander, attached to a huge cigar injected some jocularity into the Republican campaign.*

3, 4, 5, and 6 trace the development of campaign images and public participation, from George Washington's uncontested selection by the electoral college in 1789, through the hurrah campaigns of the nineteenth century and the front-porch candidacies at the turn of the century, to the pattern of decline in political participation after 1900. Chapter 7, by Edith Mayo, concentrates on a more specialized aspect of campaigning, the gradual inclusion of women in mainstream American politics and the images that appealed to them, particularly in the fifties. In chapter 8, Larry Bird writes about the effect of television on campaigning in the fifties. Chapter 9 centers on the current decline of political parties and the rise of political consultants, and the effects of new technologies.

This book derives much of its raw material from the collections of political Americana in the National Museum of American History of the Smithsonian Institution, collections largely of ephemeral objects, temporary in purpose, eminently disposable. Yet here and there, these transient objects were preserved as souvenirs. Many of them eventually came to the Smith-

McKinley pocket watch, 1900. *Portraits on the functional objects of everyday life were one way to keep candidates in the public eye. Here the Republican ticket of McKinley and Roosevelt is printed on the face of a working watch.*

sonian Institution to constitute one of the largest assemblages of political Americana in the nation. The Smithsonian collections began without fanfare or much recognition of their larger significance. The first important gift arrived in 1884, donated by one of the leading manufacturers of campaign objects, the Unexcelled Fireworks Company of New York City. The donation included examples of uniforms and regalia sold to campaign marching clubs for the presidential contest of 1884. A company official wrote regretfully, "We are sorry we were not able to send you some of the finer kinds – but they were all sold." The firm's illustrated 1884 catalogue of campaign goods and fireworks offered a wide assortment of suits, capes, caps, helmets, and other costumes, as well as torches, lanterns, and banners for the simplest or most elaborate political marching club.

That early gift represented a decade of growing campaign enthusiasm and vigorous partisanship. Manufacturers of campaign goods found a ready market for their varied wares. There is no evidence, however, that the gift to the Smithsonian Institution led to an influx of additional acquisitions or that there was any systematic follow-up to the Unexcelled Fireworks gift. Early Smithsonian curators showed little interest in electioneering. Nevertheless, campaign objects continued to trickle into the collections. Changing as campaign enthusiasm and techniques evolved, political advertising resulted in new generations of persuasive artifacts.

Campaign objects gained new appeal and significance around the time of World War II. American democracy, under pressure from adversaries abroad and critics at home, seemed

Taylor mirror, 1848. *This palm-sized mirror (3.5 in. in diameter) bears a relief likeness of Whig candidate Zachary Taylor on its metal cover. Taylor ran as a military hero rather than a politician.*

Hanson pitcher, c. 1810. *The inscription "J. Hanson and Trade forever" refers to John Hanson, first president of the Continental Congress under the Articles of Confederation in 1781. The pitcher's shape and silver-luster trim belong, however, to a later period, between 1805 and 1820. The pitcher, less than 5 inches high, may have been made in England for Federalist partisans to record their opposition to Jefferson's trade embargo from 1807 to 1812.*

Bryan game, c. 1908. *"The White House or Bust" parodies William Jennings Bryan, a three-time loser in the race for the presidency. The point of this game was to get the metal beads to land in the vanquished candidate's eyes.*

Buchanan badge, 1856.
This unusually elaborate silk badge (approx. 10 in. long), heavy with metallic-thread embellishments, was meant to be worn by James Buchanan supporters at rallies. The rooster was the symbol of the Democratic party.

Democratic sheet music, c. 1932. *By projecting an image of joy and celebration, the Democrats sought to link the repeal of Prohibition with attempts to lift the nation out of the Depression, drawing sharp contrasts between their party and the stuffy, puritanical image of the Republicans.*

Kennedy hat, 1960.
This light plastic hat was worn by delegates to the 1960 Democratic convention, though their candidate became notorious among hat manufacturers for his dislike of hats. Its old-fashioned style harks back to an earlier age of American politics when thousands of men waved hats at conventions and night rallies.

endangered. The apparatus of our political system, including the procedures and paraphernalia of electing our leaders, seemed to symbolize American free elections and therefore became increasingly valuable. In the forties, students of politics and collectors of hitherto obscure campaign devices organized themselves and began promoting their avocation. Their organization, the American Political Item Collectors (APIC), founded in 1945, is still the leading collectors' group in the field.

Although political Americana attracted the interest of collectors and students early in the twentieth century, the Smithsonian Institution's collections were little appreciated by the curatorial staff or the public. It was not until the fifties that the Smithsonian began to take the subject seriously and started intentionally acquiring the materials of campaigning. At about that same time, traditional electioneering devices were being threatened by the growing influence of television. A new unit, the Division of Political History, was established in the Museum of History and Technology in 1957 to deal with campaign history as well as with other historical memorabilia.

The collections received their greatest boost in the late fifties when Ralph E. Becker, a Washington, D.C., attorney, public official, and political activist, visited the Smithsonian seeking information about materials in his personal collection of campaign memorabilia. Following negotiations with Smithsonian officials, Becker agreed to begin donating material, and the Ralph E. Becker Collection of Political Americana became the largest single accession of campaign objects in the institution. Including more than 20,000 catalogued items ranging over the

G.O.P. plate, 1908. *Ornamental plates are a recurring campaign collectible. On this souvenir from the 1908 Republican presidential campaign, portraits of William Howard Taft and his running mate, James S. Sherman, are surrounded by images of previous Republican nominees.*

entire spectrum of presidential souvenirs and promotional devices from the time of George Washington to the age of Eisenhower, the Becker Collection is a remarkable, largely untapped source of information about American political life. As the nation's most comprehensive body of political artifacts, it has been a magnet attracting other collections to the National Museum of American History. In addition to building the museum's holdings of traditional campaign ephemera, the Smithsonian collects recent campaign devices, especially videotapes of campaign television advertising.

In 1961, when he presented his collection to the Smithsonian Institution, Ralph Becker suggested that his collection might be a form of historical archeology. The study of thousands of objects, graphics, and printed ephemera preserved in the collection would, he believed, change,

Socialist poster, c. 1932. *Few collectibles from third-party campaigns have survived because commercial novelty firms were not interested in manufacturing them and minority parties had little money to buy them. The Socialists, however, were relatively successful early in this century. In 1912 and 1920 Eugene Debs received more than 900,000 votes, and in 1932 this ticket won more than 881,000 votes.*

REPEAL UNEMPLOYMENT!

FOR PRESIDENT
NORMAN
THOMAS

FOR VICE-PRESIDENT
JAMES H.
MAURER

VOTE SOCIALIST

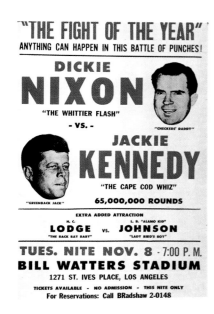

Nixon-Kennedy poster, 1960. *This whimsical poster likens the 1960 election to a boxing match between Republican Richard Nixon and Democrat John F. Kennedy. The poster may have been produced to satirize the famous debate the two candidates conducted on national television that year.*

amplify, and correct the impressions gained from a concentration on more-conventional documentary sources about American political history. Certainly the vivid character of campaign objects adds color and authenticity to exhibits about American politics. Since Becker's donation, the research use of artifacts uncovered by historical archeology has enlarged interpretations of everyday life in the past. Similarly, as he predicted, political memorabilia have begun to tell a more complete story about the history of everyday politics.

There is inherent in democratic politics a need for communicating tangible evidence of the personalities of leaders, and so, much of this book deals with image making: the deliberate creation of representations, likenesses, or ideas of a leader designed for mass distribution. At their most basic level, images – descriptions, impressions, portraits of people, associated objects – serve simply to identify leading participants in the struggle for power. Personal images simplify complex individuals, give them immediacy, and provoke emotional bonds between leaders and their publics. But as they are repeated and elaborated and incorporated into campaign devices, images offer vivid, appealing, and dynamic depictions of the people who compete for our loyalties. Many enduring images have been featured in presidential campaigns since the republic's early years. This text interprets the images projected by candidates and their political parties, the processes and different styles of campaigning, and the innumerable devices and techniques used to communicate campaign imagery and persuade voters. As one of the leading political journalists, Theodore H. White, observed, "The transaction in power by which a President is chosen is so vastly complicated that even those most intimately involved in it, even those who seek the office, can never know more than a fragment of it." Although campaigns and the electoral devices used by our leaders to project themselves are beyond the understanding of any one observer or analyst, we may hope in these pages to comprehend a fragment of the visual and tangible memorabilia of presidential contests over the years.

As with other forms of persuasion, there are few accurate measurements of effectiveness, few certainties about why the vote went one way or another. After the much-criticized contest in 1988, a thoughtful observer, Elizabeth Drew, wrote, "Whether . . . Dukakis could have won under any circumstances, we can never know. . . . After each election, we enter the land of unprovable hypotheses." Larry Sabato, a close student of modern campaign consultants, has observed: "The impact of any consultant or any technology, then, can usually only be guessed at. No one has the foggiest notion of what percentage of the vote a consultant or a piece of new campaign technology can or does add to a candidate. . . . Campaigning remains a complex, unpredictable, and very unscientific process, and one may expect and be grateful that it always will be."

Although they truly flourished for less than a century, campaign objects enriched and enlivened American political history. By studying them, we can recall a different America, more innocent, somehow more promising than the nation in the late twentieth century.

The Imagery of Campaigning
and Campaign Devices

"The hiring of presidents," as historian Clinton Rossiter calls the system by which we nominate and elect our chief executives, has never been a simple or easy process. The writers of the Constitution, hoping to minimize conflict and emphasize talent in high office, devised elaborate methods well insulated from popular control to choose the president. The Constitution provided no devices for nominating candidates, no machinery for putting candidates in touch with voters, no practical means to make a choice possible.

In the two centuries after the Constitution was written and approved, the hiring of presidents evolved into a complex series of rituals and symbolic occasions centered around popularizing the presidential choice. Broadened rights of suffrage, political parties, nominating conventions, electoral machinery, and electioneering, all unforeseen in the Constitution, made popular elections a reality. As Rossiter explains, "Our manner of choosing the President . . . has converted the election into a process of decision-making far more centralized, direct, protracted, hot-blooded and popular . . . than the framers could have imagined in their most restless nightmares." In this evolution, there was a period when popular participation and dramatic spectacle were prominent features of campaigning. More recently, changes in the process have diminished participation and emphasized the passive role of voters as spectators.

Popular participation in campaigns left a varied and vivid legacy of devices and images. Colorful, exciting, often funny, sometimes malicious, campaign objects have a special character all their own. In many instances they hardly seem suited to the sober business of electing this nation's rulers. Such is the case, indeed, because campaign devices serve a variety of functions. Beyond the immediate goals of promoting presidential candidates and their parties, campaign gadgets and gimmicks are means of communication and representation, speaking a language of their own. Often they incorporate words, but primarily they convey images with strong emotional overtones and social implications that transcend verbal discourse. For citizens who carry or wear them, or merely observe them, campaign objects embody rich and diverse meanings that may extend far beyond references to political rivalries or candidates.

Overleaf:
Presidential game, 1876.
By combining the celebration of the nation's centennial with a celebration of the presidency, this game indicates that the office was still a symbol of national faith, in spite of the scandal-ridden administrations that followed the Civil War. That faith was again tested in the election of 1876, when Democrats were accused of election fraud and a congressional commission gave the win to Republican Rutherford B. Hayes.

Electioneering devices appeared in the first hurrah campaign of the 1820s and persisted into the twentieth century, figuring prominently in every election since 1840. The range of such objects includes banners, bandannas, torchlights, marching regalia, parade floats, posters, gadgets and novelties, and paper advertising, adding, in the late nineteenth and early twentieth centuries, buttons, bumper stickers, fliers and fund-raising letters sent by mail, and other promotional items. Recently, as television has grown to dominate presidential campaigning, the variety of electioneering trinkets and gadgets has diminished noticeably. Yet to some degree, campaign items still define elections.

Campaigns and persuasive techniques have existed since the time of George Washington. The earliest political objects were not, in the modern sense, campaign devices. Instead they were tributes celebrating the distinguished reputations of political leaders. The greatest number and variety of these early items celebrated Washington, depicting the worshipful veneration conferred on our first president and father figure. Scores of rather formal, quasi-religious objects made in many forms, of different materials, honored Washington's virtues. Ceramic ware, textiles, and prints bearing the first president's image, although not created for his election, served as examples for promoting candidates who came on the scene later.

Between 1825 and 1860 campaign devices grew explosively. A two-party political system, intense popular campaigning, political advertising, festive candidate images, and a vast infusion of campaign devices appeared. Several new features of the political process were associated with Andrew Jackson's campaigns. Following his defeat in 1824, Jackson stimulated a political movement to assure his later success. Over about twenty years Jackson's followers

Democratic playing cards, 1888. *In a humorous juxtaposition of games of chance and weighty politics, Grover Cleveland and his wife decorate a deck of fancy playing cards.*

Bryan pull card, 1908.
Pull the tail, and the candidate's face emerges from the donkey's rear end. These mass-produced novelties poked fun at both parties. The Republican version pulls W. H. Taft out of an elephant.

formed the world's first modern political party, the Democratic party. During that early period, print was the chief medium of expression for electioneering. Biographies, newspapers, pamphlets, broadsides, and cartoons circulated nationally. Diverse campaign objects appeared in the Jackson period, but a great number did not survive. The real explosion, however, came in 1840.

Symbolic devices serve as one element of the political process. Through them candidates present themselves, translating their appeal into tangible, visible artifacts. In competitive politics, as in the commercial world, candidates frequently run as products in a marketplace of sophisticated, often subtle and dangerous rivals. Individuals campaign and sell themselves without shame. Numerous campaign devices are not directly aimed at selling candidates, however. Rather, they entertain, attract attention, offer a chance for people to participate; above all they serve as powerful inducements to vote, helping to make elections important. Campaigns often mobilize the electorate selectively, encouraging loyalists, offending opponents, and discouraging participation by opponents.

When we examine the imagery of campaign objects, several questions emerge. One concerns the most basic issues of form and substance. Some campaign devices convey messages through their forms. Banners, for example, were designed for display in large assemblies – rallies, parades, festivities. Thus their imagery and meanings are those of celebration. Banners often also carry intellectual or verbal messages of substance, using words and symbols. The language of banners therefore operates at several levels. Other objects, lapel devices for example, convey

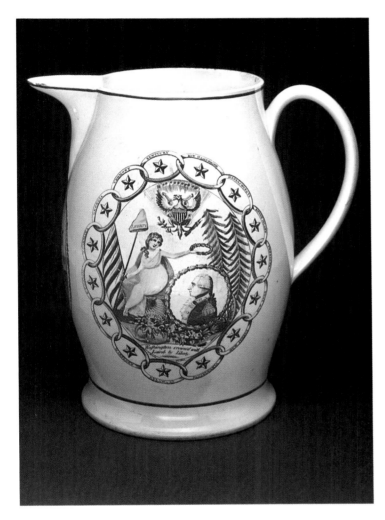

Henry Clay pipe, 1844. *Candidates were common subjects for pipe carica-tures. This one incorporates a pun as well: the bowl is made of clay.*

Washington pitcher, 1789. *Souvenirs honor-ing the father of our country were forerunners of campaign objects. This 10-inch Liverpool pitcher,* *imported from England, is richly elaborated with symbols of patriotism and liberty, including the border of stars representing the states of the Union.*

messages through their shape and material. Buttons, pins, ribbons, or badges are made to be worn and displayed, representing personal attachments and loyalty to candidates or causes. But often campaign buttons or badges carry messages in words or symbols that reinforce or even make fun of the idea of personal commitment. A lapel ribbon showing William Henry Harrison's portrait and a log cabin conveys not only a commitment to the old General but also reminds voters of Harrison's rustic imagery. The form and the substance of campaign objects often work together to create their effects.

As popular communication devices, political items are loaded with symbolism, not all of which seems to relate directly to promoting candidates. The messages in the objects suggest the central importance of presidential elections in American society. A closer look at their im-ages of festivity and celebration, of humor and laughter, of party loyalty and personal commit-ment, of candidate and partisan causes, of attack, and of promotion will illuminate the meaning of campaign items.

Jackson sheet music, c. 1828. *Andrew Jackson's campaigns were among the first to use music to project the image of the candidate. The martial music and images supported Jackson's appeal to patriotic, emotional reflexes rather than the intellect of the electorate.*

E. PLURIBUS UNUM.

FOR

HARRISON & TYLER,

And no reduction of the prices of labour

THE LOG CABIN,

The house our fathers lived in.

STONEHAM,
JULY 4, 1840.

Harrison-Tyler banner, 1840. *This is the opposite side of the eagle banner on page 7. The shoes or shoe lasts symbolize the shoemakers of Massachusetts, important artisans in the town of Stoneham. Whig partisans tried to present themselves as the friends of the workingman.*

The Imagery of Celebration

Beginning in the 1820s, political managers and ordinary people transformed presidential electioneering from contests for the nation's highest office into frenzied national entertainments – folk festivals. Instead of a thoughtful decision-making process, each presidential election became an outpouring of emotional enthusiasm, partisanship, and popular delight. And why not, for what were campaigns if not celebrations of every voter's right to choose freely among the leaders running for president? Elections were examples and rituals of freedom worth celebrating.

The ties between campaigning and the spirit of celebration become more evident when electioneering rituals are compared with other forms of festivity. A prominent folklorist, Richard M. Dorson, has vividly described celebrations as the "joyous outpouring" of the people's high spirits, the "creative play of their imagination in a variety of the performing and decorative arts." Dorson includes among his classes of celebrations: "festivals, rituals, ceremonies, spectacles, pageants, fetes, holidays, and extravaganzas. . . . A celebration . . . should fall at a fixed period and should involve, or at one time should have involved, sacred and symbolic elements." Like other important celebrations, presidential campaigns occur at regular intervals – every four years – marking recurrent occasions of profound political and social significance. Although not overtly religious in a worshipful sense, electioneering is a powerful quasi-religious observance originating from a faith in popular government that most Americans share, an element of what John MacAloon calls the nation's "civil religion."

Elections also celebrate an important rite of passage for candidates and for the nation. Like a child who must become an adult during a ritual of initiation, so a presidential hopeful endures exhausting initiatory combat and humiliation to demonstrate a capacity to lead the people and the nation. Presidential candidates temporarily suspend their real identities and take on special behavior patterns, much as adolescents must assume special identities during initiations into adulthood. Like the child, the candidate performs ritual roles and ordeals not associated with a former identity to become a full-fledged president. Election festivals can also be compared with "political and civic celebrations . . . that celebrate a rise in status, such as the festivities of kingship."

We need not wonder at the festive nature of campaign devices, for they reflect one of America's most important occasions. Since presidents, chosen by the people at large, symbolize the nation, the process of electing them is fraught with danger, enthusiasm, and emotional strain. A modern student of campaigning sums up the reasons for celebrating elections:

Our presidential campaigns . . . get leaders elected, yes, but, ultimately, they also tell us who we as a people are, where we have been, and where we are going. . . . Most fundamentally, because political institutions represent the grandest and most powerful of our social institutions in this century, campaigns at base define us to ourselves for at least a

few years. As campaigns end in the endorsement of political myths, ideologies, and derived programs of action, so also do they end in a large-scale enactment of our collective self. In a perhaps terrifying sense, by the end of the campaign, *we are whom we elect.*

Even a casual examination of certain campaign objects confirms their celebratory nature. One of the earliest and rarest political artifacts in the Smithsonian collections, the 1801 Thomas Jefferson inaugural banner, reflects the spirit of celebration. It employs several sets of symbols announcing patriotic and partisan political rejoicing. A formal portrait of the honored Jefferson is framed in a circle with sixteen stars for the states of the Union in 1801; the portrait is surmounted by an eagle adapted from the Great Seal of the United States; streamers flowing out from the eagle's beak carry the exultant message of Jefferson's triumph over John Adams. By adopting national symbolism, the banner celebrates not only Jefferson's victory as an embodiment of the whole nation but also his success as a partisan candidate.

Banners traditionally represent festive themes, special celebrations, or occasions honoring distinguished personages. As they developed in the United States, political banners thus became central objects in the expression of electoral enthusiasm during mass rallies and parades, which were such characteristic features of partisan politics beginning in the late 1820s. Many accounts of these events, such as those in A. B. Norton's reminiscences of the 1840 contest, record in detail the elaborate banners carried to represent each delegation or group in atten-

**Lincoln torch,
1860.** *Abraham
Lincoln's first
presidential
campaign gener-
ated massive
torchlight parades
by tightly orga-
nized marching
clubs. This oil-
burning torch is
15.5 in. tall.*

dance. A contemporary narrative of Baltimore's 1844 Henry Clay ratification celebration por-
trays scores of banners carried by state and local delegations. For example, Whigs from Lan-
caster County, Pennsylvania, carried five complex banners, two honoring Clay and three for
the deceased Old Hero, Harrison. The banners combined several messages: celebration, political partisanship, and candidate advertising. Studies of American political banners, especially
those from the nineteenth century, confirm the festive nature of these colorful and highly valued campaign devices. In their vivid illustrations and descriptions of political festivals, the
studies also suggest multiple purposes for the objects: their forms were inherently festive,
while their words and symbols carried messages of partisan persuasion.

Another type of object that belongs primarily to the political festival or celebration is the
campaign torch. Among the most striking events of American presidential campaigning were
the giant torchlight parades popular during the nineteenth century. Campaign torches, designed to burn oil or kerosene, were manufactured to be carried in these great celebrations.
Often borne by thousands of marching men in a single parade, masses of flickering, smoking
torches had an extraordinary festive effect. Other lighted campaign items such as transparencies and lanterns were made to carry persuasive messages.

Humor and Laughter

"Too funny to be president?" Ex–presidential candidate and humorist Morris Udall re-
members that question arising as his campaign expired in 1976. In his book *Too Funny to
Be President*, Udall argues that humor is necessary to our political system: "Political
humor leavens the public dialogue; it invigorates the body politic; it uplifts the national spirit."
Nobody is too funny to be president. Thus humor infects many successful campaign objects.
Humor, fun, and laughter are closely allied to and often combined with celebration; political
festivities commonly embody enthusiastic joy and organized hilarity. Since the time of George
Washington, humor and satire have been favorite techniques of presidential campaigners and
their managers, valuable allies in creating favorable public attention or disarming opponents.

What's so funny? Almost anything that politicians do or say can be funny. For political maneu-
verings at all levels – the eternal search for gullible voters, the masking of motives and real
intent, the weaknesses of the flesh and intellect, the vain ambitions, the intermittent changing
of political disguises and identities, the constant playacting, the sheer childishness of it all –
display the foibles of human nature. There has always been something ridiculous about the
activities of candidates for office – preening, negotiating for favors, playing roles to impress the
voters, making believe the candidate is superior to others in the contest – that leads naturally
to political fun and ridicule. "Ridicule thrives on the disparity between profession and act,"
writes historian Linda K. Kerber. And nowhere is that disparity more evident than in politics.

McKinley dolls, 1896. *Although these dolls are made of soap, they were meant to be kept, not used. They came with storage containers that carried messages, such as "My papa will vote for McKinley, gold standard, protection, reciprocity, and good times."*

I AM FOR
McKINLEY
and
SOUND MONEY,
AIN'T YOU?
No 16 to 1 for me

I AM FOR
BRYAN
and
SILVER,
16 to 1 for me
AIN'T YOU?

Taft cartoon, 1912.

Disenchanted Republicans who viewed President Taft as inept and asleep on the job argued for a vigorous federal government in the style of Teddy Roosevelt, seen here frowning through the window at Taft's tangle. In 1912 they split from the Republican party and ran Roosevelt as the Progressive candidate.

"GOODNESS GRACIOUS! I MUST HAVE BEEN DOZING!"

Political humor is effective for many reasons. Much humorous imagery incorporates elements of superiority. Seeing a caricature of a respected leader, we can feel superior and we laugh. A doll or a satirical image of a candidate may belittle an ostentatious politician who aspires to lead us, making us laugh. Another source of humor lies in incongruity. Jokes, events, and objects amuse us because their contents or forms are out of place or inappropriate to the words or context presented. A punch line or an unexpected situation takes us by surprise and makes us laugh. Campaign objects often employ irony and incongruity: a candidate's face on a paper novelty or a pipe bowl may strike us as funny because it is out of place. Surprise and extravagance are ingredients of incongruous campaign novelties.

Humor can also mask or displace aggression. Amusement is a socially acceptable outlet for venting tensions, resentments, and other fundamental human impulses. Writer Stephen Leacock suggests that laughter results from a primitive sense of exultation and delight at observing demolition. Similarly, political scientist Charles Schutz writes of the way humor can replace destructive aggression: "Humor provides a socially acceptable release of the repressed emotions of our primitive aggressiveness. Politics as a war of words is then an arena in which humor is indispensable for limiting the war to words."

The imagery of fun can be employed to attack the opposition, or it can serve to enhance a campaign. Satire and ridicule may raise doubts about a candidate's competence or integrity. But funny devices can help a candidate appeal to the public and reinforce loyalties. A good

Tippecanoe pen card, 1840. *This cardboard hand-out (3.5 in. wide) was published as a pen advertisement. It presents one of the strongest existing statements of W. H. Harrison's image as a candidate. Standing before his ubiquitous symbols, the log cabin and the cider barrel, the Old Hero is pictured as a war veteran greeting other veterans.*

example of negative ridicule turned to positive ends was the Democratic joke in 1840 about General Harrison's affection for log cabins and hard cider; it was transformed into a powerful image of rustic strength.

Since the early 1800s, every election has produced its share of campaign devices filled with humorous imagery. Cherished by collectors, fascinating to historians, these millions of gadgets, novelties, and printed items played a significant role in America's political traditions. Humor, parody, exaggeration, ridicule, and political caricature remind candidates and voters of the importance and folly of running for office. Again and again, collectors and students of politics confront appealing and intriguing examples of political Americana, seeking to understand their humorous, satirical, and often insulting intent.

The late nineteenth and early twentieth centuries witnessed a vast increase in the production and creativity of humorous campaign paraphernalia. Political items of the period between 1880 and 1916 possessed vitality and lightheartedness, vivid flamboyance, visual excitement and color, and a rich iconography. In part, the objects and their images were products of an intense yet high-spirited partisan rivalry, at a time when elections were closely fought by evenly matched Republican and Democratic political organizations. By that time party politics had to compete with other forms of entertainment. To hold the public's attention, electioneering devices needed to be showy and appealing. Some objects featured humorous themes. For example, in 1888 the Republican candidate Benjamin Harrison, grandson of the victorious log-

The Rats leaving a Falling House.

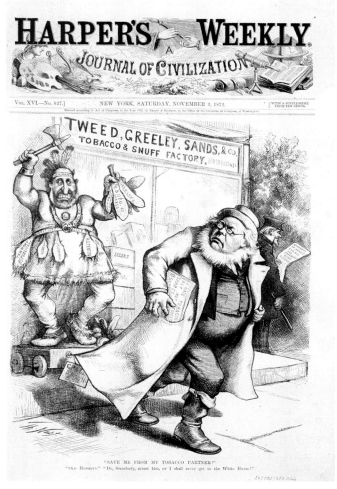

Jackson caricature, 1831. *Andrew Jackson seemed to bring out the worst in his political opponents. This cartoon, attributed to Edward W. Clay, depicts a crisis in Jackson's administration that began with the social snubbing of a cabinet member's new wife. After collecting resignations from both factions on his cabinet, Jackson reinstated Martin Van Buren (second rat from the right). Such cartoons could be purchased in printmaker's shops and bookstores, but the technology did not yet exist to print them in newspapers.*

Harper's Weekly cover, 1872. *Horace Greeley, a pioneer of American politics and journalism from W. H. Harrison's logcabin campaign, became a favorite target of the press when he ran on the Liberal Republican ticket against the corruption of U. S. Grant's administration. He is here linked with the infamous Boss Tweed of Tammany Hall in a cartoon counterattack by Thomas Nast. The Republicans' venomous tactics defeated Greeley politically and physically. He died less than a month after the election.*

cabin candidate in 1840, ran with log-cabin symbols. Quite obsolete in the Gilded Age, the cabin nevertheless appeared on many campaign devices, appealing to old-timers who remembered the exciting 1840 contest and tickling younger people who saw the fun of it. Campaign games were another humorous device of the period, including puzzles, board games, and card games. Much humor was reflected in the increased variety of smoking and tobacco materials: pipes, cigars and cigar boxes, and advertising cards. Comic ceramics and glassware reinforced the enthusiastic electioneering spirit. Posters, cartoons, and banners made funny statements about the candidates and the issues. Clever lapel devices, including ribbons, badges, pins, and novelties, also appeared in great quantities and varieties.

One of the most entertaining yet satirical campaign novelties is the candidate portrait, caricatured or distorted into a political device. Ranging from glass bottles to bottle corks, from paper caricatures to pipe bowls, from cloth dolls to face masks, candidates' funny faces serve many purposes. Like all campaign objects, they draw public attention to office seekers, reminding voters that an election is near. On the one hand, they may testify to and reinforce voter loyalties; on the other, they make subtle or broad and bawdy fun of presidential hopefuls.

Cartoons, the most abundant visual political jokes, appeared from the late eighteenth century onward. Cartoonists began attacking presidents during the time of Washington and Jefferson. Political cartooning flourished especially during the era of Andrew Jackson, after the introduction of lithography as a printing process in the 1820s. Lithographic printing enabled printmakers to produce quantities of detailed engravings for sale to a popular audience, but prints could not then be combined with other forms of printed text, so caricatures were printed and distributed individually. During the Jackson years many caricatures appeared, mainly anti-Jackson engravings.

During the Civil War era, cartooning was associated with mass-circulation illustrated magazines. *Frank Leslie's Illustrated Newspaper* and *Harper's Weekly*, the nation's earliest examples of the genre, appeared in the 1850s, taking the lead with all kinds of pictures, including caricatures. Thomas Nast, often described as the nation's greatest cartoonist, worked for both *Leslie's* and *Harper's*, inaugurating a new era in American caricature. Nast's cartoons, rendered in pencil and printed as wood engravings, helped make *Harper's* the most influential magazine of the day. The influence of Nast and *Harper's* waned in the late 1870s.

Illustrated magazines continued their dominance of the cartoon marketplace through the 1890s. *Puck*, a weekly founded in 1877 by Viennese immigrant Joseph Keppler, became highly successful because of Keppler's elaborate lithographed color cartoons of trenchant satire and lighthearted wit, which appeared on the front and back covers and the centerfold. Competition among the illustrated magazines intensified during the 1880s with the establishment of *Judge*, a Republican-leaning periodical in contrast to the Democratic preferences of *Puck*. Regular newspaper cartoons first appeared in the 1860s, but only in the nineties did they begin publication on a daily basis. Among the most biting and intellectual applications of political humor, cartooning occupies a distinguished position among American devices of electioneering and social criticism.

At a deeper, darker, more speculative level, the imagery of humorous, ridiculous, or satirical campaign devices may represent a strong ambivalence and anxiety among the electorate about the electoral process. At bottom, American democracy rests on faith, a belief that representative institutions derive from the ballot box and that elective officials can be trusted. Every four years that faith is tested and often found wanting. During each election, voters briefly have the ultimate power to support or reject one candidate or another. Hoping to believe in potential leaders but often disappointed with candidates' promises and accomplishments, the voters enjoy objects that ridicule presidential aspirants. Comical devices thus express a deep doubt about political institutions and personalities involved in elections. More bitter than laughable, the language of humorous objects may express a basic distrust of the electoral process itself.

Partisanship and Personal Commitment

During the intensely partisan era from the 1830s until the early twentieth century, many campaign objects featured images of loyalty and commitment. Scholars and observers of American political history have noted that party loyalties reached their highest levels in the middle to late nineteenth century. As historian Michael McGerr writes, "The idea of loyalty to a party, was . . . deeply imbedded in Northern society. Partisanship . . . entailed more than attachment to a particular political organization. For mid-nineteenth-century Northerners . . . found it second nature to perceive events from a partisan perspective and to imagine a black-and-white world of absolutes, of political friends and enemies." Men often inherited their partisan preferences, much as they received property and religious convictions, from their parents.

Among the objects emphasizing partisan loyalties were a wide range of artifacts and communication media whose forms almost inevitably signified personal commitment. Tokens, buttons, ribbons, and other devices were manufactured to testify to personal loyalty, as were objects to be displayed on personal property and real estate such as license-plate attachments, bumper stickers, placards and stickers for households, and posters for showing in yards and open spaces. For more than a century, before they took on the trappings of neutrality, newspapers consistently adhered to partisan loyalties and convictions. The parties also became strongly attached to certain symbolic devices that were immediately identified with partisanship.

Through the nineteenth and twentieth centuries the variety of personal partisan devices grew, diversified, changed in character, then diminished as party loyalties weakened. They did reflect personal choices, however. Voters chose to carry or wear the earliest such devices – political coins, medalets, tokens – to honor individuals, not parties. After 1820, as party politics became more pronounced, medalets were less honorific and more competitive.

After 1896 the modern style of pinback button replaced most other lapel devices, becoming the most prevalent and most popular of all campaign paraphernalia. In the presidential campaign of 1896, political buttons became primary emblems of personal and party loyalties. During the following half-century, dozens of manufacturers of advertising novelties entered the button business. Cheap, durable, easily distributed and handled, buttons could convey an astonishing range of messages and symbols. By wearing campaign buttons, loyalists could easily announce their partisan and candidate preferences. The buttons became the most convenient and most widely used of all personal campaign items. In the heat of campaigns, candidate images portrayed on buttons often became the embodiments of partisan affection, bearers of party traditions and virtues.

The imagery of party loyalty persisted, despite a gradual reduction of partisan enthusiasm. New classes of objects for personal display appeared in the 1920s for use on automobiles. First, when cars carried their spare tires outside, there were political spare-tire covers. Later, license-plate devices bore political messages, and after car bumpers were streamlined they became ideal locations for the display of political images on bumper stickers (and of messages reflecting protest and commercial interests). Besides their automobiles, political loyalists often decorated their houses and yards with stickers, placards, and posters that testified to their commitment.

Although generally forgotten today, one of the leading devices for promoting party loyalty during most of the nineteenth century was the partisan newspaper. From George Washington's administration until William McKinley's, the majority of American papers retained strong, one-sided partisan affiliations. As early as 1830 the United States had about 1,200 newspapers, most of them narrowly partisan, dominated by party editorials and invective. Jacksonian Democrats led in the formation of the partisan press, followed soon by the Whig party and, later, the Republicans. By the mid nineteenth century most cities and even counties supported at least two papers, each one representing a major party and subsidized by the party.

At its most extreme level the partisan press appeared in the form of special newspapers published strictly for the purpose of partisan electioneering. Printed in the years between 1828 and the 1860s only during presidential campaigns, scores of these small sheets presented biased campaign information and partisan promotion exclusively. They used catchy slogans as titles, such as the Democratic *Hornet, Rough-Hewer,* and *Sober Second Thought,* or the Whig *Log Cabin, Old Tip's Broom,* and *That Same Old Coon.* A man's politics could be readily identified by the paper he read. Moreover, party news sheets were among the chief organs of partisan loyalty.

Still another set of partisan symbols appeared to reinforce and give vitality to political loyalties during the nineteenth century. These were the animal emblems associated with politics, the Democratic donkey and the Republican elephant. The precise origin of the donkey as a Democratic party symbol is unknown. Donkeys were seen on anti-Jackson coins during the 1830s, and a cartoon from 1837 depicts Andrew Jackson riding an unhappy ass, apparently representing his party. But the donkey had competitors as the Democratic symbol. The rooster appeared often on campaign devices for more than forty years, and cartoonist Thomas Nast depicted the Democratic party sometimes as a tiger, especially as the Tammany tiger of New

Roosevelt banner, 1940. *This oilcloth banner combines a plain black-and-white portrait of Franklin Roosevelt with the simple and forceful graphic style of the New Deal. With pressures mounting to enter the war in Europe, it encourages voters to break tradition and elect him to a third term.*

York, other times as a fox, a dog, a wolf in sheep's clothing, and a snake, before settling on the donkey. Nast and other critics imagined the Democratic party as an obstinate, backward, slow, and dull-witted creature, like the donkey. Nast also created the elephant as a symbol for the Republican party, first appearing in a *Harper's Weekly* cartoon on November 7, 1874. Nast's elephant, according to a student of his work, represented the cartoonist's disappointment with the Grand Old Party: "During the 1874 campaign . . . [Nast] introduced the figure of the Republican elephant. At first labeled 'the Republican vote,' his was a cumbersome, purposeless beast: in effect, what Nast feared his party had become." Although Nast depicted the two party animals as denigrating caricatures, the symbols evolved into happier, more appealing creatures. First as cartoons, later incorporated into countless campaign devices and novelties, Democratic donkeys and Republican elephants became instant, cheerful indicators of political loyalties. People who loved the parties cherished the party beasts.

Some Account of some of the Bloody Deeds of
GEN. JACKSON.

 Jacob Webb.  David Morrow.  John Harris.   Henry Lewis. David Hunt.   Edward Lindsey.

Poor JOHN WOODS; he was a generous hearted, noble fellow as ever lived, who had volunteered for the service of his country...

Gen. Jackson, detailing his progress among the Indians.

FRANKLIN, Tenn., September 10, 1828.

THOMAS HART BENTON, Lieut. Col. Thirty-Ninth Infantry
And now a member of the Senate of the United States.

THE MODERN BALAAM AND HIS ASS.

Candidate Imagery

Jackson cartoon, 1837.
In an early use of the donkey as a symbol of the Democratic party, Andrew Jackson rides while the new president, Martin Van Buren, meekly follows. The drawing mocks Jacksonian banking and financial policies, which critics believed brought on the Panic of 1837.

Since the time of Andrew Jackson, images of candidates have been among the most common and appealing ingredients of campaign objects. Candidate images consist of deliberately created representations, likenesses, or concepts of a leader designed for mass distribution. At their basic level, images – descriptions, impressions, portraits of people, image-bearing objects – serve simply to identify leading participants in the struggle for power. Personal images simplify complex characters, give them tangible substance, and stimulate emotional bonds between leaders and their publics. As they are repeated and elaborated, images offer vivid, attractive, and dynamic depictions of the people who compete for our loyalties. Incorporated into campaign devices, images become reflections of, even substitutes for political leadership and symbols of loyalty for most of the voting public.

Images are probably essential to a system of popular democracy, for in few other ways can the millions of voters in the electorate learn about individuals seeking their support than through impressions or images conveyed by the visual media. Using available means, most American presidents cultivated and established public images. We remember most of our presidents through the shorthand of simple images. George Washington was a disinterested, heroic patriot, Jefferson a natural aristocrat, Jackson the hero of New Orleans and man of the people, Harrison the log-cabin, hard-cider hero, Lincoln the rail-splitter and representative common man, Ulysses S. Grant the great general and leader, and so on. Some presidential images bore relationships to the leaders' lives, but others were largely contrived. Whether or not their images had realistic dimensions, the language of imagery enabled voters to gain some sense of the candidates' supposed achievements.

Several images have been especially durable in American politics. One is the image of the general or military hero. Associated with noted generals such as Washington, Jackson, Grant, and Eisenhower, and with more-obscure officers like William Henry Harrison, Zachary Taylor, Winfield Scott, Franklin Pierce, Rutherford Hayes, James A. Garfield, even William McKinley, the military hero image had wide appeal, especially in postwar eras. After the Civil War, the Republican party ran a series of ex-officers. Grant, the most renowned, appeared as a classic American success story, an ordinary man who had risen from obscurity to high responsibility through natural talent and the democratic rags-to-riches process. His weak presidency, unfortunately, contrasted image and reality. Grant's successors, former Union army officers, also ran on their military records. Keeping alive the memories of war, every four years the Republican party "waved the bloody shirt" by sending its legions of Boys in Blue to parade through the nation's cities and towns, reenacting their defense of the Union.

The opportunities for contriving candidate images have generated some of the most imaginative of all campaign devices. The central themes of the log-cabin and hard-cider contest of 1840 gave political managers and manufacturers of campaign devices wonderful chances to create appealing objects for electioneering. Another vivid example of inspired presidential image making is that of Theodore Roosevelt. Elected vice president in 1900 and becoming president after McKinley's assassination, Teddy Roosevelt created his own image as Rough Rider, ex-cowboy, and energetic outdoorsman. The active, outgoing, exhilarating president had a gift for self-created imagery. He uttered several distinctive political phrases calculated to convey an ebullient spirit: "Speak softly and carry a big stick – you will go far"; "muckraker," referring to journalistic crusaders; "bully pulpit," for use of the presidency to inspire; and "strong as a bull moose." His images were translated into campaign objects, producing a positive impression of Roosevelt as audacious, physically aggressive, a lover of the outdoors, a moral leader.

Modern interpretations of campaigning associate image politics with television and political advertising. Historically, however, candidate images were present at the beginning of American political life – from the creation of our first and most durable political image, that of George Washington. The founding fathers had no clear idea of a political image; instead they used the term "reputation." Today we associate imagery in politics with unsavory, even unethical practices and unscrupulous manipulation. The negative connotations of imagery may apply in some instances, but certainly not always.

Scott handbill, 1852. *Large numbers of German and Irish immigrants arrived in the United States in the 1840s, and by the time of Winfield Scott's unsuccessful campaign, they had become naturalized citizens. This handbill appeals to those German speakers, although nativists in the Whig party didn't want to allow them to vote. Many anti-immigrant Whigs wound up in the Know-Nothing party. The caption refers to the popular slogan "First in war, first in peace, and first in the hearts of his countrymen."*

Teddy Roosevelt

Rough Rider tray, c. 1900. *This quite ornamental but utilitarian metal tray may have been intended for serving beer. It reflects the unprecedented intensity that Teddy Roosevelt brought to the cultivation and exploitation of his image as a leader.*

Johnson button, 1964.
While Lyndon Johnson's presidential campaign used television to portray opponent Barry Goldwater as a trigger-happy monster, other media, like this button, cast Johnson as a gentle and thoughtful visionary, a fitting successor to John Kennedy, and the steady hand needed in the aftermath of Kennedy's assassination.

As American politics developed, political images arose from many different sources. Heroic images emerged from military service in wartime and were embellished, sometimes almost beyond recognition. Other kinds of images grew out of the experiences and personalities of the candidates, as for example the rail-splitter candidacy of Lincoln. Some strong images, such as Harrison's log cabin, were invented almost by accident. Often, however, the circumstances of an image's origin were used creatively and were greatly enriched to enhance the candidate's appeal.

Although they did not call themselves public relations experts, the men who created and circulated political imagery through most of the nineteenth and the early twentieth centuries were thorough professionals. Campaign managers, political writers, artists and cartoonists, and editors, they learned by experience how to project their party and "product" (the candidate) in the most attractive manner, through information and by means of powerful appeals to the emotions of the voting public.

The candidate imagery was conveyed through campaign devices of many varieties, all aimed to achieve similar goals. The graphic portraits and caricatures carried by millions of mass-produced ribbons, buttons, textiles, and paper objects encouraged voters to see connections, similarities of preferences and beliefs, between themselves and presidential candidates. Publications such as broadsides, pamphlets, newspapers, and campaign biographies developed narratives and pictures that established and reinforced certain public perceptions about candidates. Long before television, other media presented vivid images to the electorate – images important to the conduct of government.

Devices of Attack

One campaign technique that makes Americans uncomfortable is the form that attacks, or as it is best known in the late twentieth century, negative campaigning. Devices of attack are not inevitable in politics, although they have always been by-products of American electoral competition. Often disguised as humor and caricature, negative images are present in numerous campaign devices. Contrary to the assumption that it is recent, negative campaigning – and derogatory, insulting electioneering devices – go back to the beginning.

Smears against the president began during the time of George Washington, with accusations of incompetence in the president's administration and even the circulation of lies accusing the first president, who steadfastly refused a crown, of plotting to establish a hereditary monarchy. During the first competitive presidential election, between John Adams and Thomas Jefferson in 1796, there was widespread use of invective, accusations, name-calling, and outright lies. Again, when Adams and Jefferson met in the campaign of 1800, many of the same smears and accusations circulated, as well as new attacks on Jefferson's private conduct and character. Electoral publications, reaching new heights in quantity and invective, disseminated hostile

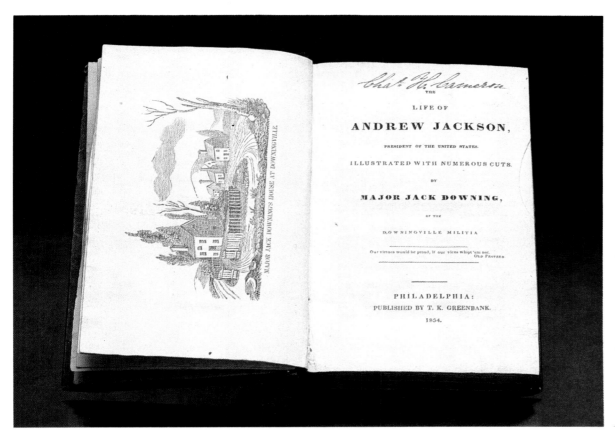

The Life of Andrew Jackson, 1834.
Jackson was the subject of the first campaign biography, in 1824. Later the genre and the president were satirized in this comic biography, which originated as a series of letters by the fictitious Major Jack Downing, a creation of humorist Seba Smith. The book remained popular for twenty years as a telling commentary on American politics.

messages. A typical anti-Jefferson pamphlet of the 1800 contest predicted "that if Jefferson is elected, and the Jacobins get into authority, . . . those morals which protect our lives from the knife of the assassin . . . [will] be trampled upon and exploded."

A generation later, in 1828, when John Quincy Adams and Andrew Jackson battled each other for the presidency, the candidates exchanged smears and mudslinging. Jackson was denounced for wanting to be emperor and for murder, dueling, and adultery, among other evil deeds. One of the worst attacks accused Jackson's adored wife, Rachel, of bigamy, adultery, and promiscuity. It was during this contest that some of the first celebrated negative campaign devices appeared, the notorious coffin handbills, which accused Jackson of murdering militiamen under his command and committing other misdeeds. Several versions of these lurid broadsides were published and circulated around the time of the 1828 campaign. In return, the Jacksonians denounced Adams as a monarchist, an effete snob, and a procurer of American girls for the Russian czar when Adams was minister to St. Petersburg.

Negative campaigning against Jackson continued by means of numerous satirical and bitter cartoons during his presidency. The Democratic party and Jackson were also satirized in political tokens, whose language of attack, in the words of Edmund Sullivan, consisted of "coarse and critical allusions to Jackson through the device of a jackass, a hog and legends which continually repeated the word, 'My.'" Subtler attacks took place in humorous publications, including a burlesque campaign biography by the fictitious character Major Jack Downing, posing as an intimate Jackson friend and advisor. The real author, New England humorist Seba Smith, ridiculed Jackson's presidency and scoffed at his heroic exploits. Curiously, smears against Jackson apparently had few harmful effects on his popularity.

Serious attacks also appeared against Jackson's successor, Martin Van Buren, during the campaign of 1840. An effective slur on "little Van" accused him of extravagance and misuse of public funds for decorations and high living in the White House. The lies were surprisingly popular, circulated in a variety of campaign media, and were translated into at least one campaign device that depicted Van Buren as a foppish dandy sipping "White House champagne." Less obvious attacks on Van Buren appeared through campaign media such as music. In turn, the Democrats attacked the Whig candidate, Harrison, as a fraudulent hero and indulged in name-calling, but their slurs were relatively ineffective.

Taking different forms, negative campaign devices appeared in most election contests during the nineteenth century. Abraham Lincoln, for instance, was the victim of scores of caricatures, emphasizing his awkward frame and his unorthodox sympathies for African Americans. An-

Grant pig charm, 1872.

A tiny picture of Ulysses S. Grant is set inside the hole under the pig's tail. This novelty was created to make money for an independent manufacturer, not to promote a political party.

Cleveland cartoon, c. 1884. *With its implication that Grover Cleveland had fathered an illegitimate child, this Victorian-age cartoon represents a notorious episode of campaign mudslinging. Cleveland's opponent was the victim of an even more damaging bribery scandal.*

other victim of attack, President Ulysses Grant, became involved in several scandals that justified some of the criticism against him. A particularly interesting anti-Grant object is a silver charm in the form of a pig. An observer looking into a small opening below the pig's tail will see a portrait of Grant inside. Grant's unlucky opponent in the election of 1872, Horace Greeley, was devastated by the language of attack, especially in savage cartoons from the pen of Thomas Nast.

The presidential contest between James G. Blaine and Grover Cleveland in 1884 was particularly unpleasant. Both candidates had serious liabilities that were translated into campaign devices. The Republican Blaine was implicated in railroad graft that prompted a campaign broadside comparing his old homestead before he became a national politician and his great mansion in Washington, D.C., after he profited from national politics. Under attack, Democratic contender Grover Cleveland admitted having fathered an illegitimate child, an error that received wide publicity in cartoons, campaign songs, and printed devices. Few elections have seen more negative campaigning.

Presidential contests of the late nineteenth and early twentieth centuries seem to have been more mannerly than some of their predecessors. But in 1920, the Republican candidate, Warren G. Harding, who had been dogged since childhood by tales of illicit ancestors, was attacked with vicious and unfounded stories concerning his alleged African American ancestry.

During the election of 1940, scores of different campaign buttons attacked or ridiculed President Franklin D. Roosevelt, his family, his New Deal programs, and his third-term presiden-

Johnson dart game, c. 1967. *This game was probably not a campaign novelty but rather an expression of opposition to Lyndon Johnson's escalation of the war in Vietnam. Still, it does crystallize the attitude behind the ugliest campaign attacks, and it may mark a change for the worse in America's view of politics in general.*

tial race. Most of these fascinating negative buttons are favorites with collectors. A few are reminiscent of anti-Jackson tokens of the 1830s, attacking Roosevelt for his supposed arrogance by emphasizing the word "my," as in "*my* friends" and "*my* ambassador." Eleanor Roosevelt, a vivid personality in her own right, came under attack, as did several other family members.

In later elections the language of attack flourished through novelties such as "hos-til'-ity: The 'anti-hero' dart game," advertised as a "great new game in the great American tradition," whose target was President Lyndon B. Johnson. Even more recently, the medium of television has provided extensive opportunities to treat voters to the language of attack. Conventions of attack and politeness have alternated from time to time in American politics. In the late twentieth century, with artistry from the wizards of television politics, we observe new dimensions to the fine art of attack and negative campaigning.

Convergences: Promoting the Candidates

Long before there were national radio and television networks, voters were mobilized and rallied by campaign gadgets and persuasive devices whose purposes converged on the goals of promoting candidates, their programs, and parties. All forms of campaign devices thus centered around political rivalry, campaigning, selling candidates as complicated products, to achieve victory at the polls.

The varieties of political devices often come together during the great events of presidential contests. In the mass gatherings of the last century, which included banners, torchlights, ribbons and other lapel devices, music, and the pageantry of electioneering, all campaign media were concentrated, focusing the voters' attention on the next presidential contest and encouraging voter participation. Campaign historian Michael McGerr assesses the effect of those devices: "The widespread acceptance of . . . campaign spectacle . . . helped make possible the record turnouts in the North during the nineteenth century." Even in the late twentieth century, national party nominating conventions carried on the tradition of mass party celebrations by employing a wide range of campaign devices.

Critics of contemporary presidential contests complain about a neglect of substantive issues and a preponderance of shallow imagery. With the overwhelming influence of television commercials in contemporary campaigns, an impression has fixed itself in the minds of intellectuals and commentators on the media that modern elections, unlike those in the past, are decided on the basis of imagery instead of issues. As Wilcomb Washburn observes, however, electioneering has long been "essentially a matter of symbols and images, not issues. . . . Yet this has been so for more than a century and a half, and it has long been understood by the ordinary voter." Perhaps the point is not that imagery replaced issues as the central focus of electioneering but that campaign managers have always sought to transform issues and personalities into appealing devices to attract the voting public.

Campaign devices are not so different from the other elements of campaign processes and behavior. By their nature, visual devices and novelties are a shorthand for attitudes and emotions, not means of expressing arguments about campaign issues. Issues are often complicated, controversial, and divisive, whereas political objects are intended to simplify, to soothe and reinforce the party faithful. When dealing with issues, campaign items almost invariably translate them into celebration, humor, loyalty, imagery, or attack.

Issues sometimes appear indirectly in campaign devices, such as the Whig party's manner of handling the depression issue in the campaign of 1840. Aware of the influence of persistent economic troubles on voters, the Whigs staged campaign spectacles and created positive campaign devices, suggesting that a new administration, based on old virtues and simple living, might resolve the economic downturn. Slogans about "Harrison and reform" implied the need for change, and campaign festivities anticipated how the country would prosper under Whig rule. Alternately subtle and festive, Whig devices and behavior offered implicit promises of better times. Thus the feel-good campaign became a dramatic statement of one of the day's leading issues.

Electioneering with gadgets, although not unique to the United States, flourished in this country as in no other political system. Whatever their imagery, campaign devices were vital elements of a lively and changing political culture in America from the early nineteenth century onward. For about a century these objects proliferated, popularizing politics, attracting and engaging millions of participants, giving American presidential elections a high-spirited fascination. Later they became nearly obsolete as other communication media grew to dominate presidential campaigning. Their history includes some of the leading characters and movements in American politics during the past two hundred years.

Origins: Emblems of Honor and Glory

When a reluctant George Washington, feeling somewhat like "a culprit who is going to the place of his execution," traveled to his first inauguration in the spring of 1789, he observed the "joyful acclamations of every party and every description of citizens" – in short, the earliest celebrations of the American presidency. Among all the festivities there were objects, the oldest examples of presidential commemorative emblems, honoring Washington, America's most popular leader, and through him celebrating the nation's glory and achievements.

Washington's election was unlike any other in American history. For one thing, the winner had no serious competitors for the highest office. Another unusual circumstance was the absence of any popular vote. Instead, the electoral college, chosen in some states through general elections, in others by different procedures, voted unanimously for George Washington. Elected to a second term in 1792, again unanimously, Washington indeed seemed to be "first in the hearts of his countrymen."

As there was no real campaign, there were no campaign devices exhorting people to vote for the Revolutionary hero. Nevertheless, George Washington's astonishing popularity stimulated the creation of a wide range of commemorative and celebratory objects. Among the few surviving early American political artifacts are souvenirs that celebrated Washington's inauguration. Highly desirable as political collectibles, Washington commemorative buttons began to appear shortly after the inaugural ceremonies, manufactured by New York and Connecticut button makers. Stamped or engraved, made from coins or round pieces of solid brass or copper, some forty distinct varieties of Washington buttons have been identified. Many were inscribed with patriotic symbols, such as eagles and thirteen stars, with the president's initials, "G.W.," and with legends such as "Long live the President" or other appropriate messages. These inaugural souvenirs were forerunners of countless millions of devices honoring American presidents or urging citizens to vote for certain candidates.

Veneration of George Washington began during the Revolution. A contemporary, President Ezra Stiles of Yale University, captured the public's worshipful attitude toward the hero when he exclaimed: "O Washington! how do I love thy name! How have I often adored and blessed thy God, for creating and forming thee the great ornament of human kind! . . . Our very enemies stop the madness of their fire in full volley, stop the illiberality of their slander at thy name, as if rebuked from Heaven. . . . Thy fame is of sweeter perfume than Arabian spices in the gardens of Persia." A host of sermons, panegyrics, essays, toasts, and other expressions of praise, during and after Washington's life, expressed the public's esteem for Washington. Uncounted visual representations – portraits, prints, statues, and other mementos of the nation's hero – were created, distributed, and treasured across the United States. During his lifetime, Washington was the center of a cult of adoration, becoming the first and, in the early years, the foremost personal image assimilated by the whole nation.

Overleaf:
Washington pitcher, c. 1800. *George Washington had always been the country's most popular subject of deification, but after his death in 1799, memorial objects like this transfer-printed pitcher proliferated. It shows the first president's final apotheosis. The pitcher was made in Liverpool.*

The First Presidential Image Maker

Long before his election as president, Washington cultivated a distinct image as military leader and gentleman-politician. Historian Paul K. Longmore has shown how Washington's apparent modesty concealed a powerful ambition and how his reluctance to compete for office helped make his public appeal more pervasive. John Adams expressed concern about the excessive admiration of Washington: "I have been distressed to see some members of [the Continental Congress] disposed to idolize an image which their own hands have molten. I speak here of the superstitious veneration that is sometimes paid to General Washington." A

Philadelphian commented on the people's attitude at the time of the Constitutional Convention: "General Washington is among them . . . but the commonpeople dont know how to admire without adoring him." A legend, almost a myth in his own time, Washington became a demigod.

In a perceptive analysis, historian Marcus Cunliffe discusses four mythic dimensions of Washington's reputation: the hero of nearly perfect character and integrity; the father of his country and model president; the nation's greatest patriot, comparable to the Roman hero Cincinnatus, who left his plow to save the Republic, then returned to the land, a simple farmer; and the revolutionary leader, renowned at home and abroad as the "chieftain, the liberator, the champion of nationalism, and the victor in the first revolution of modern times."

Highly self-conscious of his public role, Washington conducted himself as "a figure upon the stage" of life, confirming his mystique. Whatever he did, he behaved with a dignity appropriate to his rank as a planter, a general, or a president. When he led the army, as Barry Schwartz has shown, General Washington made a public spectacle of his pure intentions, conducting a careful campaign of "image management." He projected images combining authentic courage

Salute to General Washington in New York Harbor, c. 1875
(L. M. Cooke, oil on canvas, 27 x 40.5 in.).

George Washington, 1780

(Charles Willson Peale, mezzotint, approx. 10 x 12 in.).

Washington inaugural buttons, 1789.

More than forty varieties of Washington inaugural buttons are known. Many were later sold by independent vendors to commemorate the first president's first inauguration, on April 30, 1789. Their association with that landmark event places them among the most valuable items of political Americana. Although they did not figure in a campaign, they are considered ancestors of the modern campaign button.

and majesty with symbolic elements he or others embellished from the realities. It was as though he deliberately played the part of Cincinnatus.

Even before his election as president, Washington's heroic image had grown larger than life, as that of a leader of superhuman integrity and courage. Living close to his troops during the war, he shared their hardships and combined a common touch with a reputation for unusual dignity and self-control. Critics during the Revolution attacked his decisions as arbitrary and often erroneous and his conduct as overbearing. Despite opposition, he emerged from the struggle as a hero. His disinterested conduct as president of the Constitutional Convention in Philadelphia reassured the delegates. They easily imagined Washington as the perfect president under the new constitution.

Although he was elected in February 1789, the absence of a quorum in Congress postponed the first inauguration. Not until April did Washington make his ceremonial journey from his home at Mount Vernon, Virginia, to be installed as president in New York. Traveling by horse-drawn carriage, he was greeted everywhere by throngs of people and, in many places, formal ceremonies. His trip was akin to a royal procession. Delegations of horsemen from each town or city on the route escorted Washington as guards of honor, carrying special flags and banners made to celebrate his presence. He was feasted and toasted in many places, and in the larger cities his carriage passed under celebratory triumphal arches. Again and again he listened to welcoming addresses, special poetry, and musical greetings from assembled dignitaries and groups of citizens. Although recorded in newspaper reports and memoirs and, in a few cases, preserved visually by illustrations, the artifacts associated with Washington's inauguration have mostly vanished.

On his arrival in New York, he met an elaborate ceremonial barge with twenty-six oarsmen to carry him across the Hudson River, to rounds of salutes by cannon and music from bands and choruses. The president's inauguration on April 30 was no less stirring and admiring than his journey to the inaugural. His image had reached its apex of splendor.

Inevitably, opposition arose among countless ordinary people and scores of influential leaders. Denounced as a would-be monarch, a tyrant, a traitor, and a hypocrite, Washington endured withering press hostility, especially during his second term. The increasing polarization of Americans on issues of foreign relations between partisans of France and English sympathizers put Washington in the middle, damned by one side or the other. By the time he retired from office, Washington had become personally bitter, his image tarnished. His presidency produced a counterimage, cultivated by his opponents: the pompous, imperious, dangerous monarchist.

The Presidency and Partisan Politics

Inadvertently George Washington had become embroiled in the emergence of America's first political parties. Following the Constitutional Convention, two interest groups formed in the states to argue over the charter's ratification. Federalists, who supported a more centralized government, fought for approval against antifederalists, who feared the centralizing, undemocratic tendencies of the Constitution. But the two sides never organized as parties; they "were simply two sets of individuals holding different opinions about adopting the Constitution; they were not parties because they lacked the organizational structure." George Washington and most other founders discouraged and deplored political parties, believing them to be founded in corruption and greed, productive of disunity and strife. Nevertheless, serious partisan rivalries arose during the first administration of George Washington, and two rival political organizations formed into what some modern scholars call the first American party system. As President Washington labored to organize a government in Philadelphia, he set in motion the basic sources of political parties – disagreements over foreign and domestic policies, and struggles for power and position.

Parties, almost by definition, are natural components of competitive politics; Austin Ranney and Willmoore Kendall define them as "autonomous organized groups that make nominations and contest elections in the hope of eventually gaining and exercising control of the personnel and policies of government." Diversity of wealth, power, and position among the citizens led to competing interests and disagreements. But of all the incentives toward lively national partisan activity, none was more compelling than the contest for chief executive. Nominating and electing presidential candidates became the most important perceived goal of the parties and their followers.

The first two parties formed around Alexander Hamilton and Thomas Jefferson, reflecting the different domestic and international views held by the two leading members of President Washington's cabinet. Hamilton proposed ambitious economic plans and favored a strong national government. He feared the "turbulent" masses and would give the rich and well-born a "destined, permanent share in the government." His supporters became known as Federalists. Jefferson, on the other hand, "felt the farmers to be the most valuable citizens and dreamed of an agrarian America." His party, known as the Jeffersonian Republicans, advocated states' rights and majority rule. In foreign affairs also, the Hamiltonians and Jeffersonians were sharply divided. Sympathetic to the French Revolution, Jefferson and his partisans became its enthusiastic supporters. Hamilton feared that revolution's radical tendencies and favored an American alignment with England against France. Jefferson had by 1794 left the administration and was cooperating with James Madison and others in the House of Representatives to form an opposition political movement.

One of the first tangible products of the new partisan spirit was the political press. An administration or Federalist paper, the *Gazette of the United States*, was followed by an opposition

Alexander Hamilton, 1804 *(William Rollinson, stipple engraving, approx. 17.5 x 14 in.). Although he did not run for the presidency himself, Hamilton was the leader of one of the nation's first political parties, the Federalists.*

sheet, the *National Gazette*, which attacked Hamilton's programs and defined positions for Jefferson's Republican party. In 1793 Jefferson's partisans began organizing Democratic-Republican societies, anti-Federalist political and fraternal groups that were active in party affairs until the late 1790s.

As Federalists and Republicans squared off for the presidential campaign of 1796, George Washington announced his retirement from office, warning in his farewell address "against the baneful effects of the spirit of party. . . . It agitates the Community with ill-founded jealousies and false alarms, kindles the animosity of one part against another, foments occasional riot and insurrection." Despite his warning, there was no way to avoid a battle over the presidency. For the first time the highest office served as the focal point of political rivalry. Techniques of promoting candidates for popular appeal appeared in the form of vigorous name-calling. Jeffersonians branded Adams as an "avowed Monarchist," and Federalists denounced Jefferson as a religious disorganizer, a Jacobin, and the leader of a "French faction." Despite superior organizing by Jeffersonian Republicans and a divided Federalist party, Adams won the close presidential contest by three electoral votes.

By the next presidential contest, in 1800, both Federalists and Republicans were organized as parties, naming partisan presidential candidates, Adams and Jefferson, in congressional caucuses – party meetings of congressmen who met specifically to nominate candidates. The Jeffer-

New Orleans, 1803 (*Boqueto de Woieseri, oil on canvas*). *This panorama was painted in the year of the Louisiana Purchase, one of the surprising events that made Thomas Jefferson's presidency pivotal in American history. When Jefferson proposed to buy New Orleans from the French, a cash-strapped Napoleon gave him a bargain on the entire Louisiana Territory, doubling the size of the new nation.*

sonian Republicans sponsored unprecedented outpourings of printed propaganda through newspapers, broadsides, pamphlets, and printed election tickets. Both parties engaged in name-calling and innuendo. With Republicans far better organized than their rivals, the race was a vigorous, hard-fought party battle for both sides.

The Republican party won with an electoral vote of 73 for Jefferson and 65 for Adams. But a tie between Jefferson and Aaron Burr in the electoral college required the House of Representatives to decide which of the two would be president and which vice president. After a torturous struggle, Jefferson took the prize. The parties had succeeded in producing a peaceful change of administration, called by Jefferson a "revolution," using campaign machinery not provided by the Constitution. The election of 1800 climaxed the first American party system.

Few tangible reminders exist from Thomas Jefferson's victory in 1800. Perhaps the rarest survivor is a cloth banner celebrating the inauguration of Jefferson, one of the earliest American political artifacts to carry a strong partisan message. Unlike the neutral souvenirs of Washington's inauguration, the banner depicts the bitter rivalry between Jefferson and Adams.

Early in 1801, when the House finally announced Jefferson's election, his partisans were relieved and elated. Across the country victory rallies, parades, and celebrations took place, as happy Republicans danced and marched and hastily created devices to honor their standard-bearer. Among the objects created to commemorate Jefferson's election was probably a banner with a portrait of the new president and the triumphant message: "T. Jefferson President of

Thomas Jefferson, 1798-99
(Michel Sokolnicki, hand-colored aquatint, approx 10 x 8 in.).

Jefferson banner, c. 1800. *This handpainted portrait of Thomas Jefferson is no doubt based on a printed image. The linen banner, 37 in. wide, was found near Pittsfield, Massachusetts, the home state of opponent John Adams.*

the United States of America / John Adams is no more." Other than the message carried on the banner and the data that can be pieced together from circumstantial evidence, little is known about the object or its origin. We know that "Republicans throughout the country were . . . caught up in a wave of festivities celebrating the inauguration of Jefferson as President." Therefore this mysterious object probably came from one of the many inaugural festivals. We know that it was discovered in Massachusetts, suggesting the tantalizing possibility that it was made for a pro-Jefferson celebration in New England, the region that opposed his election most vigorously. Possibly the Jeffersonian minority in the region flew this victory symbol to taunt the supporters of local favorite Adams. The message "John Adams is no more" would surely have infuriated them, and in the minds of Jeffersonians, it must have seemed a fitting reward for the straitlaced Yankees who favored the Massachusetts native, known to his rivals as "His Rotundity."

In the educated judgment of historian Noble Cunningham, the object represents the earliest employment of a Jefferson portrait in a political device. Another scholar identified the banner's portrait as based on an engraving taken from a lost 1800 portrait of Jefferson by Gilbert Stuart.

The cloth's fiber content and condition are consistent with the dates 1800–1801. The explicit message of triumph suggests that the banner was used at a rally or public gathering to celebrate the results of the election. Its later history gives little help in solving the mysteries, for until 1958, the banner was unknown to historians.

The Jefferson banner recalls one of the most important and bitter presidential elections in American history. A leading student of the period, Merrill Peterson, argues that the election and inauguration of Jefferson

> completed the first democratic transfer of power in the nation's history, indeed in the history of modern politics. When the Jeffersonians went outside of government and built a political party in the broad electorate, thus giving voice to the "silent democracy," they set up a different ideal, one that saw in the agitation and organization of public opinion the vital principle of American government. Because the Jeffersonians were successful, the Constitution became an instrument of democracy. . . . The election of 1800 was therefore critical in the most basic sense: it secured all the elections to come.

Thus the fragile textile announcing Jefferson's election and John Adams's eclipse carries one of the most significant statements ever delivered in the history of American politics.

Following Jefferson's election, partisanship began to wane. Several factors contributed to its decline, including a severe falling off of support for the Federalists. The Federalists sealed their doom as a party by calling the Hartford Convention, in 1814, in opposition to the War of 1812. The convention, in which every delegate was a Federalist, recommended that New England begin to cut its ties to the Union. Shortly afterward the war ended, bringing condemnation of the Hartford Convention. The Federalists' loss of support meant that they could not compete on a national level with the Republicans.

The Cult of Washington

As party politics flourished and then waned in the early years of the new century, the reputation of George Washington soared to unearthly heights. His death in 1799 stimulated a new round of admiring patriotic imagery to commemorate the man and his heroic achievements. Godlike virtues were translated into countless literary products and visual artifacts. First came an outpouring of mourning expressions of all sorts, sermons and orations by the hundreds shortly after Washington's death and on his birthday in 1800. These speeches were often incorporated into elaborate ceremonies with processions, simulated burial rites, feasts, and other formal commemorations. Sometimes as part of these ceremonies, sometimes separately, complicated prints, textiles, ceramics, and other mourning devices were produced in large quantities and widely circulated. The worship of Washington's memory thus took on tangible form.

Commemoration of Washington, after 1800.
This picture was made by applying glass over an English print and vividly coloring the figures to create a semi-transparent effect (16 x 13 in.). The plumed goddess represents mourning America paying tribute at a marble memorial to Washington.

An EMBLEM of AMERICA.

Daniel Boorstin and others have noted the extraordinary circulation of popular Washington biographies during the years after his death. Their most enthusiastic purveyor, "Parson" Mason Locke Weems, promoted and sold his cheap, imaginative biographical sketches by the thousands between 1800 and 1825. Weems celebrated Washington's resemblance to the Roman patriot Cincinnatus and enlivened his tale with moral fables about the hero's pure virtues. It was Weems who invented and propagated anecdotes of Washington and the cherry tree ("I can't tell a lie, Pa; you know I can't tell a lie. I cut it with my hatchet"), along with many other exploits of the hero. Innumerable other volumes, both popular and learned, exploited Washington's memory and added to his image. In effect, Washington's popular biographers had invented a posthumous campaign biography. Although Washington was not running for office, the numerous stories of his life campaigned him into the nation's memory.

Washington's image gained political content as it spread through the nation. In particular, the Federalist party, during its gradual demise from 1800 until the 1820s, appropriated the name and reputation of Washington. Federalists formed several partisan societies dedicated to the first president's memory and the perpetuation of his principles, taking his ideals as theirs. Beginning about 1808 this development took the form of a Federalist movement known as the Washington Benevolent Society. During the next decade Federalists established several hundred local branches of their Washington society.

Most units of the Washington Benevolent Society were devoted to supporting Federalist party candidates and projects. Although open to anyone able to vote, the society attracted primarily young men of the better sort. One of its principal public activities was to hold parades, usually on Independence Day, Washington's Birthday, and the anniversary of the first inauguration. Branches of the society aided the Federalist party by raising money, electioneering, and sponsoring propaganda. Among their other projects, the members circulated documents and artifacts commemorating Washington, including many editions of Washington's Farewell Address. Silk ribbons bearing Washington's portrait issued by the society are among the earliest mass-produced partisan objects in American political history.

Americans were reminded of Washington's image again in 1824–25 when the General's beloved friend and helper in the cause of our revolution, the Marquis de Lafayette, returned to the United States for a national tour. Lafayette's reputation resembled Washington's. Nearly half a century after he had fought beside Washington, "The Nation's Guest" received a hero's welcome with countless processions, ceremonies, and mass demonstrations of affection and remembrance. Lafayette's visit brought to local communities everywhere a sense of the nation's history and a chance to honor a national symbol. As historian Fred Somkin describes it, the French patriot inspired "a kind of republican worship. . . . The practical deification of Lafayette opened new paths of contact between the heroic model and his republican admirers." Some of those paths achieved tangible, material results; Lafayette, like Washington, inspired the manufacture of artifacts – china, glassware, badges, ribbons, apparel bearing his portrait and image – as souvenirs of the visit. There were "LaFayette boots – LaFayette hats –

Le Général Lafayette, c. 1825
(Achille Moreau, aquatint and etching, approx. 16 x 21 in.). Lafayette's image in America represented the epitome of the romanticized military hero and served as a model for many politicians.

LE GÉNÉRAL LAFAYETTE.

LaFayette wine – and LaFayette everything." And these artifacts, like those honoring Washington, were models for a host of political devices soon to appear.

As it evolved, Washington's image had a long-lasting influence on other presidential image-making. Portraits of Washington abounded on medals, on ceramics, in popular prints, and on ribbons and other textiles during the first half of the nineteenth century. His image adorned varied secular campaign devices promoting a number of causes. Washington imagery proliferated into a vigorous posthumous campaign spreading enthusiasm for the hero and providing direct examples for live presidential candidates during the era of popular politics between the 1820s and 1840s. Direct links between the first president and campaign devices of later years are found in ribbons and novelties dating from the 1830s, the 1840s, the early 1900s, and the mid twentieth century. His image reappeared in curious forms to celebrate the hero's birthday and other occasions. Souvenir hatchets, recalling the cherry tree legend, found a ready market in 1889 at the time of the centennial of his inauguration. Such promotional artifacts are evidence of the continuing effectiveness of Washington's image.

Grand in Peace, Brave in War,
Lovingly in the Hearts of His Countrymen.

First in Peace, First in War,
First in the Hearts of His Countrymen.

Politics Without Parties

Elections after 1800 drew relatively little serious competition for the presidency, and ordinary voters played only indirect roles in the process. For the most part candidates behaved as "patriot kings" or "mute tribunes," above the unseemly quarreling and self-promotion of everyday politics. The disappearance of partisan politics between roughly 1816 and 1824 was only temporary. The so-called Era of Good Feeling concealed furious factional rivalries among a growing number of men who aspired to be president.

In the election of 1824 those rivalries came out into the open, disrupting the contest and reflecting the unsettled political conditions of the time. Four major candidates competed in the final race: John Quincy Adams, Henry Clay, William H. Crawford, and Andrew Jackson, each receiving some electoral votes. Andrew Jackson secured the most popular votes but not an electoral majority, and the House of Representatives had to decide the results. After a series of trades and maneuvers the House chose John Quincy Adams. President Adams then named Henry Clay as Secretary of State. Jackson, furious at his defeat in the House, insisted that his victory had been denied through a "corrupt bargain" between Adams and Clay. Two new factions then developed, consisting of Jackson's supporters against those favoring Adams. Throughout Adams's term in office, Jacksonians openly fought against the president's policies.

Bryan novelty, 1908. *More than a century after the first president's death, campaigners were still exploiting Washington's image. When this paper card is folded, the face of Democratic candidate William Jennings Bryan appears in a hole in Stuart's famous Washington portrait. Even as late as 1952, supporters of General Douglas MacArthur were casting their potential candidate in the Washington mold.*

New rivalries and circumstances called for stronger political institutions. More liberal suffrage requirements meant that nearly all adult white males were eligible to vote for president in most states. The addition of new states to the Union also expanded the electorate by many thousands of voters. In 1828 all states except one chose electors by popular vote of the whole state, demanding new political machinery to appeal to a greatly expanded and more influential voting public. By the late 1820s national politics had entered an era of partisanship and electoral competition unprecedented in the nation's brief history. The emblems of honor and glory that had celebrated George Washington and other national heroes would soon take on new functions in the struggle for the nation's highest office.

Mobilizing the Multitudes

Presidential politics began a fundamental change during the 1820s. Historians now recognize that the period between 1825 and 1860 was probably the most inventive time in American history for political parties and campaign techniques. Partisan organizers mobilized masses of people to participate and vote in contests for offices at all levels of government. New institutions and practices, unknown in 1825, provided mechanisms for organizing voters, identifying political leaders, and mobilizing public opinion. Factional rivalries that dominated presidential politics in the early 1820s gave way after the election of 1824 to a new partisan competition, known to historians as the second American party system.

Political innovations of the time included campaign techniques and devices originating from three influences: new men, new institutions, and a new electorate. The new men included Andrew Jackson, a military hero, resolute and popular, a westerner, and a self-styled man of the people. Along with Jackson came scores of other new political operatives who helped put together the most effective new institution of the period, the Jacksonian coalition. The best-known and most skilled of these men, Martin Van Buren, helped build the organization at the local, state, and national levels. Jackson, Van Buren, and others designed new electioneering techniques to bring out thousands of first-time voters – the new electorate. Enfranchised during the 1820s and consisting of a majority of white males in most states, the new voters more than doubled the number of popular ballots cast for president between 1824 and 1828.

The Jacksonian organization developed rapidly between its candidate's first defeat and the election of 1828. Central committees assembled in several states, and active correspondence began among state leaders. Jackson's supporters established a network of strategically placed state newspapers, which served as organizing centers in several states for political committees headed by party editors. As the election of 1828 approached, it became a contest between two candidates, President John Quincy Adams and the challenger Jackson.

The First Popular Campaign

Mass mobilization of the American electorate occurred in 1828. Bitter after his loss of the 1824 election to Adams and the "corrupt bargain," Andrew Jackson aimed to defeat his rival at any cost. Jackson and his followers invented new devices and adapted old ones to popularize elections, creating an explosive new political style. More parades, rallies, and symbolic devices than ever before encouraged enthusiastic participation by Jackson's partisans and made the race unlike its predecessors. Abandoning any pretense of dignity and formality, Jackson's partisans openly cultivated emotional appeals in the style described by historian David Potter as the "hurrah" campaign.

Many features of the hurrah campaign had appeared earlier. Jacksonians learned to adapt rituals of the principal national celebration, Independence Day, into spectacular political events. Cities and towns everywhere sponsored patriotic festivals and ceremonies, more or less elaborate, to honor American freedom. In time these joyous displays, with their processions, speechifying, feasts, and hearty good times, were directly appropriated by political managers and converted into party rallies. Other patriotic events with their rallies and parades were adapted for partisan political purposes. An eyewitness description of a political rally of this period comes from a French visitor, Michael Chevalier, in his account of a celebration by New York City Democrats: "The procession was nearly a mile long; the democrats marched in good order to the glare of torches; the banners were more numerous than I had ever seen them in any religious festival; all were in transparency on account of the darkness. On some were in-

Jackson sewing box, 1828. *Thought to be French in origin, this colorful box is handmade of soft materials, probably cardboard and paper. As usual, Andrew Jackson is depicted as a dashing military hero.*

scribed the names of the democratic societies or sections." That such demonstrations occurred by the hundreds is almost certain. For example, popular parades in Philadelphia included both official ceremonial processions and burlesque types that mocked the respectable parades. These demonstrations were significant ingredients of popular political culture throughout mid-nineteenth-century America.

The election of 1828 also marked the arrival of a more vivid kind of campaign imagery associated with Andrew Jackson. Appealing to the people's emotions and interests were Jackson's military exploits and his appearance as a man of the people. His campaigns revived and adapted the Washington image, still alive in the 1820s, depicting General Jackson as a "New Washington" or "Second Washington" and praising him as a "Modern Cincinnatus." Indeed, long before he ran for the presidency Andrew Jackson was an authentic military giant and a popular figure, known as the hero of New Orleans for his defeat of British forces in 1815. Stories were told, songs sung, orations and tributes offered, and myths created to celebrate his military exploits. Jackson was an aggressive westerner and expansionist; his nickname "Old Hickory" derived from an unbending disposition and powerful will as a military leader. Possessing great confidence and a fierce temper, he could be politically shrewd and personally charming. Unlike earlier presidents, Jackson had little formal education and had achieved his considerable wealth by

Jackson pitcher, c. 1820.
On this elegantly glazed ceramic piece from England, Andrew Jackson is shown in civilian dress, as a white-haired statesman, but the legend celebrates his military victory at the Battle of New Orleans.

his own efforts. He was the sort of personality who might appeal to the new masses of ordinary voters in the South and West.

Jacksonian editors and orators issued a barrage of rhetoric that today would certainly be called image-making, emphasizing Jackson's achievements as the Old Hero and Old Hickory and depicting him as the people's candidate in opposition to the aristocratic Adams. In reality a wealthy planter and slaveholder, Jackson was pictured in the political press as a simple, brave, and pious frontiersman, a figure larger than life. Adams, in contrast, was presented as effete and corrupt.

Artifacts celebrating Jackson, similar to those commemorating Washington, were made soon after his victory at New Orleans. Imported English lusterware extolled his exploits before he

Jackson crock, 1825. *Inscribed with "25,000 majority," this ceramic crock protests the 1824 election results, which gave the presidency to John Quincy Adams, even though Andrew Jackson had won a plurality of popular votes in the four-way race. That disastrous election sparked a revolution in the American party system and reform of the electoral process.*

was a presidential contender. Although primarily commemorative, such objects indirectly promoted Jackson's candidacy. They are early examples of the transitional object dedicated both to celebrating and selling presidential candidates. Not surprisingly, since Jackson and Napoleon were contemporaries, many Jackson items imitated Napoleonic imagery. Ceramics and other celebratory objects carried portraits of Jackson in uniform with a dashing French look.

Jackson also presented himself as the virtuous candidate wronged by the conspiracy of an eastern aristocrat, John Quincy Adams, and a western opportunist, Henry Clay. A ceramic crock made in New Haven, Connecticut, between 1825 and 1828 carries the legend "25,000 majority Gnl Jackson," representing the stolen election in 1825 (the actual margin was close to 40,000 votes). Jackson's opponents endowed him with a counterimage as a man of violence, a brutal, immoral frontiersman, and a tyrant, "King Andrew the First." Some of those themes were reflected in the savage coffin handbills issued for the 1828 campaign. Such accusations probably aided Jackson among many voters.

As conducted by the Jacksonians, the canvass required an immense organization and a level of participation that could be assembled only by a structured political body and a hierarchy of local, county, state, and national activists. Jackson's supporters raised and spent more money than had been expended in any earlier political contest, including probably half a million dollars (a huge sum in those days) for the press. Funds were raised at all levels, from a few pennies and dollars obtained and spent by local groups to large contributions given to city and state committees. One of the campaign's largest expenses, the cost of mailing, was defrayed by members of Congress, who used their franking privileges to send out large quantities of propaganda at federal expense.

In the summer of 1828 the Jackson campaign reached its climax, taking the form of a national mass celebration. Capitalizing on Old Hickory's nickname, his partisans erected countless hickory poles in village squares and alongside roadways throughout the country. By helping to erect the poles, local enthusiasts could join directly in celebrating and promoting their hero. Typical of this style of participation was a scene in New York City shortly before the election: the local Jacksonians gathered to erect a hickory pole. "The beer-barrels were rolled out; and it required no vivid imagination to distinguish in the uproar the yell of the hyaena, the cry of the panther and the whoop of the Winnebagoes." Music was composed to help raise campaigners' spirits, and mementos made of ceramics, metal, glass, and other materials reminded the people of their hero's exploits. Political propaganda issued forth in thousands of printed forms, mostly emphasizing the hero's personal qualities – his image.

The well-organized Jacksonians won the presidential contest with 56 percent of the popular vote and 178 electoral votes to 83 for Adams. Jackson's new coalition had done its job, recruiting a winning candidate, organizing public support for him, and decisively capturing the presidency. The Jacksonian strategy of 1828 signified a permanent shift in electoral competition toward partisan politics and campaigns of mass participation. Successive elections in 1832 and 1836 continued the development of party organizations, political devices, and popular campaigning.

The new political styles were not universally popular. Jackson's opponents found the hero's popular electioneering distasteful, debauched, and demagogic. To critics, the emphasis on emotional appeals, mass participation, and festivity seemed to contradict traditions of rational republican discourse. But the new style appeared to offer an attractive and winning formula. By dramatizing elections, hurrah campaigns excited the voters and attracted their interest. With more people than ever qualified to vote, the political spectacle stimulated a high turnout at election time.

The Log Cabin Campaign of 1840

In elections after 1828, the new political techniques slowly gained favor. It was not until the formation of a strong opposition to the Jacksonian Democrats, however, that an organized political body had sufficient energy and direction to take full advantage of the hurrah campaign style. Through the 1830s, this opposition developed in the form of a national political party that took the name "Whigs." By 1840 the Whigs were prepared to carry the new styles of electioneering to their greatest potential, in the "Log Cabin and Hard Cider" presidential campaign. In terms of organization, recruitment of participants, hullabaloo, pageantry, enthusiasm, and outright fun, the canvass far outclassed the Jackson campaign of 1828 or any other preceding popular political spectacle. The massive Whig party show became a model for later presidential races.

The contest featured an old military hero, General William Henry Harrison, running for president under the banners of the recently formed Whig party, an upsurge of popular enthusiasm and participation, and a cluster of images concentrating on the hero candidate and his association with the rustic log cabin. Political collectors and historians agree on the spectacular quality of the log-cabin and hard-cider campaign circus of 1840, and collectors especially appreciate the profusion and variety of campaign techniques and gimmicks it produced. Many skeptical historians complain, however, that the absence of reasonable deliberation and concern about substantive issues, as well as the demagoguery, hoopla, and festivities of the campaign, misled the electorate. "So the campaign became a volcanic eruption of volatile and unintelligent sentimentalism," writes Albert Beveridge. Despite differences of opinion among scholars and collectors, the circus of 1840 was a watershed event, the first classic and fully developed expression of the enthusiastic hurrah campaign for America's highest office.

From the contest's beginning, Whig party leaders planned a campaign of exciting displays and mass participation. Thurlow Weed, Whig organizer in New York State, planned the party's political strategies, much as Martin Van Buren had for the Democrats a decade earlier. Editor of the *Albany Evening Journal*, Weed himself never ran for public office but served several Whig candidates as a campaign manager. Weed and Thaddeus Stevens of Pennsylvania were determined to win the 1840 contest and rigged the party nominating convention to secure the prize for General Harrison of Ohio. Passing over longtime politicians Henry Clay and Daniel Webster, the Whigs nominated Harrison, who seemed relatively popular, had few enemies, possessed a military record, and could be molded – "designed" – according to political needs. Almost incidentally, they gave the vice presidential nomination to John Tyler, balancing the ticket with a Virginian. The convention issued no election platform, being insufficiently united to risk taking a stand on policy issues.

The Whig leaders presented their candidate as General Harrison, the Old Hero, and farmer Harrison, the rustic log-cabin dweller. The heroic Harrison was an old soldier and leader in battle during the War of 1812 and earlier Indian wars. Throughout the campaign Whig publi-

Whig sheet music, 1840.
The Whig campaign of 1840 was famous for its music. Sheet music and songsters were produced for the masses of marching bands and glee clubs that turned out for rallies.

W. H. Harrison

Written by

WILLIAM HAYDEN, ESQ.

and respectfully dedicated to the

Whigs of the United States.

BOSTON.

Price 25 cts.

Published by PARKER & DITSON, 135 Washington St.

Harrison covered dish, 1840.

The domestic scenes decorating this English-made dish were meant to evoke everyday life in the United States, surrounding W. H. Harrison with comfortable, homey images. They also reflect early notions of Victorian sentimentality.

cations and political devices boasted of Harrison's heroism, endlessly describing his achievements in battle and his generosity toward war veterans, or comparing his abilities to those of George Washington. Like Washington, Harrison left his farm to save the country. But Whig presentations of Harrison's heroism surpassed and shifted the heroic traditions associated with Washington and Jackson. Harrison's military qualities were sentimentalized by allusions to his generosity toward visiting strangers and old soldiers. The latchstring always out, the cider barrel always ready with cooling yet temperate refreshment, the hero's cabin was pictured as the home of benevolence. Unlike the fierce, impulsive disposition of Jackson, Harrison's character was tempered with sympathy and wisdom, endowed with the down-to-earth virtues of frontier cabin dwellers and farmers. Such domestic and agrarian aspects of Harrison imagery coincided with growing domestic, sentimental trends in American culture.

Harrison's association with the log cabin and hard cider grew out of a joke from a Democratic newspaper sneering at "Old Granny" Harrison, who, the paper declared, would be content with "a barrel of hard cider, and . . . a pension of two thousand a year [to] sit the remainder of his days in his log cabin." Whigs gleefully converted that sarcastic estimate of their candidate into a central theme of their campaign. Harrison was no log-cabin boy, however, having been born on a great Virginia plantation, the son of Benjamin Harrison, a signer of the Declaration of Independence. Whig publicists identified Harrison's ample residence in Ohio as a log cabin and endowed the candidate with the rural simplicity of the frontier cabin owner and farmer. The "farmer of North Bend" became one of his many identities.

The cabin and beverage were devices of astonishing inspiration and great emotional power, calculated to appeal to ordinary Americans, especially in the rural West. Log-cabin symbolism transformed the Harrison campaign into an emotional spree, a celebration of the common people. Evoking memories among millions of Americans who had ties with the frontier, either in their own experience or one or two generations removed from the edge of settlement, the log cabin tapped strong sentiments of home and origins. Along with symbols and images, this extravagant political battle focused around the slogan "Tippecanoe and Tyler Too." The folksy term "Tippecanoe" was a reference to Harrison's 1811 victory against the Indians at the battle of Tippecanoe.

Another important feature of Harrison imagery in artifacts was the widespread depiction of the candidate's portrait. Pictorial representations of Old Tip, based on engraved portraits, graced every imaginable device and material. On medals and tokens made of metal, textile banners, bandannas, ribbons, ceramics and glass, and paper devices of all sorts, Harrison's face appeared. Harrison was shown sometimes as a genial grandfatherly figure, other times as a uniformed general resembling Napoleon. By the time they voted, the majority of Harrison's supporters surely knew what their favorite looked like. Modern voters take candidates' appearances for granted. For a people unaccustomed to seeing pictorial representations of their leaders, however, the circulation of images of Harrison provided a new kind of vision. Not just a name but a face, the candidate gained a genuine, tangible identity.

Harrison cane head, 1840. *Found in the estate of Admiral George Dewey, this cane is probably one of a kind. Its ivory head, in the shape of a cider barrel, is inscribed "Tippecanoe" and "Hard cider." The crude and rustic imagery superimposed on a walking cane – a symbol of upper-class elegance and privilege – sums up the strategy behind Harrison's campaign.*

Harrison brush, 1840.

This painted brush may have been intended for use by women, but its primary campaign purpose – the purpose of all the other household tools and ornaments emblazoned with W. H. Harrison's portrait and log-cabin scenes – was to insinuate the Whig cause into the voter's every-day life. More than one hundred years later, this brush was rescued from the trash by a custodial worker who found it still attractive and useful.

As he had done earlier in New York State elections, organizer Thurlow Weed hired Horace Greeley to edit the principal campaign newspaper. Greeley began planning a network of Whig newspapers even before Old Tip's nomination. His weekly paper, appropriately named the *Log Cabin,* led the newspaper brigade, provided material for a system of campaign papers, and reinforced all the campaign symbolism depicted during rallies and processions. From May to November it carried endless sentimental stories of Tip's heroism, his kindness to the troops who fought under him, and his generosity to visitors at his North Bend "cabin." Battle stories endowed the general with a heroic image similar to that projected by Andrew Jackson in the campaign of 1828. Every edition of the *Log Cabin* published lengthy descriptions of rallies and celebrations to illustrate the progress of the Whig cause, its popularity, and the general enthusiasm it aroused. Dozens of other campaign papers appeared briefly during the contest, filled with electoral trivia, attacks on the opposition, and rollicking fun. The *Log Cabin* also featured texts of speeches by the great Whig orators – Clay, Webster, Harrison himself, and others – some of them focused on issues in the campaign, such as the economic hard times and alleged abuses of executive power. Greeley also engaged in negative campaigning, printing attacks on the Democrats along with lies about Van Buren and other opponents. Each week 80,000 copies of this lively campaign paper circulated across the country.

An unprecedented aspect of Whig enthusiasm was the encouragement offered to participation. Typical of the chances for plain people to help were the "cabin raisings" that took place in hundreds of communities. Men with modest rural skills joined together at a central place, perhaps a county seat, bringing logs from their farms. At an appointed time, the farmers assembled their cabin, which became the local Harrison meeting place and Whig party headquarters. Women also helped by offering refreshments and often presenting a flag or banner. The Whig managers thus gave people a physical chance to "re-form," to build anew a house representing their candidate, in the name of "Harrison and reform." Miniature cabins were carried in parades, and full-sized cabins appeared on parade floats. Hard cider was much in evidence as the favorite campaign beverage, celebrating the hero of Tippecanoe and his many virtues.

The campaign itself can be likened to a series of popular celebrations taking place around the country. First there were ratification meetings in the states, then George Washington's birthday rallies and partisan festivals. An example of one of these spectacles was the Ohio State Convention on Washington's birthday, 1840. A "grand procession . . . surpassed in enthusiasm anything ever before or since in the history of Ohio." From everywhere in the state came the "stalwart Buckeye boys" to set "the ball a rolling on for Tippecanoe and Tyler too." Like "an army with banners moving through streets whose walls were hung with flags, streamers and decorations to honor a brave old patriot and pioneer," the people congregated. Participation and drama were the order of the day, and Whig assemblies of cabin boys and ciderites spread through the country. Similar scenes were enacted hundreds, perhaps thousands of times during the political season between February and November. A contemporary account of a New York State rally suggests the power and enthusiasm of the party gatherings. At the rally site in an

Harrison miniature cabin, 1840. *The log-cabin image saturated the nation in 1840. Great numbers of miniature cabins were made to carry in parades, hoisted on poles like banners. This one, 17 in. high and 12 in. wide, is made of wood.*

upstate city, "Never were the foundations of popular sentiment so broken up! The scene, from early dawn to sunset, has been one of continued, increasing, bewildering enthusiasm. The hearts of TWENTY-FIVE THOUSAND FREEMEN have been overflowing with gratitude and gladness and joy. . . . The People . . . poured in from the Valleys and rushed in torrents down from the Mountains . . . vocal with Eloquence, with Music, and with Acclamations. Demonstrations of strength and Emblems of Victory and harbingers of Prosperity are all around us."

The log-cabin campaign was one of the most original of all American presidential confrontations, a contest of electioneering firsts. It was the first presidential campaign in which two competitive nationally organized political parties battled one another at nearly every level. Both the Democratic and Whig parties were established and evenly matched in many states and even in local areas.

The contest was one of the first true image campaigns, concentrating on the use of imagery and advertising techniques to sell a party leader. Slogans and rich verbal descriptions – especially negative writing and distortion – had appeared before but never as widely as in 1840. Negative images of "Van, Van the Used-up Man," the candidate of champagne and rich living, are only a tiny sample of the brilliant twists of Whig image-making. Visual images circulated everywhere, including countless portraits of the heroic general and depictions of log cabins and hard cider.

Whig campaign newspaper, 1840. The Log Cabin, *edited by Horace Greeley, was the leading campaign newspaper of 1840, with a circulation of 80,000. It reported on fun and entertainment along the Whig campaign trail, on speeches and cabin raisings, and advertised W. H. Harrison's heroism. After the campaign, Greeley transformed the paper into the* New York Tribune.

The campaign may be the first American national advertising campaign of any kind. Candidate Harrison was one of the earliest products to be marketed vigorously and imaginatively across the land. The whole nation could visualize the candidate from portraits on cloth ribbons, printed ceramics, publications, medals, and other devices. The canvass included many elements of a latter-day Madison Avenue production: slogans, jingles, and testimonials circulated through the media.

The log-cabin extravaganza was also the first comprehensive media campaign. Although earlier contests had used newspapers and publications, in 1840 the Whig party mobilized a range of media as no party had attempted before. Whigs saturated the country with words and images before the appearance of communication technologies such as the telegraph. The Whig party conducted a successful experiment in 1840, demonstrating that people everywhere would respond to the election show. Both Whigs and Democrats adapted many media and events from other festivals and patriotic celebrations. Processions and parades had served for centuries as expressions of public attachment to civic and religious institutions. Whig strategists appropriated many elements from Independence Day celebrations, until the entire summer took on the character of a giant Fourth of July festival. Whig partisans also adapted some of the tactics that had served so well in Andrew Jackson's 1828 campaign. Demonstrations and souvenirs were not new, but Whig managers used them more than ever, in unprecedented ways, financed with ample funds raised by party leaders.

The Legacy of Tippecanoe

For collectors, remembering the campaign of 1840 means recalling and preserving the vast body of artifacts that survive from that presidential contest. Assessing the election, historian Roger A. Fischer writes, "The 'Tippecanoe and Tyler Too' campaign inspired a harvest of souvenir items seldom if ever surpassed in quantity and variety in nearly two centuries of American politics." Experts estimate that more than two hundred distinct Harrison campaign ribbons were probably made during the campaign year. No campaign before and few since have left such an imaginative, colorful array of political items. They are chief among the treasured memories of this election. The objects were not just ordinary campaign devices, however. In their vast numbers and enthusiastic imagery, they were forerunners of similar items that would be integral parts of American political culture for the next 150 years. That is why they have a special place in the story of American politics and political Americana.

To understand these devices it is important to view them in the context of campaign rituals and practices. Although they survive today as separate, collectible antiques isolated from their origins, during the summer of 1840 the gadgets were elements of an intense, festive process. Defined and called into being by the campaign, endowed with the imagery and high emotions of the log-cabin contest, they should be understood as parts of the whole. Whatever their functions – to call attention to the Whig cause, help rally support, reinforce existing loyalties, cre-

Whig rolling ball, 1840.
One of the most spectacular contraptions in the Harrison campaign was the Great Ball from Allegany County in western Maryland. Made of buckskin and adorned with a long rhymed message, it was rolled through the state by costumed mountain boys.

ate warm feelings among the voters, or convince the public that changes or reforms in government were needed – the banners, ribbons, novelties, and the festivities in which they appeared were all of a piece. All grew out of and contributed to the overall political strategy.

Symbols appeared on thousands of novelties and devices, many of them mass-produced, such as ribbons, ceramics, sheet music, and banners. Great campaign balls were rolled from place to place around the country. In ways never before seen, campaign artifacts were incorporated into celebrations, becoming integral parts of every event. Participants wearing ribbons, badges, and medalets, carrying flags and banners, helping with cabin wagons and floats, thus demonstrated their loyalties to the partisan cause. Their souvenirs represented serious political commitment.

Among the devices of the log-cabin campaign were large and small things, from huge leather balls inscribed with slogans and mottoes to tiny medalets and clothing buttons. Elegant examples of decorative arts or useful objects coexisted with things cheap, simple, and mundane. Humor and satire were explicitly or subtly reflected in many campaign novelties. But nearly all the devices depicted one or both of Harrison's dual images as military hero and simple farmer. Good examples are the many Harrison medalets that show a military bust of the General on the obverse side and a log cabin on the reverse. Inscriptions on these coins also emphasize the dual image with such legends as "The Hero of Tippecanoe," "The People's Choice," "The Log Cabin Candidate," and "He Leaves the Plough to Save His Country." Some twenty distinct examples of medalets were struck carrying portrayals of the hero, the log cabin, and appropriate legends.

Political items from 1840 include elegant decorative and useful objects that might have appealed to well-to-do gentlemen and ladies. A handsome silver spoon probably made for the

Harrison snuff box, 1840. *Made of a soft metal, possibly pewter, this snuff box bears a particularly sentimental rendering of the Harrison log cabin, perhaps playing on nostalgia for a lost rural simplicity.*

campaign bears a log-cabin image. Other finely decorated items include a metal snuffbox, bearing a detailed log-cabin illustration, and a unique thornwood cane surmounted with a hand-carved bone or ivory head in the shape of a miniature cider barrel inscribed "Tippecanoe" and "Hard Cider." Many examples of ceramicware survive, such as mass-produced and specialty pieces with transfer-printed images of log cabins or portraits of General Harrison. Glassware with images of Harrison or the log cabin probably received broad distribution. These elegant items are of special interest in illustrating the circulation of log-cabin imagery among people of wealth and influence, as well as among members of the general public. In curious and ambiguous ways, the Whig theme of log-cabin simplicity captivated even wealthy partisans, juxtaposing rustic imagery and stylish decorative objects.

Reflecting extensive mobilization of the electorate, mass-produced Whig ribbons and parade items served as symbols to identify and rally Harrison supporters. Advertisements in campaign newspapers from several different printers boasted of their excellent ribbons and badges. Valentine's engravers and printers of New York addressed a notice "To Tippecanoe Clubs, Conventions, &c., throughout the United States," recommending "appropriate Tippecanoe badges, (suitable for any occasion or place in the United States,) with a splendid likeness of Gen. Wm. H. Harrison . . . engraved . . . to be a correct likeness of the brave Hero." Typical ribbons display images of the noble General ready to save the country, the log cabin, patriotic symbols, and messages praising the hero. Many of these small textiles, made for specific rallies or festivals, carry the name of the place where they were worn. Other devices to inspire Harrison's "troops" include emblematic parade objects such as banners, flags, and miniature log cabins made to be mounted on poles and carried in parades. Campaign sheet music and song-

Harrison ribbon, 1840. *Ribbons, worn on the lapels of supporters at rallies, emphasized W. H. Harrison's military career. This silk ribbon delivers a triple image, comparing the candidate to George Washington, casting him as a military hero in the romantic French style, and picturing his devotion to the defense of the common people.*

#104   08-31-2012 2:23PM
Item(s) checked out to p1107399.

TITLE: Mickey Cohen, in my own words : t
BARCODE: 3 1220 00091 2508
DUE DATE: 09-21-12

TITLE: The new new rules : a funny look
BARCODE: 3 1220 00973 3541
DUE DATE: 09-21-12

TITLE: Hail to the candidate : president
BARCODE: 3 1220 00462 9090
DUE DATE: 09-21-12

2012 POV Summer Documentary Series
Wednesdays @ 5:30pm through August

sters encouraged strident Whigs to test their vocal cords for the old General. Campaign managers assumed, probably correctly, that happy voters would support the party that promoted their joy.

The proliferation and refinement of Harrison campaign imagery can be examined by surveying a few examples of 1840 political ephemera. For instance, a complicated ribbon published in Baltimore carries three illustrations, each with its separate text. An engraving at the ribbon's apex depicts Baltimore's Washington Monument surrounded by a ring of stars, with a text to identify the Baltimore Young Men's National Whig Convention. Beneath the image is the legend: "Washington the Father of His Country. Harrison a Chip of the Old Block." Below those words is an engraving of General Harrison, in full uniform with raised sword, mounted on a prancing horse, with the legend "The Hero of Tippecanoe, the Farmer of North Bend." Under that line lies an illustration of a log cabin, somewhat in the Greek Revival style, a barrel marked "hard cider," and two human figures, representing Harrison and a disabled war veteran. Those elements reflect the full standard expression of hero and farmer imagery as depicted on thousands of mass-produced campaign objects.

Some ribbons added portraits of Lafayette and Washington to the image of Harrison, all identified as "Founders and Defenders of American Independence." In each one the log cabin appears, as if to prove the hero's rural authenticity. Other forms of political ephemera, campaign stationery for instance, depict a letterhead with a portrait of the General and an engraving of the log cabin. Through such devices, images of Harrison and the log cabin circulated throughout the United States.

An unusual Whig party device from 1840 foreshadowed a whole family of campaign novelties: an anti-Democratic pull card depicting candidate Van Buren as a smiling, sandy-whiskered dandy holding "a beautiful goblet of White House champagne." When the card tab is pulled the candidate's expression changes to a frown and the message to "an ugly mug of log-cabin hard cider." One of the earliest humorous mechanical devices, this paper caricature becomes even funnier when its joke is revealed by manipulation of the object. Over the next century numerous other examples of animated paper devices appeared. Among the utilitarian domestic devices of 1840 is an elaborate Harrison brush bearing the General's portrait surrounded by floral decorations. An overwhelming array of images and symbols conveyed visual reminders of the election, creating a political frenzy.

Campaign music, to cite another device, had never been more enthusiastic. Political music had been around at least since 1800, and songs were prevalent in Jackson's 1828 contest. In 1840, however, music was everywhere. At least twenty small music booklets, called songsters, containing words and indicating the popular tune to be used, appeared for mass distribution at rallies and festivals. The largest songster was *The Harrison Medal Minstrel*, published in Philadelphia with 192 pages and about 120 songs. A young politician of the period later remembered, "But the most distinguishing feature of the campaign was its music. The spirit of song was everywhere, and made the whole land vocal. The campaign was set to music . . . and poured

A BEAUTIFUL GOBLET OF
WHITE-HOUSE CHAMPAGNE

AN UGLY *MUG* OF
LOG-CABIN HARD CIDER

Van Buren pull card, 1840. *This novelty, made of light cardboard, shows Democratic incumbent Martin Van Buren as a grinning aristocratic dandy who sips White House champagne. When the tab is pulled on the card, his expression changes to repugnance as he tastes hard cider from a Harrison mug. Such caricatures implied that Van Buren's elitist, spendthrift habits were responsible for the country's economic depression. Devices such as this, decorated by engravings, appeared at least as early as 1837.*

itself forth in doggerel rhymes which seemed to be born of the hour, and exactly suited to the crisis." Some observers argued that Harrison was "sung into the White House." Perhaps they remembered some of the hundreds of Whig ditties of the season, such as this popular one:

What Has Caused This Great Commotion?
Tune, "Little Pig's Tail"

What has caused the great commotion, motion, motion,
　Our country through?
　It is the ball a rolling on, on.

Chorus
　For Tippecanoe and Tyler too – Tippecanoe and Tyler too,
　And with them we'll beat little Van, Van, Van,
　Van is a used up man,
　And with them we'll beat little Van.

Like the rushing of mighty waters, waters, waters,
　On it will go,
　And in its course will clear the way
　For Tippecanoe and Tyler Too – Tippecanoe and Tyler too.

See the loco standard tottering, tottering, tottering,
　Down it must go,
　And in its place we'll rear the flag
　Of Tippecanoe, *etc.*

Don't you hear from every quarter, quarter, quarter,
　Good news and true,
　That swift the ball is rolling on
　For Tippecanoe, *etc.*

The Buckeye boys turned out in thousands, thousands,
　Not long ago,
　And at Columbus set their seals,
　To Tippecanoe, *etc.*

And on for many more verses.

Harrison campaign devices extensively employed the imagery described earlier – celebration, humor, party loyalty and personal commitment, candidate and partisan imagery, attack, and merchandising. Countless banners, songs, and rallies embodied celebration. Those same devices, other objects, and satirical novelties conveyed humorous messages, as did the central images of cabins and cider, based on a Democratic joke that backfired. Thousands of ribbons and medalets worn or carried by Whig partisans signified their enthusiastic political commitments. The language of imagery emerged as one of the campaign's most enduring contributions to popular politics. Languages of attack figured prominently in Whig smears against the "Little Magician," Van Buren. Throughout the contest, converging in all its complexity and emotionalism, there was an atmosphere of salesmanship.

Amid all the celebrating, what became of the public issues of the campaign? Both Whigs and Democrats avoided the most threatening and divisive issues of the period – slavery, expansionism, and sectional antagonisms. But Whig propaganda and electioneering devices touched on several fundamental problems and Democratic weaknesses – depressed economic conditions, government mismanagement, and questionable executive conduct. On the positive side, the log-cabin circus united style and substance. The Whigs' enthusiasm and feel-good campaign sent a message to the electorate that there were alternatives to the financial depression. On one level the slogan "Harrison and reform" implied economic reconstruction and national optimism. At another level the sense of renewal was simulated dramatically and physically through processions, rallies, and political festivities.

Democrats were baffled, dazzled, and dispirited by the log-cabin and hard-cider campaign and the magnitude of the Whig organization. Again and again in writing to President Van Buren, Democratic partisans expressed skepticism and surprise at the high spirits and success of their opponents. They voiced contempt for such "silly devices" as log cabins and complained of the "zeal" and "fanaticism" of ciderite crusading. For months Democratic leaders could not believe that they were being outmaneuvered.

Another significant innovation appeared in 1840. Harrison was the first presidential aspirant to go out on the stump in his own behalf. At a time when candidates acted as though they had no desire for office, Harrison made twenty-three speeches, all in his home state of Ohio. These appearances were unprecedented efforts at displaying the candidate to the electorate, additional evidence of the democratization of American politics. The voters expressed curiosity and delight at seeing and hearing their hero in the flesh.

The Harrison campaign established a sequence of campaign events that served as rituals of American politics from the mid nineteenth century to the present. The struggle contributed as much to American popular culture as it did to the nation's politics. Historian Daniel Walker Howe comments perceptively: "Party politics was our first national sport, and the public played and watched the great game with enthusiasm. Torchlight parades, electioneering songs and slogans, debates, and speeches were popular entertainment." With few sources of entertainment and excitement available to a widely dispersed, heavily rural people, Americans in 1840 found satisfaction in the dramatic, crowd-pleasing experiences of the campaign. Politics filled a yearning for mass entertainment and spectacle later provided by spectator sports and show business. It was the best show in any town.

The massive Whig effort in 1840 brought out more voters by far than had cast ballots in any previous election. Voter turnout rose from 57.8 percent of adult white males in 1836 to 80.2 percent in 1840. Competition between the parties was closer and more intense than it had ever been. The Whigs' great commotion had done its job, attracting new voters to the polls by the thousands. Complaining about their opponents' successful appeal to the people, Democrats sneered with some justification that the people had been tricked.

The log-cabin campaign helped give the Whig party a distinct campaign style. While the pageantry, showmanship, riotous entertainment, mass participation, and exhilaration may have appeared somewhat coincidentally, they became deliberate elements of the Whig campaign style. Through the use of countless electioneering devices the Whigs became the party of positive symbolism, more than their Democratic opponents ever were. Aside from their successful application of the hurrah campaign style, the Whigs had good reasons for sticking with dramatic techniques. Whig candidates were often underdogs, usually running against Democratic incumbents. And Whigs tended to nominate leaders not closely identified with partisanship, such as old generals.

Historians have ridiculed the Whig circus in 1840, some simply calling it the "jolliest" among our presidential sweepstakes. A more severe view interprets the campaign as all form and no substance, contrived to disguise the true Whig purposes of capturing the government away from the people to enhance the manufacturing, banking, and commercial interests. Yet the hurrah devices of 1840 created extraordinary interest among the electorate. This, then, is the paradox of the wild antics of the Whigs: a demagogic, seemingly irrelevant political excitement was successful beyond comparison with any preceding presidential contest. In this election, even its severest critics admit, the Whig organization successfully outfought the Democratic party and popularized presidential electioneering.

Presidential campaigns after 1840, especially those of the Whigs, took the log-cabin campaign as a model. Having perfected the hurrah campaign, Whig partisans hoped to repeat their victory with Henry Clay as their nominee in 1844. As with Harrison, the Whigs organized a campaign of mass participation and saturation with political devices, expecting Clay to be paraded, sung, and celebrated into the presidency. Electioneering festivities began in Baltimore with a massive ratification convention, procession, and rally, replete with excitement and elaborate ceremonial atmosphere. The parade route was ornately decorated with flags, banners, draperies, and giant triumphal arches. One of these, 42 feet high at its center and 39 feet across, was inscribed with "Whig Principles," words such as "Union, Peace, Encouragement to Industry, Sound Currency," and rich festoons of flags, an eagle, colored draping cloth, surmounted by portraits of the immortal Clay with the legend "A Nation's Choice." Another arch spanned a different intersection, and other immense constructions of cloth were spaced along the parade route. To those complex decorations were added patriotic symbols and words, abundantly depicting Whig principles. No observer could doubt the party's devotion to "Domestic Industry," "Order," and Henry Clay. The abstract ideas were made as vivid and tangible as possible, spelling out the party's commitment to conservative, enthusiastic enterprise.

Henry Clay, 1844
(Nathaniel Currier, hand-colored lithograph, approx. 13 x 9.5 in.). The 1844 nomination was viewed as the righting of a wrong by those who believed the 1840 Whig nomination should have been Clay's.

Whig parade arch, 1844.
For a parade celebrating Henry Clay's nomination, Whig managers in Baltimore embellished the city center in magnificent style, erecting two large arches. This wood engraving shows the Grand Triumphal Arch, forty-two feet high and decorated with all manner of patriotic motifs and sculptures, which stood on Baltimore Street. Inscriptions on the base proclaim the Whig principles of union, peace, and distribution of the public lands.

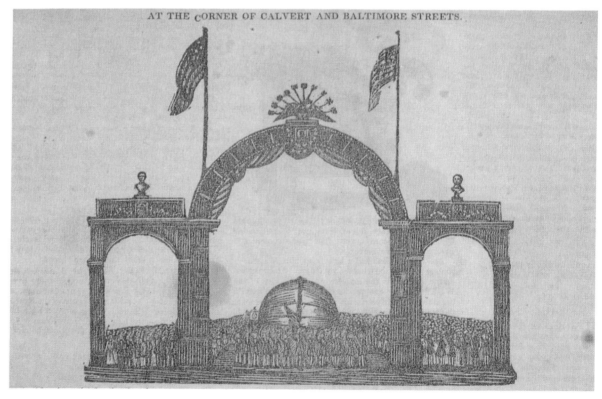

Specialized symbolic objects included a great ball similar to those rolled through the land in 1840. From Allegany County in western Maryland, the buckskin ball was adorned with long campaign messages and pushed by costumed mountain boys, "several hundred strong, all dressed in their hunting shirts." Unique among all the extravagant devices was a precious flag, the Star-Spangled Banner flown in 1814, which had inspired Francis Scott Key to write the verses that later became the national anthem. The family of Major Armistead, defender of Fort McHenry, displayed the massive flag. A richly designed prize banner for the state sending the largest proportional delegation to the convention went to "the gallant Whigs of Delaware, . . . every fifth Whig in the State being here, and from some townships every voter." Delegates and participants sported handsome ribbons and campaign medals to commemorate their attendance and reaffirm their partisan loyalties. As in 1840, campaign memorabilia linked individual participants with the collective performances.

An immense procession of Whigs marched through the city along the festive parade route toward a meeting ground on the Baltimore outskirts. Delegations from state after state marched in order, each with its banners, followed by city delegations in order by ward, with a banner for each. Several ward organizations had received their banners from ladies of the district. Baltimore's first ward also pulled a float, "a beautiful and gallant Ship – the Tariff," manned by a crew from the ward. The convention finally assembled, 65,000 strong, to hear addresses from distinguished Whigs, including Daniel Webster. A sympathetic writer reported: "No language can fully describe the excitement and grandeur of the occasion."

Later events in the Clay campaign repeated rituals and themes similar to the Baltimore ratification convention. Through the summer, Whigs in small towns as well as cities organized Clay clubs, held conventions, listened to speeches, and waved banners for Clay. In what was then the far West, in Illinois, the young Whig Abraham Lincoln was a leading activist for Clay. Lincoln spoke at Whig meetings at Peoria in June and at Vandalia in July. These rallies and meetings attracted crowds of thousands with parades and feasting. On returning to Springfield from one rally the delegation was met by a band and escorted through the streets to the "Clay cabin," where Lincoln spoke. Later that summer the Whigs of Springfield erected a liberty pole more than two hundred feet high. Attending many rallies during the summer, often taking a leading role, Lincoln behaved like a typical prominent loyal Whig of the 1840s.

Whigs and Democrats alike committed enormous resources to the campaign in 1844. *Niles' Register*, a leading journal of the period, reported that both parties were more involved in election enthusiasm during this year than they had been in 1840: "Standards are erected not only at places for holding elections – places of party meetings, and before public hotels, but hundreds are to be seen in every county at private residences towering far above the forest trees and decorated with the names, ensigns or flags of the partisans. Processions – standards – transparencies – bands of music – thundering artillery – burning tar barrels – and all the other paraphernalia of electioneering warfare are in active requisition." In this campaign the Whigs had a financial advantage, with more wealthy donors in their camp. They distributed more

Clay ribbon, 1844. *One of Henry Clay's nicknames was "Old Kentucky," but like W. H. Harrison, Clay was a rich aristocrat. Unlike Harrison, he never found an effective rustic image. The Whig party tried to give him a woodsy appeal by creating this raccoon caricature. On this ribbon, he triumphs over the Democratic rooster.*

electioneering devices than their rivals. About ninety different styles of Clay campaign ribbons survive from 1844, but there are only twenty-six for James K. Polk, the Democrat.

Running against a divided Democratic party and campaigning in the style shown to be successful in 1840, Clay and the Whigs were confident of victory. Although he was too well known to pose as a rustic farmer, Clay needed to cultivate an image as attractive to plain rural farmers as the log cabin had been four years before. Thus on some devices he was pictured as "The Farmer of Ashland," a simple plowman, while other items featured Clay's rustic symbol the raccoon, taking off on the slogan "that same old coon." All sorts of campaign objects illustrated the Whigs' contradictory images, appealing to wealth and conservative order on one hand and to simple farmers and plain people on the other. But Clay never gained the common touch that Harrison had in 1840.

In 1844 issues overwhelmed imagery. During the campaign Clay faced a serious problem, the Texas annexation issue. If he were known to be against annexation he would lose southern votes, but if he favored expansion he might repel northerners opposed to the addition of another slave state to the Union. So he tried to straddle the issue, writing several contradictory letters for and against Texas. Behind the Texas issue lay a more dangerous question, slavery. For his opponent, James K. Polk, there was no doubt about Texas. Polk was for immediate annexation and was certain to capture the majority of southern electoral votes. Despite his image-making, Clay's ambiguity about Texas cost him the presidency when New York went for Polk by more than five thousand votes. The contest illustrated the close competition between parties; Polk led Clay in the popular vote by only 1.4 percentage points.

Polk banner, 1844. *The Democratic candidates in 1844, James K. Polk and George M. Dallas, were represented by many fewer campaign objects than the Whigs Clay and Frelinghuysen. This cotton flag banner (51 x 29 in.) is similar to Clay's banners except that it includes an extra star, outside the blue field, symbolizing Texas. Polk, an ardent expansionist, campaigned for the admission of Texas to the Union.*

Taylor stove, 1848. *This richly ornamented parlor stove advertised the Whig candidate Zachary Taylor. Naming the sites of his victories in the War with Mexico, it reminded the* *voters of his military leadership only a few years earlier. Similar stoves were made to represent Taylor's opponent, Lewis Cass.*

The Bay and Harbor of New York, 1855 *(Samuel B. Waugh). Between 1845 and 1889, three million Irish immigrants arrived in the United States; this painting shows a stream of immigrants disembarking at the Battery in New York. About half were refugees from the Great Famine, bringing no money and few industrial skills to their new home. Large numbers of them congregated in the cities of the Northeast and voted for the Democratic party.*

The campaigns of 1848 and 1852 saw renewed use of party rallies, special political newspapers, and other accepted techniques adapted from the hurrah campaign style. But apparently fewer examples of political devices were made for these contests than for the elections of 1840 and 1844.

In 1848 the Whigs nominated a hero of the War with Mexico, General Zachary Taylor, Old Rough and Ready, with the idea of repeating General Harrison's success in 1840. The choice of Taylor was intended to rise above partisanship and factionalism, to present another general who had few partisan ties. Indeed, in Taylor's case, there was little evidence even of partisan commitment. He had never voted and had trouble deciding whether he was a Whig or a Democrat. Finally, in published letters, he avowed himself "a Whig but not an ultra Whig." Although a slaveholder and resident of Louisiana, and identified with the South, he straddled sectional issues adroitly at a time of growing animosity between North and South.

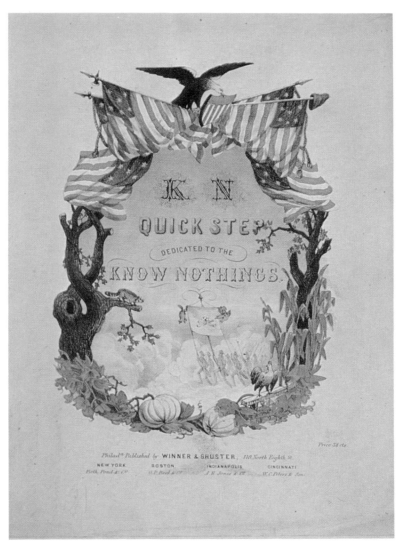

Know-Nothing sheet music, 1854. *One of the few surviving political devices relating to the Know-Nothings is this sheet music for the "K. N. Quick Step." The Know-Nothing movement, sometimes called the American party or the Native American party, opposed immigrant voting during the political tumult of the 1850s.*

Opponents of the Whigs were divided. Lewis Cass, the Democratic nominee, former governor of Michigan Territory, prided himself on many years of service to the Democratic party. His support of "popular sovereignty" was sympathetic to slavery in the territories, making him attractive to southern slaveholders. For many northerners that view was a drawback. Opponents of slavery expansion had another option because a former Democratic president, Martin Van Buren, offered himself as candidate of the Free Soil party. That gave the advantage to the hero, General Taylor.

As the contest evolved, paraders marched, banners flew, songs rang out amid the usual festive atmosphere. Responding to the influx of German immigrants in the 1840s, many campaign publications appeared in German, praising the various candidates. The Whigs shouted for old Zach, the military hero, making great noises in the general's behalf, and the hero himself, although politically innocent, conducted himself with discretion. Campaign objects and novelties for this contest included at least one substantial new artifact: identical campaign stoves bearing likenesses of Taylor or Cass.

The next presidential contest, that of 1852, found both the Democratic and Whig parties severely divided. The principal contenders were known as "doughfaces," northern men with southern principles. In making nominations, both parties struggled mightily at their national conventions, the Democrats agreeing on dark horse Franklin Pierce after 49 ballots, and the Whigs choosing General Winfield Scott after 52 long ballots. Despite his mediocre performance, Pierce won the election handily. The divided, dispirited Whigs were too weak ever again to contest a presidential election. Two new parties arose on the ruins of the Whigs, the nativist Know-Nothing party, which survived only a few years, and a new Republican party, which quickly replaced the old Whig organization as the Democrats' chief opposition.

A Republican Revival

Campaigning in the late 1850s gained renewed vigor and enthusiasm from the partisan realignments. After its formation in 1854, the new Republican party nominated its first candidate for the election of 1856. Rejecting several former Whigs and Democrats, the Republicans chose the explorer John Charles Frémont, a young, romantic, nonpolitical figure who might, like old General Harrison, appeal to the widest range of voters.

As inheritors of the hurrah tradition of the Whigs, the Republicans far outdid the Democrats and the Know-Nothings in their campaign endeavors. The Republicans promoted their candidate as an authentic hero and created symbols representing his western exploits. Remembering the festivities of 1840, Republicans revived the log-cabin symbol to go with their attractive candidate. For example, in the college town of Hanover, New Hampshire, the Frémont Club erected a 130-foot-high mast with a "Rocky Mountain cabin" constructed partway to the top. Elsewhere party cabins were erected, and some political clubs took the name "Rocky Mountain Club," to symbolize their hero candidate.

Mass meetings occurred on a scale reminiscent of the 1840 election. In Indianapolis a monster rally was described as the largest meeting ever held west of Ohio, and a county convention in New Jersey attracted 15,000 participants. The parades seemed endless. Near the campaign's end a grand rally and Frémont torchlight parade in Boston was made up of 240 sections. Participants carried flags, lanterns, torches, and transparencies, and they pulled floats, including one holding a California delegation that enacted life on the frontier. Often the parades included a wagonload of thirty-one young women dressed in white, representing the states, and one additional woman clothed in mourning to represent the territory of Kansas, where the dispute over slavery centered. Reports of a mass rally in Pittsburgh described a parade seven to nine miles long. The various trades – blacksmiths, printers, and others – marched together carrying banners and symbols of their vocations. Banners and flags were evident everywhere; in Albany,

PRIZE BANNER
OBTAINED BY THE REPUBLICANS OF THE TOWNSHIP OF PEQUANNOC,
Sept 18th
1856.

FOR PRESIDENT
JOHN C. FREMONT,
FOR VICE PRESIDENT
WILLIAM L. DAYTON,

OUR STANDARD BEARER THEN,
THE BRAVE PATH FINDER BE!
FREE SPEECH, FREE PRESS, FREE SOIL,
FREE MEN,
FREMONT AND VICTORY.

E. Krautch, Pnt.
Morristown

Frémont banner, 1856. *In its first presidential contest in 1856, the new Republican party carried on some traditions of its predecessors, the Whigs, including the awarding of banners to local political clubs. At a mass meeting in Morristown, New Jersey, this prize banner was won by Republicans from the rural township of Pequannoc, which sent 53 percent of their voters to the rally.*

New York, the Young Frémonters hung a thirty-by-eighty-foot banner, called the largest in the nation. At a Deerfield, Massachusetts, rally a reporter stated: "Flags were streaming, and banners bearing significant and pertinent mottoes, were planted in every quarter."

Inheriting much of the old Whig organization, the Republicans apparently improved on the Whig legacy. Party leaders urged that every village and every township organize a Frémont club with central union clubs in each county. Clubs had many duties, but they were challenged to put the success of national and congressional tickets above local issues and quarrels. Evidence from New York City indicates the existence of Frémont clubs in each of the city's wards, which met frequently and had active programs. Even more than the Whigs, Republicans appealed for women's support in promoting their candidate. John C. Frémont's wife, Jessie Benton Frémont, was something of a romantic celebrity in her own right, and Republicans made use of her name and image. Party rallies often featured a "Jessie pic-nic" for women and made a place for women as spectators.

The Republican struggle took on some of the trappings of a religious revival. In rural New York a campaign rouser and preacher named Van Wagoner, the "Poughkeepsie blacksmith," toured northern counties with a tent for revival-style tent meetings, holding one-day or two-day political rallies in important towns. Accompanying the blacksmith was the Sherwood family glee club, three brothers who sang campaign songs between Van Wagoner's speeches. So the campaign went, sometimes more like a festival of religion or entertainment than a political movement. In response to this outpouring of high spirits for Frémont, the Democrats ran a veteran politician of the old school, James Buchanan, in a conventional campaign.

In that emotional atmosphere occurred one of the most memorable of all American political episodes, the Lincoln-Douglas debates of 1858. In an election for the Illinois state legislature, a nationally known Democratic senator, Stephen A. Douglas, debated with a little-known Republican rival, Abraham Lincoln. Out of this dusty campaign, with its typical country rallies and speechifying, came one of the legendary confrontations in American history. Seeking to persuade Illinois voters to elect state representatives who would choose Douglas or Lincoln as U.S. senator, the candidates debated the issues of slavery and its expansion. Although not the first time that leading candidates engaged in debate, the Lincoln-Douglas rivalry carried the debate process to a new intellectual and political level.

By 1858 the political parties had learned how to mobilize great numbers of people, and the seven Lincoln-Douglas debates, scattered around the state in rural county seats, attracted huge and lively crowds. An eyewitness described the first debate: "The next stage brought us to Ottawa. . . . Here the crowd was enormous. Crowds were pouring into town from sunrise till noon in all sorts of conveyances, teams, railroad trains, canal boats, cavalcades, and processions on foot, with banners and inscriptions. . . . The town was covered with bunting, and bands of music were tooting around every corner, drowned now and then by the roar of cannon."

Although Lincoln lost his bid for the Senate, he impressed the voters of Illinois and made himself known across the nation. Events developed quickly after the Lincoln-Douglas contest.

Senator Stephen A. Douglas, c. 1859
(James Earle McClees and Julian Vannerson, photograph, salt print, 7.25 x 5.25 in.).

Two years afterward, on the eve of the 1860 presidential campaign, the nation was poised for a grave, contentious electoral struggle. After a decade of political turmoil, change and defiance were in the air. But, although under intense pressure, the competitive two-party system had been confirmed and tested by experience.

By the late 1850s campaign rituals, like the two-party system, were in place and accepted by most contenders for the presidency. The voting public, by all evidence, had grown to expect a dramatic show. Custom, however, dictated that presidential candidates maintain the fiction of staying aloof from the campaign. Taking little active part in electioneering, candidates typically behaved as though the office should seek the man, not vice versa. Those practices and attendant objects would shortly be tested as never before. The multitudes had become thoroughly engaged in the political drama. As historian Roy F. Nichols has observed about the 1850s, the constant occurrence of political campaigning was almost hazardous: "The incessant procession of artificially ordered electoral conflicts . . . had become dangerous. The campaigns of that critical decade focused public attention too sharply upon conflicting attitudes. . . . Election campaigns thus became the catalytic agents which fatally hastened the processes that brought on secession and civil war." Among the elements of politics that aroused an excited electorate were the myriad campaign objects circulating during every presidential contest.

Partisan Campaigning, 1860–1896

Some elections stand out among America's presidential encounters. Certainly the contest of 1860 was one of the most extraordinary. It had drama, spectacle, campaign innovations, a host of unexpected events and results, and ultimately, it produced tragedy. Beginning with a disastrous split between northern and southern Democrats at the party's national convention, the campaign featured a four-way struggle in which the Republican, Abraham Lincoln, received essentially no southern support. Three other candidates, Stephen A. Douglas of the national Democrats, John C. Breckinridge of the southern Democrats, and John Bell representing the Constitutional Union party, also ran. Under those conditions of intense political instability, the 1860 campaign set the stage for a new era of lively two-party competition and vigorous partisanship. Near the year's end, after Lincoln's election, the state of South Carolina withdrew from the Union, beginning a process that led to the Civil War.

The Wide-Awake Campaign Armies

The Republican campaign, in keeping with other momentous events of the year, made significant departures from earlier contests. "The greatest feature of the campaign," according to the *New York Herald*, was the Wide-Awake movement, a national organization of local political marching clubs enrolling hundreds of thousands of members. With the appearance of this immense political force, hurrah-style campaigning entered a more disciplined stage of partisan activity.

The Wide-Awakes composed a military-style political group. Most historians trace the movement's origins to Hartford, Connecticut, where a club appeared early in 1860 to escort and protect a controversial Republican antislavery speaker from Kentucky, Cassius M. Clay. Its armylike stance may have arisen from a desire to appear militant in the face of fierce and growing hostility to "black Republicans," so-called because of their opposition to slavery. The Hartford club typified the Wide-Awakes, as one of its founders remembered: "The enthusiasm . . . was such that it was at once decided that we form a club, appointing officers, procuring new torches, enamel cloth capes, glazed caps, and be ready for the next meeting. It was suggested that we have a name for our club, . . . as the papers said that Hartford was wide awake, we adopt the name 'Hartford Wide Awakes,' which was at once adopted." Months before his presidential nomination, Abraham Lincoln spoke at Hartford and received an escort from the original Wide-Awake club.

Before the summer of 1860 ended, Wide-Awake Republican clubs had been formed in cities and towns throughout northern states, with approximately 400,000 young party loyalists as members. Local clubs developed elaborate parade styles, executing complex maneuvers and following highly structured marching orders. The effect of a nighttime parade – thousands of torches lighted, row after row of uniformed marching men, with a background of fireworks – was both inspiring and ominous. For although they were engaged only in political warfare, the Wide-Awakes had the appearance of an army.

Overleaf:
Republican banner, 1860. *As an image of power, the eagle is used to provoke emotional bonds between leaders – or would-be leaders – and their publics.*

Wide-Awake clubs immediately stimulated their own varied material culture. Torchlights, although common in earlier campaigns, defined the Wide-Awakes. Never had campaign torches been so expressive. Rifle torches were noteworthy in reinforcing the military bearing and appearance of many Wide-Awake clubs. As Herbert R. Collins has shown, campaign torches became commercially successful in 1860, with several different types patented and thousands marketed. Others were apparently homemade for individual use in parades. One expressive torchlight, attributed to the 1860 contest, was beautifully shaped to resemble an eagle. Parade

Wide-Awake parade, 1860. *The Wide-Awakes, pictured here in a New York parade, first marched for Abraham Lincoln and attracted huge numbers of people. Their drill routines and torches made in the shape of rifles foreshadowed an event that was soon to follow the election – the Civil War – and a martial style that would dominate campaigns for decades to come.*

Wide-Awake marcher, 1860. *The Wide-Awakes generated a brisk retail trade in parade regalia. Marchers wore capes to protect their club uniforms and bodies from hot torch oil, and this costume became the un-official uniform for the Lincoln faithful.*

Republican banner, 1860. *The Ladies of Downers' Grove, a small town west of Chicago, presented this banner to a Republican marching club called the Plow Boys. It was painted on silk, probably by a professional artist.*

Its farm images reflect the ideology of "Free soil, free labor, and free men."

transparencies, consisting of wooden frames covered by cloth and lighted from within, carried appealing slogans, symbols, and messages visible in night marches. Symbolic lanterns also served Wide-Awakes and their opponents.

Besides carrying illuminated devices, Wide-Awake club members wore uniforms of several types. Almost always topped off by oilcloth capes designed to shed hot torch oil, uniforms were more or less elaborate matching outfits, including shirts, trousers, and caps or helmets. The garments added drama and precision to the Wide-Awakes' appearance, enhancing the warlike maneuvers of Lincoln's "troops." But festivity, not combat, was one of the main qualities of the campaign, promoted by the colorful painted and printed Lincoln banners. Although most authentic Lincoln banners have disappeared, some survive in institutional and private collections. Expressive banners came from small towns and rural areas as well as cities. One example, from Downer's Grove, Illinois, depicts a farmer or plowboy prepared to campaign for Lincoln. A brightly decorated banner from Maine, the home of Lincoln's running mate, Hannibal Hamlin, carries a legend promising triumphant success.

From Maine to Illinois, Wide-Awake clubs demonstrated their high spirits. At Springfield, Massachusetts, for example, a rally ratifying Lincoln's nomination brought out enthusiastic participants and a band, escorting Republican speakers to their meeting with torchlights and a "procession of the Wide Awakes which excited great attention through its course." As in the log-cabin raisings of 1840, Wide-Awake participation helped to symbolize partisan loyalty and created a crowd-pleasing spectacle. Formation of a young women's Wide-Awake club was reported in upstate New York, "comprising the 'beauty and fashion' of some of the first families. . . . The uniform worn is a drab cambric dress, a cape of the same material, and a striped apron of red, white and blue, each color bearing a single letter of the word 'Abe.'"

No part of the country organized more enthusiastic Wide-Awake celebrations than Lincoln's home state, Illinois. An immense gathering in Chicago boasted spectacular displays of paraders, illuminations, and fireworks. Trainloads of delegates assembled from across the state to hear Republican speakers and honor their nominee. One account reported: "The Wide-Awake torch-light procession is undoubtedly the largest and most imposing thing of the kind ever witnessed in Chicago. Unprejudiced spectators estimate the number at 10,000. Throughout the whole length of the procession were scattered portraits of ABRAHAM LINCOLN. Banners and transparencies bearing Republican mottoes, and pictures of rail splitters, were also plentifully distributed. Forty-three bands of music were also in the procession." Even more impressive than the big-city rallies were partisan demonstrations staged in downstate Illinois. At Jacksonville, a county seat of about 5,500 people, an all-day rally in September attracted an estimated ten thousand participants, thought to be the largest political crowd ever assembled there. An evening torchlight parade, including "Wide Awakes . . . from almost every precinct in the county," numbered nearly two thousand torchbearers. Farther north, in the county seat of

Wide-Awake parade, 1860. *The first Wide-Awake club was organized in Hartford, Connecticut. Lore has it that the name came from a newspaper line,* *"Hartford is wide awake for the Republicans." The eye painted on the lantern suggests the organization's alertness to the dangers to the Union.*

John Bell lantern, 1860. *John Bell, a southern Whig, was the candidate of the Constitutional-Union party in 1860. He was pro slavery but also pro Union. The lantern is from Salem,* *Massachusetts, but that does not mean that Salem was a hotbed of support for Bell. It does serve as a reminder that we cannot generalize about politics from the mere survival of artifacts.*

Princeton, a day-long Republican rally, described as "the largest and most imposing political meeting ever held" there, attracted club members from throughout the county for "a grand Wide-Awake display" in the evening.

In October the New York City Wide-Awakes invited clubs from far and near to join in a great torchlight parade. Hoping for twenty thousand or more torchbearers, the organizers were disappointed when just over twelve thousand appeared. Nevertheless, the effect of the marching throng and their flaming, smoky torches, captured in *Harper's Weekly* and *Leslie's* engravings, was impressive. Defending the Wide-Awakes from critics, the *New York Times* praised the marchers for their good order and peaceful, not military, purposes. Yet in the volatile atmosphere of 1860, thoughtful observers might have been uneasy. Besides the Wide-Awakes there were other Lincoln marching groups known as Rail-Splitters or Rail-Maulers. Lincoln's rival candidates had their own marching groups – Little Giants, Little Dougs, Ever Readys for Douglas; Bell Ringers, Union Sentinels, Minute Men, and others for Bell and Edward Everett on the Constitutional Union ticket.

The Republican Wide-Awakes perfected a participatory model of campaigning described by historian Richard Jensen as the army-style campaign. Characterized by strong partisan organization and mass mobilization of voters in parades, army-style campaigning in Jensen's view had become the predominant campaign type earlier in the nineteenth century. But from 1860 on, the army style reached the height of its effectiveness and influence.

The Wide-Awake movement revived a complex series of campaign languages similar to those of the great 1840 log-cabin and hard-cider contest. The language of celebration was especially evident in the long parades with thousands of marchers carrying brilliantly lighted torches and transparencies, and the music and festivities that accompanied the paraders. The language of loyalty and commitment was repeated and reinforced by Wide-Awakes regaled in partisan uniforms, bearing party banners, wearing badges and other devices of personal commitment. Republican parades revived the imagery associated with Whig log cabins and other rustic symbols of the common people, celebrating Abraham Lincoln's simple origins and reviving the mythic traditions of 1840. In subtle and not-so-subtle ways, the Wide-Awakes conveyed a language of attack, of an army on the march, ready to fight for its party and candidate. And as they had in 1840, the languages of campaign devices converged in the drive to promote and sell the Republican candidate.

"Abraham Lincoln the Rail Candidate for President in 1860" – this slogan appeared with two ancient wooden fence rails carried into the Illinois State Republican Convention in May 1860. The relics were described as being from a group "made by Abraham Lincoln and John Hanks . . . in the year 1830." After their appearance and Lincoln's nomination as an Illinois favorite son, the convention crowd arose as one man in approval of the Rail Candidate: "The cheering was like the roar of the sea." From those simple objects and their associated pun began one of the nineteenth century's great campaign images: Abraham Lincoln, the Prince of Rails. Thus

Lincoln ribbon, 1860.

This primitive ribbon is hand-made of leather. It is the only one known to exist today. Lincoln liked the photograph glued to this ribbon and often signed prints of himself for admirers.

Lincoln axe, 1860.

One of Abraham Lincoln's most popular images was that of rail-splitter, and thousands of rails were distributed during the campaign, each one allegedly split by the candidate. This wooden axe was meant to be carried in parades; besides showing enthusiasm for Lincoln and his humble beginnings, it symbolizes the notion that industry and sobriety would allow humble men to rise on the social ladder.

was campaign imagery transformed from the semiregal splendor of Washington to the back-woods simplicity of farmer Lincoln.

By 1860 candidate images were accepted as natural ingredients of presidential electioneer-ing. Identities adopted by presidential contenders reflected the hopes and values of many Americans in the nineteenth century. Political issues sometimes influenced image campaigning, but often they were subordinated to the appeal of personalities or good feelings about candi-dates. Image campaigning became increasingly effective because of new technical means for reproducing and distributing visual information. Diverse campaign objects and printed items, mass-produced and broadly distributed in the Civil War and postwar era, carried political im-agery throughout the North. Image campaigning, like other promotional techniques, flourished especially among Republicans.

After Lincoln's presidential nomination, celebrations of his homespun virtues multiplied. A native of frontier Kentucky and son of early Illinois, he was presented to the voting public as Honest Abe, man of the people and frontiersman. The rail-splitter image gave Lincoln a vivid campaign identity, repeating the simple yet powerful appeal of the log cabin twenty years ear-lier. Lincoln's rustic common-man image matched Republican party appeals to free labor, in behalf of free men working their own land. Posters, parade devices, cartoons, and other 1860 campaign objects reinforced the imagery.

Important ingredients of the Lincoln contest were campaign portraits. Not as well known as some other Republicans, Lincoln needed name recognition, and the public wished to know what he looked like. Filling those needs, popular prints and photographs of Lincoln were nationally distributed. Publishers like Currier and Ives advertised prints of Lincoln at twenty cents apiece, six for a dollar. Printed images of Lincoln's plain but dignified facial features, coupled with stories of his rise from humble beginnings, gained him national recognition and respect-ability.

Besides their innovations in the Lincoln campaign, Republicans utilized the usual parapher-nalia of presidential campaigning. Liberty poles more than one hundred feet high were raised in many towns. In an Illinois village a Lincoln banner more than eighty feet across could be seen. In many places Republicans built rustic and folksy wigwams as local party headquarters, similar to Whig log cabins in 1840. Rallies took place everywhere, with long processions passing through cities and countryside. In Lincoln's hometown of Springfield a procession culminating in a rally at the fairgrounds attracted 75,000 people.

During the campaign Lincoln avoided any personal involvement in the contest, remaining at home in Springfield and refusing almost every plea to comment on issues or personalities. Fol-lowing the tradition of "mute" candidates, it was, he declared, "imprudent, and contrary to . . . reasonable expectation" that he should take a position on issues during the campaign. Of Lin-coln's three rivals, John C. Breckinridge and John Bell took the established candidate's position and remained silent. Stephen Douglas Democrats held rallies and parades, but their efforts lacked the intensity and enthusiasm of Lincoln's partisans. In a forlorn effort to unite behind Douglas, New York Democrats staged a mammoth "fusion" parade not long before the election. The party of Jackson seemed incompetent and obsolete.

Douglas himself, fearing the possibilities of southern secession, felt compelled to conduct an unprecedented personal tour. Traveling through the states, speaking endlessly for the Union, he reassured the South that the region had little to fear from Lincoln, if he should be elected. As the campaign progressed, evidence mounted that Douglas would lose, and the Democratic candidate returned South, hoping to prevent catastrophe. Exhausted from his efforts, physically sick, certain of failure, he carried his message to the slave states. On the night before his defeat in the election, he was defending the Union in Mobile, Alabama.

The March to the Polls

The years after the Civil War witnessed another revival of the two-party system much as we know it today, with major competitive parties, the Democrats and Republicans, in the field. The period also saw the perfection of army-style parades modeled on the Wide-Awakes, serving as vital symbols of loyal enthusiasm and vehicles for political expression. With thousands of Civil War veterans available as participants, it is little wonder that parades, especially torchlight parades, became memorable political events of the postwar years.

Given the Republican claim to be the party of the Union and the only truly patriotic political body, many Union veterans understandably joined with that party. In countless communities around the nation, veteran Boys in Blue marched by the thousands every four years in behalf of Republican candidates. At Indianapolis in 1868 a reporter described participants that included "the Grant Guards, cavalry and infantry, the Grant Tanners and Fighting Boys in Blue, uniformed and bearing banners and emblems." Another account expressed the "greatest enthusiasm" for more than eight hundred German veterans who paraded in New York City in 1868, "uniformed in oil skin caps and cloaks like the Wide Awakes of old," carrying lanterns, Civil War battle flags, and transparencies. One transparency bore the message: "The cartridge box has saved, the ballot box will save."

The Republican party set out on a southern strategy, hoping to win regional support in the South. In Richmond, Virginia, partisan marchers carried banners with messages such as "Grant and Peace, or Blair and War," "Let Us Have Peace," "We Are Coming, Johnny Reb," and "Malice Towards None," articulating the party's pacific but firm intentions. Images of Grant and Lincoln, faces by then familiar to nearly all the people, reassured southerners that they could trust in leadership that had won the war.

Republicans also made explicit appeals to newly enfranchised black voters, mostly former slaves in the southern states. Such cultivation of the new voters showed up in a startling innovation, the employment of black people as marchers in Republican campaign parades. In Atlanta, Georgia, a Grant procession included seven hundred black marchers, making the point that Republicans were the party of civil rights. Prominent features of an 1868 Grant ratification parade in Virginia were "various colored societies and quasi-military organizations, in regalia or uniform" with "flashing swords and sabers in the hands of colored marshalls and military." A wagon carried "a loom, a plow, an anvil and several other implements of industry," explicitly portraying Republican free-labor ideology. Although temporary, the involvement of black people in campaigning was a radical and provocative departure from southern traditions. It would end after the conclusion of Reconstruction with the enforcement of Jim Crow laws and the disenfranchisement of African Americans.

Military and ideological messages were prominent in later Republican campaigns, emphasizing the political influence of military reconstruction. A demonstration in 1872 at Raleigh, North Carolina, included "2,000 Republicans in a torch-light procession" carrying banners with legends such as: "Grant and Wilson," "Let Us Fill the Bloody Chasm," "Equal Right to All," "Let Us Have Peace," "No Intimidation," "Charity for All, Malice Toward None." At a grand ratification meeting in Greensboro, "Cheer after cheer and wild huzzahs filled the air. Tarbarrels, pine torches and rockets furnished such an illumination as has never been seen in the city of Greensboro before." Besides carrying their masses of torchlights, Republican paraders wore brightly colored uniforms or regalia depicting their unity and loyalty to the Union cause. Salutes of gunfire, bonfires, and fireworks reminded voters of the war and the Republican defeat of the rebels. They appealed to former slaves who could vote because of the war.

Similar patterns of Republican parading persisted in later campaigns. In New York City in 1876 grand torchlight processions of Boys in Blue marched frequently. On one occasion, "The band struck up a national air and the procession started up 5th Avenue presenting a picturesque appearance in their blue capes, red collars and regulation army caps with blue tops and red bands while the column was lighted on its march by torch bearers and Chinese lanterns." Again and again, parades reminded spectators of the recent war. Blue uniforms resembled the colors worn by members of the Union army, cannon fire and rockets simulated a battlefield atmosphere, and messages on banners revived wartime attitudes and prejudices.

Democrats were at a disadvantage in the business of parading because of their association with the South during the Civil War. They could not readily take advantage of the Boys in Blue and other war-related symbolism. Nevertheless members of the Democratic party staged many political parades and demonstrations during the postwar years. In 1868 Democrats for Seymour and Blair organized political clubs and carried torchlights for their candidates. Some southern meetings even included partisan clubs with black members. Seymour and Blair meetings in Brooklyn included colorful "banners, transparencies and lanterns and the usual music," along with the firing of a "beautiful brass cannon."

Democrats paraded without much enthusiasm for Horace Greeley in 1872 and again for Samuel J. Tilden in 1876. They demonstrated much more zeal during the successful contest of

"The First Vote," 1867.
This print from Harper's Weekly *pictures a southern polling place during the state elections of 1867. Many southern whites were so outraged by the prospect of former slaves voting that they joined the Ku Klux Klan and other organizations to terrorize the new voters.*

Democratic parade, 1868.
This magazine illustration shows a New York parade for Democratic candidate Horatio Seymour, whose platform called for lower taxes and more greenback money. The lanterns were popular in campaigns and marches between 1860 and 1890.

Grover Cleveland in 1884. When Cleveland returned home to Buffalo late in the campaign he was greeted with an immense parade: "All the principal streets of the city were decorated with flags, transparencies, and pictures of the Governor. Chinese lanterns were burning all over the front of many buildings and upon ropes stretched from one building to another across the streets. The scene was such as had never been witnessed before in Buffalo."

The 1880s saw increases in the business of marketing mass-produced campaign devices for paraders, including uniforms, badges, flags, bandannas, posters, and paper devices. Firms such as the Unexcelled Fireworks Company, Eagle Fireworks, A. G. Spalding and Brothers, and many others manufactured and sold great varieties of apparatus intended for use in political campaigns. Catalogs issued by campaign equipment dealers illustrated these objects, showing similar or identical items made to represent opposing candidates. An advertising circular of 1880 promoted "Badges! Beautiful Campaign Badges of the Democratic and Republican Presidential Candidates . . . [with] life-like photographs of the candidates."

In 1884 a publisher announced, "Something Everybody Will Buy," elaborate campaign portraits, identical for both parties except for the faces, for door-to-door agents: "Of course, where the politics of a family are known, an agent should show only the Republican picture to Repub-

Harrison-Morton bandanna, 1888. *The great era of bandannas was the 1880s. This one presents the Republican party's campaign issues: high tariffs to protect American industry, and civil-service reform. It is unusual because it has no candidate portraits, only issues.*

licans and the Democratic picture to Democrats. Every householder will want this magnificent souvenir of the Presidential Campaign, but of course he will want the one that suits his political views, hence the advantage to agents of having two different editions for sale." A Chicago firm announced a silk bandanna "appropriate for either Republicans or Democrats" and described a marching-club badge: "It can be used by either Democrats or Republicans and will be equally popular with each." Every four years campaign paraphernalia became objects of vigorous commerce.

Among the period's favorite mass-produced campaign devices were printed cotton bandannas. Several manufacturers copyrighted textile designs for Republicans Garfield and Arthur and for the Democratic candidates, Hancock and English, in 1880. Again in 1884 nearly identical bandannas were worn or carried for both Republicans and Democrats. More varied partisan textiles than ever appeared in 1888, with increasingly elaborate designs, patriotic symbolism, and partisan messages. Republican bandannas were among the few campaign items to mention or depict a campaign issue, the tariff, with the slogan "Protection to Home Industries." Among Democrats, the use of these devices gained credibility from their association with vice presidential candidate Allen G. Thurman, a bandanna carrier, known as the "Knight of the Red Bandanna." Mass-produced by the thousands, these items were widely advertised in popular colors such as "Turkey red."

The mass demonstrations and their associated political items were important ingredients of a style of politics that had its heyday in the late nineteenth century. As Richard Jensen has written:

> The parties were army-like organizations, tightly knit, disciplined, united. All the voters, save for a few stragglers and mercenaries, belonged to one or the other army, and the challenge of the campaign was the mobilization of the full party strength at the polls on election day. To heighten the morale of the troops, the generals employed brass-band parades, with banners, badges, torches and uniforms. Chanting sloganized battle cries, waving placards and flags, the rank and file marched for hours before smiling, waving politicians, who invariably thought the men would appreciate a two-hour speech.

Parades and rallies of this sort contributed to incredibly high turnouts of eligible voters in presidential elections. In some areas 80 to 90 percent of the qualified electorate voted for president. Dramatic public events displayed the strong party loyalties in this period. People affiliated with one of the two major parties early in life and maintained their loyalties during their lifetimes.

Images Heroic and Silly

The language of imagery in campaign devices was widespread from the late 1860s to the 1890s, ranging from quite exalted candidate images to ridiculous depictions of competitors for president. Quasi-military parades emphasized a leading image of post–Civil War candidates, that of the war hero. The Republican nominee in 1868 and 1872, General Ulysses S. Grant, embodied both heroic and democratic virtues. As the chief Union general, Grant immediately took on a heroic character, gaining immense stature and popularity as the commander who won the recent war. Simultaneously, the people admired Grant as a magnanimous victor, the successful leader of vast armies whose principal slogan for the election of 1868 was "Let Us Have Peace."

Grant's image, like Lincoln's, offered a classic affirmation of the American belief in success. The great general was renowned as a simple man who had risen from obscurity to high responsibility and prestige through the democratic rags-to-riches process. His achievements, demon-

Grant and His Generals, 1865
(Ole Peter Hansen Balling, oil on canvas, 120 x 192 in.). Ulysses Grant is the hatless rider in the center.

strated in war, were proof that ordinary talents could triumph over the skills of the aristocratic southern generals who opposed him. Campaign devices exploited the candidate's heroic and democratic image, emphasizing General Grant as a successful hero and a man of peace.

After Grant, a series of Republican nominees – Rutherford B. Hayes, James A. Garfield, Benjamin Harrison, and William McKinley – ran on their war records. Heroic images or simply service to the Union were ascribed to these rather bland middle-American gentlemen while every four years the Republican party "waved the bloody shirt" and reminded voters of Union blood shed by southern rebels and traitors. The party mobilized its dwindling legions of Boys in Blue to parade through cities and towns, recalling the receding Republican war in defense of the Union. Meanwhile, in Washington and in many state capitals, "the great barbecue" of business and political corruption took place.

Beginning in the 1870s, Republican leaders replaced the worn-out bloody shirt with a new partisan image, protection. The party inherited devotion to protective tariffs from the old Whigs and Henry Clay's American System. Originating as an issue by which Republicans distinguished themselves from Democrats, the protective tariff grew into a defining image of partisanship in the 1880s. Devotion to protection was the life of the party for Republicans, above and beyond candidate identities.

The effects of a Tariff exclusively for Revenue as laid down in the Democratic Platform and which the Democratic Congressmen tried to enact last winter at Washington.

The effects of Protection to American Industries as guaranteed by the Republican Party and Platform.

Democratic Free Trade Means low wages, children in rags and ignorance

If you are satisfied with this picture vote for Cleveland and Hendricks.

Republican Protection Means good wages, happy homes and education for your children

If you prefer this picture vote for Blaine and Logan.

Republican poster, 1884. *The Republicans argued that high tariffs were in the interest of work-ingmen because they kept the products of cheap foreign labor out of the United States. This is an endur-ing theme in American politics, today aimed at products from Japan and the Pacific Rim.*

The image of protection had several advantages. At a time when presidential contestants were indistinct the protective tariff clearly separated Republicans from Democrats, appealing strongly to most business constituencies. It was less powerful among working people, but its supporters made a convincing case to many labor groups that high tariffs led to higher wages. Protection appealed to patriotic motives, offering an image of Americanism: American produc-tion favored over foreign goods, the party of pro-Americanism versus the party of un-Americanism (Democrats). Basically, like most images, protection was a matter of belief, faith, and emotional commitment.

Protection also implied Victorian domestic values and sentiments: it suggested protection of the household, the hearth, and the abode of virtue. Some campaign devices of the late nine-teenth century presented candidates as domestic characters, protectors of women and the fam-ily. In the case of Grover Cleveland, who married an attractive young woman while in the White House, the domestic image and the first-lady image presented an appealing picture, almost certainly adding to Cleveland's political attraction. William McKinley, whose wife, Ida, was sickly throughout his presidency, played the role of the faithful husband and defender of the household.

As they cultivated domesticity, campaigners also took advantage of nostalgia. When promot-ing an unexciting candidate, Benjamin Harrison in 1888, Republicans recalled their man's grandfather, William Henry Harrison, old Tip, the log-cabin candidate of 1840. Many 1888 cam-paign items revived the Harrison cabin connection, even though the younger Harrison had no

Cleveland poster, 1888. *Although Grover Cleveland lost the presidential race in 1888, his beautiful young wife, Frances Folsom, was a great asset in his campaigns. Their portraits are printed here on a campaign poster; they were also popular on product advertising.*

Harrison paper lantern, 1888. *Through this and many other throwbacks to the 1840s, Benjamin Harrison appropriated his grandfather's hurrah campaign symbols, complete with log cabin, cider barrel, and "Tippecanoe" slogan, to promote the 1880s issue of protective tariffs.*

association whatsoever with the frontier. Campaign lanterns vividly presented cabin symbols and proclaimed loyalty to "Tippecanoe and Morton Too." Devices of personal commitment such as ribbons and lapel pins bore log-cabin images, and rolling balls reminiscent of the 1840s were moved around the country.

The closely fought campaign of 1888 was a banner election for imaginative and humorous political artifacts. For example, along with the log-cabin revival, the Republican campaign included broom and dustpan lapel pins to demonstrate how Washington would be cleaned up, should young Tippecanoe be elected. But, not to be outdone, Democrats too associated broom images with their candidates, Cleveland and Thurman. Among satirical items of the time were political playing cards ridiculing players in the game of presidential politics such as Cleveland, Harrison, Blaine, and others. An interesting and ambiguous 1888 "scale" depicts the candidates as ceramic babies, each wrapped in the flag as if being delivered by the political stork. With two such identical competitors, how was the voter to choose?

Additional novelties issued in the 1880s and 1890s ranged from toy horns, for partisans who wished to toot for protection, to pipes, for smokers favoring Bryan or McKinley, to canes with heads resembling McKinley and Bryan. Identical button novelties in 1892 asked who "R-U" for. Donkey and elephant pin-the-tail parlor games enabled loyalists of both sides to play with their favorite partisan animals. Despite the strength of party loyalties, voter skepticism about recent and recurring public scandals persisted, enabling manufacturers of campaign gadgets to appeal to doubts and distrust of politicians through satirical objects.

An exciting ingredient was added to the political mix of the early 1890s with a new third-party movement, the People's, or Populist, party. Arising primarily among disaffected and needy farmers and rural leaders in the South and West, the Populist movement advocated a variety of economic and political reforms such as nationalization of the railroads, a graduated income tax, currency reform, the direct election of senators, and other radical reforms. In 1892 the Populist nominee for president, James B. Weaver, received more than a million popular votes.

For all its importance as an insurgent movement, the People's party, like other third parties, left little in the way of political images and artifacts. Why? It appears that enduring campaign images were largely phenomena of mainstream politics, of the two-party system. In cultivating partisan loyalties, developing vast campaigning and communication networks, the major parties had found imagery and tangible devices to be important and useful organizational tools. Third parties, however, were generally short-lived and centered their efforts around the kinds of causes that did not immediately lend themselves to image creation. Often movements like Populism had such inherent moral authority and emotional appeal that images and objects might be regarded as corruptions of their ideals. There was in addition a practical reason for the absence of ephemera representing Populism and, later, Socialism. Insurgent movements seldom had the financial resources even to support an adequate press, and never a surplus to spend on electioneering devices. The relationship between campaign imagery and political causes can be explored by considering the election of 1896.

The Battle of the Standards

In a quite remarkable way Populism infected the lively campaign for the presidency in 1896. Among its wonders, that contest is remembered for its concentration on one Populist issue, the money question, gold versus silver. William Jennings Bryan and his horde of Populist and insurgent Democratic followers rejected the gold standard of conservatives like Cleveland and McKinley, came out for the unlimited coinage of silver at a ratio of sixteen ounces of silver to one ounce of gold, and captured control of the Democratic party. It was the gold standard against silver, the battle of the standards. But in the process the Populist movement was corrupted by the passion for silver; a great cause was transformed into an image.

The money question had been one of numerous issues in American politics for many years, partly because countless rural debtors believed they were being cheated and driven into bankruptcy by a shortage of currency and the greed of urban bankers and creditors adhering to the gold standard. Silver coinage also appealed to thousands of western mine owners, miners, and entrepreneurs who expected to prosper from the demand for their precious metal. As a result of the mystical, simplistic appeal of inflation and the silver coinage issue, various rural and western interests settled on silver as a panacea for America's economic and social troubles. Thus the crusade for silver coinage became a great political battle and one in which specific industries were willing to invest.

The silver issue energized the manufacturers and distributors of political campaign devices. Abstract aspects of the controversy were translated into vivid and concrete images for and against the coinage of silver at sixteen to one. Hundreds of different objects – novelties, buttons, ribbons, and artifacts of all description – appeared bearing slogans and messages relating to the money question. Never before or since has a political issue been converted so widely into images for use in campaign devices. A favorite item was the bug emblem, made in several forms

Democratic campaign buttons, 1896. *The modern pinback button first appeared in 1896. These early examples show much more color and variation than those of later years. The slogan "16 to 1" refers to the Free Silver faction's demand that the government increase the money supply by coining sixteen ounces of silver for each ounce of gold.*

Republican gold bugs, 1896. *Republicans who supported the gold standard and opposed the coinage of more silver were called gold bugs. Originally a derogatory term, it was embraced by Republican organizer Mark Hanna and turned to the party's advantage. This inexpensive metal device was worn as a lapel button. When the wings are pressed down, they pop back up and display portraits of candidates William McKinley and Garret Hobart.*

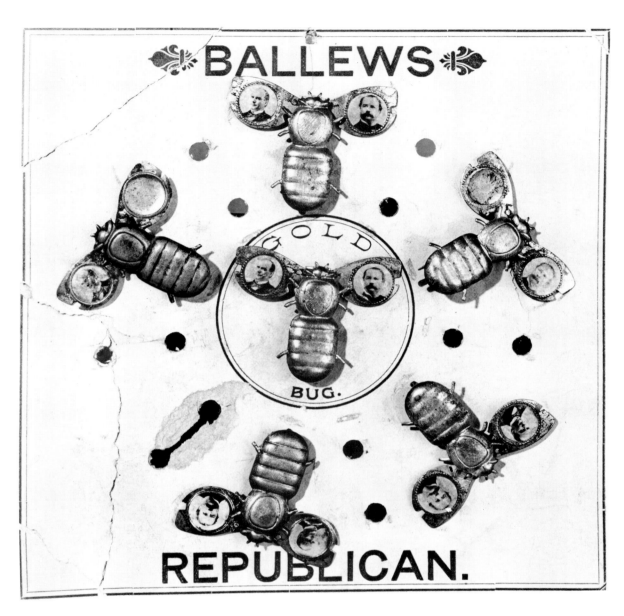

to appeal to silverites (silver bugs) or to loyalists of the gold standard (gold bugs). Partisans of silver or gold could find bugs made into pins, printed on lapel buttons, or made to stand on a flat surface.

Other examples of issue-related items included vivid McKinley novelties bearing slogans such as "Sound Money," "Protection and Prosperity," "In Gold We Trust," and others. Among the dozens of gold-related novelties are a small McKinley bucket (a dinner pail, perhaps) and a pin cushion with the legend "Pin Your Faith to Honest Money." Anti-Bryan "dollars" carried negative messages ridiculing simpleminded faith in the free-silver panacea and took occasional vicious shots at the Democratic candidate. The Republican message countered Bryan's appeal by identifying the party of McKinley with patriotism, prosperity, and sound thinking. Identical

soap dolls for McKinley and Bryan carried messages of support for gold or silver, and printed propaganda included posters and cartoons for both sides. Although Republicans had much more money to spend, large quantities of devices represented both sides.

The election was enlivened by an important new campaign lapel device, the pinback button, which quickly became the most ubiquitous of all electioneering gadgets. The history of button manufacturing has been told elsewhere but can be summarized briefly here. One material of early political buttons, celluloid, appeared in the 1860s, but it was not until the first patent for a pinback button design was issued to Amanda M. Lougee of Boston in 1893 that all components of button production became available. The 1893 patent and two later ones were acquired by the Whitehead and Hoag Company, printers of advertising novelties. From 1895 on, the Whitehead and Hoag firm produced advertising buttons of many varieties, and in the presidential campaign of 1896, the political button became a primary indicator of personal political commitments. Dozens of other makers of advertising novelties entered the button business from 1896 into the mid twentieth century. Cheap, durable, easily distributed and handled, buttons could convey an astonishing variety of messages and symbols. Some of the most vivid political buttons ever created carried messages for and against the coinage of silver.

Candidate image-making, like many other features of the 1896 contest, gained vigor over the shopworn symbolism of earlier elections. Both Democrats and Republicans treated the cam-

McKinley dinner pail, 1896. *This tiny, metal novelty was meant to be worn on lapels. The Republican party hoped to attract the votes of working-men by promising them "a full dinner pail," along with the gold standard and sound money. The power of the dinner-pail image was intensified by the lingering effects of the 1893 depression.*

paign as a crusade about the money question. Representing industrial America, McKinley openly courted working people, arguing that the laborer's wages benefited from high tariffs and a sound, gold-based money supply. He branded Bryan's moral evangelism as un-American anarchy, opposing it with his own images of true prosperity for the whole nation.

Toward the end of the McKinley campaign, chairman Mark Hanna arranged two brilliant strokes. He unleashed a mass of 1,400 party speakers who traveled through the critical states denouncing free silver, free trade, and Democratic anarchy. A few days before the election Hanna promoted a national celebration of Flag Day, which wrapped his candidate and party in the patriotism of the national colors. Across the country Republican groups, led by aging Civil War veterans, staged parades and sentimental demonstrations for McKinley. The whole Republican campaign effort was planned and carried out with care and preparation. What it lacked in spontaneity it gained in mass involvement and appeal.

The 1896 contest was memorable for the enthusiasm and excitement it stimulated, partly as a result of Populism and free silver. But it was also a great partisan battle, presenting the two major parties, Republicans versus Democrats, as unequal but worthy rivals. In another respect it had unusual importance, for it carried to new levels the active involvement of both major candidates as participants in the contest.

Personal Campaigning

THE NATION'S CHOICE.

BLAINE.   LOGAN.

N.S. BROWN

E very American presidential campaign is a new festival of electioneering, emerging out of new conditions and fresh influences while remaining faithful to past practices for much of its conduct. After 1840 all elections for the highest office reflected memories of and employed elements derived from hurrah campaigning. But during the 1880s new techniques of running for office began to appear and fall into a pattern. Although it may not have been clear at the time, hindsight shows that a new style of campaign emerged in the late nineteenth century.

As M. J. Heale and other scholars have shown, for much of the century presidential candidates did not usually speak or actively solicit public support for themselves during the campaign. Abraham

Lincoln was the perfect example of a candidate who followed a tradition of silence. After his nomination in 1860 he almost dropped out of sight, making no direct comment on the campaign or issues of the day. There were exceptions to the custom of candidate silence, as we have noted. In a limited way William Henry Harrison took to the stump during the log-cabin and hard-cider election of 1840. Stephen Douglas, Lincoln's chief rival in 1860, campaigned hard for the Democratic ticket in that momentous election. Yet the convention of mute candidates was largely observed. From 1880 onward, however, campaigns began to break with tradition, and candidate participation grew to be the norm.

Candidates on Display

O ne of the leading features in campaigning of the late nineteenth century was a tendency among candidates to become directly involved in the contest. The trend was evident in the Republican campaign of 1880. After a bruising nominating convention, the Grand Old Party (G.O.P.) chose James A. Garfield as its standard-bearer. During the campaign Garfield followed custom by staying at home. Nevertheless, people wanted to see their candidate, so they began calling at his house in Mentor, Ohio, until eventually visits became daily occurrences. Some came informally in small groups; others came in delegations with banners, flags, and spokesmen. They brought gifts, trampled on the lawn, drank lemonade or other liquid refreshments, and carried off souvenirs. Candidate Garfield obligingly met many of the visitors, entertained them with brief remarks, and satisfied their curiosity. In that somewhat casual way was born the original front-porch campaign.

Four years later Republican candidate James G. Blaine took an active role in the presidential contest but was a good deal less successful than Garfield had been. Both Blaine and the Democratic nominee, Grover Cleveland, found themselves on the defensive. In Blaine's case, letters were discovered incriminating the candidate in a railroad fraud. For Cleveland the problem was a rumor, proved true and admitted by the candidate, that he had years earlier fathered an illegitimate child. Cleveland could claim, truthfully, that he had supported the child and its mother. In response to these scandals, an observer is supposed to have remarked: "We are told that Mr. Blaine has been delinquent in office but blameless in private life, while Mr. Cleveland has been a model of official integrity, but culpable in his personal relations. We should therefore elect Mr. Cleveland to the public office which he is so well qualified to fill, and remand Mr. Blaine to the private station he is admirably fitted to adorn."

The disclosures hurt Blaine far more than they did Cleveland, and the Republican campaign suffered. In part to repair the damage, Blaine went out on the stump, making the first personal campaign tour since Douglas's ill-fated stumping journey in 1860. For about six weeks Blaine toured several states where the election promised to be close, delivering more than four hundred speeches. At the close of his tour in New York City the exhausted candidate heard a

Overleaf:
Republican banner, 1884.
James G. Blaine was a leading presidential aspirant for two decades. A skillful and popular politician, he had a reputation for graft and shady dealings. A campaign verse described him as "Blaine, Blaine, James G. Blaine, continental liar from the State of Maine." Abundant campaign devices, such as this handpainted banner, tried to present him as a patriotic and respectable statesman.

Protestant minister, the Reverend Samuel D. Burchard, slander the Democrats as the party of "Rum, Romanism, and Rebellion." Blaine was too tired or too insensitive to disavow the remark, and within a day the national Democratic press attacked him for it. In the next few days Blaine probably lost thousands of Catholic votes through that miscalculation. His campaign trip may have cost him the election because he lost New York, with its thousands of Catholic voters, by just over one thousand votes.

Whatever its outcome, Blaine's personal campaign moved presidential candidates closer to participating directly in the struggles for election. Four years after the Blaine fiasco, during the campaign of 1888, Republican nominee Benjamin Harrison – young Tippecanoe – was active through much of the contest. Instead of going out to the people as Blaine had, however, Harrison remained at home in Indianapolis for a front-porch campaign. The candidate met 110 delegations of visitors, nearly 200,000 persons. He greeted the majority of the delegations, offered brief remarks, and impressed his admirers with his geniality and respectability. Historian Richard Jensen describes his efforts: "Without notes, although not without careful preparation, he delivered seventy-nine major speeches, short, pithy, warm and gracious, and well suited to the needs of the daily press." His campaign climaxed on October 11 with a giant parade including 25,000 marchers, forty bands in uniform, floats, and at least a thousand veteran Boys in Blue.

The next important front-porch presidential campaign was that of Republican William McKinley in 1896. In that election Major McKinley, the last of a generation of Civil War officers to run for the highest office, proved to be an almost ideal front-porch candidate. In taking such an active role, McKinley responded to efforts of William Jennings Bryan, the vigorous insurgent Democrat from Nebraska. Bryan, as the nominee of a bitterly divided Democratic party, conducted an unprecedented personal campaign, the first true whistle-stop electioneering trip, traveling 18,000 miles by train, appearing in hundreds of communities around the country.

With few financial or organizational resources to command, the "Great Commoner" conducted an exhausting journey, stumping for approximately one hundred days through twenty-seven states and making about six hundred speeches, most of them from the rear car of the train. Visiting important cities and insignificant hamlets alike, the young crusader provoked the curiosity and engaged the emotions of his listeners. Twelve-, fourteen-, even sixteen-hour days were common. As he reached the end of his travels, Bryan neared physical exhaustion and collapse. Yet he was an appealing figure to pious folk as he addressed them in the language of the Bible and the missionary.

Bryan's opponent in some ways represented the exact opposite of the stirring westerner. McKinley of Ohio had developed a solid political career in the Republican party. Admired as a devoted partisan of the protective tariff, McKinley believed firmly in the conservative principles of eastern industrial Republicanism. His chief henchman in the party, Marcus A. ("Mark") Hanna, made a fortune in iron, coal, and Great Lakes shipping, then retired from industry to devote himself to advancing McKinley's political career. Together the tariff advocate and the industrialist made a powerful team.

Roosevelt whistle-stop speech, 1902. *One of the century's most vigorous campaigners, Theodore Roosevelt was also one of the first presidential candidates to take his campaign out to the people. Before the late 1800s, presidential nominees were expected to stay out of the limelight while their parties campaigned for them. As transportation improved, the popularity of personal appearances and whirlwind train tours grew, and "hitting the campaign trail" became a cliché of American politics.*

**William
Jennings
Bryan, 1908.**
*Democratic
candidate Bryan
is perhaps best
known as a
brilliant, impas-
sioned speaker.
He ran for presi-
dent three times
and lost each race.
His 1896 contest
was the most
intense personal
presidential
campaign of the
nineteenth century.*

In response to Bryan's unprecedented personal campaign effort, the Republican leadership –
Hanna and McKinley – settled on an unprecedented campaign of their own. Hanna raised at
least $3.5 million for the national Republican effort, not including the many thousands raised
by other leaders. That sum was substantially more than the funds raised in any earlier presidential contest. Although the Republican financial headquarters remained in New York City,
campaign operations were centered at a special headquarters in Chicago, closer to the center
of the country, where the money would be spent.

McKinley, playing a critical role as front-porch candidate, offered a dignified yet effective
alternative to Bryan's dramatic tour. Perfecting the front-porch style that had served other
Republican candidates, McKinley addressed admirers from his homey, spacious front steps in
Canton, Ohio. Nothing was left to chance. Each delegation scheduled its visit, making an ap-
pointment, indicating its interests, and providing copies of any remarks to be made. Prepared
ahead of time, the stately candidate could respond appropriately to each separate group. It is
estimated that nearly 750,000 visitors made the journey to Canton, assisted with free passes
or reduced fares on the railroads serving that city. Thus McKinley, too, conducted a personal
campaign but preserved his dignity and his physical strength.

In Chicago Hanna organized a highly skilled, businesslike staff with specialized subcommit-
tees appealing to particular interest groups such as black voters or bicycle riders. The Republican literary bureau's staff of editors, writers, and statisticians produced nearly two hundred
"educational" pamphlets and publications, providing a sober, reasonable case for McKinley and
sound money, with a total circulation of more than 200 million copies. The Chicago office also
sent out millions of posters, besides additional millions of campaign buttons, novelties, and
gadgets. Republican publicists provided thousands of newspaper articles and press releases for
insertion in local newspapers.

Bryan and McKinley, pursuing the presidency in different styles, fought an original and
memorable campaign. At the outset Bryan was the underdog. He had to energize a discredited,
depressed Democratic party, and he needed to win the support of many thousands of Populists,
disgusted with both the old parties. Having alienated old-line conservative Democrats, Bryan
was severely handicapped by the absence of their money for the campaign. To overcome his
disabilities, Bryan embarked on a new style of personal crusade for the presidency. His aggressive pursuit of the office contradicted the principle that "the office seeks the man" and the
assumption that personal solicitation of votes and hunger for office made the candidate appear
undignified and unworthy of the electorate's support.

The result of this spectacular contest was a victory for the skillful campaign management of
Hanna and the dignified performance by McKinley. McKinley won the election by more than
600,000 popular votes, scoring 271 electoral votes to Bryan's 176. Stimulated by the exciting
battle, the turnout was outstanding; nearly 80 percent of eligible voters cast ballots in the
election nationally, and some state turnouts were much higher than that. In the end many
voters, disgusted with the economic depression that had occurred during Cleveland's adminis-

Republican national headquarters, 1896. *By the late 1800s campaigns were professionally organized, relying on large bureaucratic staffs and highly skilled management. This staff meeting at the* *Republican party's national headquarters in Chicago is presided over by Mark Hanna of Ohio (on the platform to the left), the party's principal manager and chairman of William McKinley's 1896 campaign.*

McKinley front-porch visitors, 1896. *The railroads gave special rates and free passes to thousands of Republican voters to encourage them* *to visit candidate William McKinley in Canton, Ohio. Here an Italian brass band from Buffalo, New York, poses with the candidate in front of his house.*

tration, probably voted against the Democrats. Others from immigrant and Roman Catholic backgrounds apparently found Bryan's evangelical Protestantism unattractive.

The election of 1896 moved campaigning procedures forward in several respects. Bryan's unprecedented tour and McKinley's perfection of front-porch techniques increased attention given to the candidates. The traditional disinterest of the candidate in seeking office was now obsolete. By emphasizing the personal involvement of the candidate, the campaign of 1896 reduced the attention paid to parties and party labels. Both Bryan and McKinley urged voters to disregard their old party loyalties. The contest set new precedents for organization, advertising, and whistle-stopping. As historian Michael McGerr observes, three political styles converged in this unusual election, the "spectacular, educational, and advertised." The last presidential campaign of the nineteenth century set important precedents for electioneering in the twentieth century.

In early twentieth-century elections, torches, uniforms, banners, bandannas, ribbons, and other central symbols of partisan enthusiasm and participation continued in use. Shortly before Theodore Roosevelt's victory in 1904, a popular magazine writer was impressed by the many electioneering devices made for the campaign: "a mighty fortune in flags, banners, uniforms,

McKinley campaign workers, 1896.
These campaign workers, in the Republican head-quarters in Chicago, were probably charged with communicating with voters and distributing literature in African American communities. This office – equipped with the latest technology, including typewriters and telephones – is in keeping with the well-funded business approach of the Republicans.

torches, buttons, canvas, and muslin and paint, in crude creations that are ruined by the rains, ripped by the winds, and utterly useless after election day." Despite appearances, spectacular campaigning was already in decline as parades and other exciting features of presidential contests began disappearing.

The Perpetual Campaigner

One of the leading practitioners of the new, more personal style of campaigning was Theodore Roosevelt. More than any other individual of his era, Roosevelt reformulated electioneering as an extension of the candidate's personality. Already a colorful independent Republican in the 1890s, Roosevelt fought in the Spanish-American War in 1898 and returned as a popular hero. His dramatic leadership of the volunteer Rough Riders regiment and his flamboyant, highly publicized charge at San Juan Hill helped promote Colonel Roosevelt as he battled vigorously and personally in a successful race to be governor of New York. An observer of his gubernatorial campaign commented: "There were immense gatherings of enthusiastic people at every stopping place. . . . [At an upstate stop] there were three thousand people. . . . The speech was nothing, but the man's presence was everything. It was electrical, magnetic."

In 1900 circumstances of Republican politics led to Roosevelt's nomination for vice president with William McKinley. William Jennings Bryan again headed the Democratic party ticket, and the popular Rough Rider was assigned by campaign manager Mark Hanna to go out to the people, serving as the Republican answer to Bryan's aggressive whistle-stop tour. After a joint Labor Day appearance with Bryan in Chicago, Colonel Roosevelt set out on an exhaustive two-month campaign trip into the West, crisscrossing the country, visiting important cities and tiny

McKinley paper hat, 1896. *This cheap novelty was mass-produced and marketed as an insert in daily newspapers. It was meant to be worn at conventions and on the street but probably appealed to children as well.*

hamlets. He out-campaigned even Bryan, making 673 speeches, visiting 567 towns in 24 states, and traveling 21,209 miles. In contrast to Bryan's appeal to labor to vote for its interests, Roosevelt supported "fellow feeling" among Americans of different classes. "On the whole we shall all go up or down together," he declared at Chicago. A popular and showy speaker, he aroused the interest of people everywhere.

Theodore Roosevelt surpassed in energy and personal charisma any presidential aspirant of his generation. He revived the traditional imagery of the war hero and leader of men, remembered from the times of Washington and Jackson, Harrison and Grant. But Teddy's heroic image came to be more closely associated with his personality than the heroism of earlier leaders. Campaign devices promoting Roosevelt dramatized his identity yet made him seem closer to the people and gave him an abiding humorous appeal.

Campaign objects symbolizing celebration and festivity, formerly associated with spectacular mass events, reflected Theodore Roosevelt's vivid personality and exciting deeds. Many promotional artifacts glorified Roosevelt's western cowboy image and his Rough Rider wartime heroics. Images of Roosevelt as a Rough Rider appeared on bandannas, campaign badges, souvenir trays, playing cards, and scores of other objects.

Roosevelt gave humorous campaign language a decidedly personal turn. In many respects he was fun. Bouncy, full of enthusiasms and frenzies, he was a natural and delightful subject for campaign spoofing. Varied objects depicted his teeth, so noticeable when he smiled or laughed that they became a trademark. A whistle novelty, Teddy's Teeth, advertised as "The Hit of the Campaign!" gave its owners "more fun in a minute than a barrel of monkeys" and enabled them to whistle for their favorite candidate. The teeth were also featured on a Rough Rider doll novelty. Other aspects of Roosevelt's persona were built into funny creations: his captivating nickname, "Teddy," and numerous Rough Rider objects emphasizing the wide-brimmed western hat.

Campaign devices representing the language of partisan loyalties, partisan candidates, and partisan issues were overshadowed by objects centered on commitment to the individual candidate. The most popular devices featuring symbols of political loyalties, campaign buttons, showed the trend. By their nature, campaign buttons carried simpler messages than those on badges or ribbons. Still, early buttons from 1896 and 1900 consisted of varied designs, offering some attention to partisan appeals and issues. By 1904, when campaign buttons had become all-important as emblems of political commitment, they carried few messages except portraits and names of the candidates. Personality rather than partisanship dominated these symbols of political enthusiasm.

Campaign devices emphasizing personal imagery celebrated the candidate's strong achievements and personality. A more benign and sympathetic image was associated with the Teddy bear. Although accounts of the toy bear's origin vary, the standard version of the story traces the stuffed animal's source to a hunting trip in 1902 on which President Roosevelt refused to shoot a bear that had been captured for him. The president's refusal caught the interest of newspaper cartoonist Clifford Berryman, who drew the president and the bear. Based on the incident and the cartoon, a stuffed toy was made and a whole series of souvenirs, novelties, and bear stories was created, many of them starring Teddy Roosevelt. The identification of Roosevelt with the bear figure had a complex series of meanings: his love of the outdoors and wildlife, his sympathy for wild things and their conservation in contrast to the manly hunter image, with its allusions to Roosevelt's cowboy and Rough Rider experiences. The stuffed bear associated Roosevelt with a lovable and cuddly identity, corresponding to and reinforcing Roosevelt's love of his family, the lively and appealing children who lived for nearly eight years in the White House. In the end, the bear associations helped to domesticate Roosevelt's complex, controversial personality.

The language of attack in campaign devices seems, on the whole, to have diminished during the Theodore Roosevelt era. One of his legacies was that of cheerful, enthusiastic campaigning. A progressive follower of the Rough Rider remembered the fun of local electioneering and the "rollicking crowd" who stumped for Roosevelt and the changes that he advocated. One unpleasant group of political memorabilia stands out among the cheerful campaign items of the time. In 1901 Roosevelt invited the African American leader Booker T. Washington to the White House for dinner. Two years later, a print and a button were made commenting favorably on the dinner. Thereafter, anti-Roosevelt racist and Jim Crow imitations of the Roosevelt-Washington buttons mocked the dinner and the president's sympathy for Washington.

Despite some evidence to the contrary, it appears that three-dimensional objects became less central to the process of electioneering as personal contests and candidates' personalities grew increasingly dominant. Parades and demonstrations, marching clubs, and mass festivities gradually disappeared from early twentieth-century campaigns, diminishing the elaborate range of symbolic objects and regalia formerly devoted to the great torchlight parades of the nineteenth century. The campaign devices of the early twentieth century celebrated personalities rather than causes or partisan commitment.

Ideal Toy teddy bear, early 1900s. *The teddy bear probably originated in a cartoon by Clifford Berryman based on a story told about Teddy Roosevelt. On a hunting trip, the president was presented with a young bear to shoot. Finding it repugnant to his code of sportsmanship to shoot a captive animal, he refused. Ideal was one of the first toy manufacturers to capitalize on the quasi-political symbol of the bear.*

Teddy's Teeth whistle and advertisement, c. 1904. *Theodore Roosevelt's good humor and lively style, typified by his trademark grin, inspired many novelties and products, which were not necessarily associated with a political campaign. The teddy bear is the most famous and enduring. This whistle, though, became popular as a campaign noisemaker.*

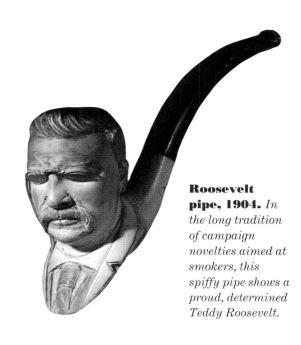

Roosevelt pipe, 1904. *In the long tradition of campaign novelties aimed at smokers, this spiffy pipe shows a proud, determined Teddy Roosevelt.*

Theodore Roosevelt and Booker T. Washington lithograph, 1901. *At the nadir of race relations in America, Teddy Roosevelt became the first president to invite a black man to the White House. This crudely manufactured lithograph celebrates the meeting of renowned educator Booker T. Washington and Roosevelt as an endorsement of racial equality, recalling the spirit of Abraham Lincoln.*

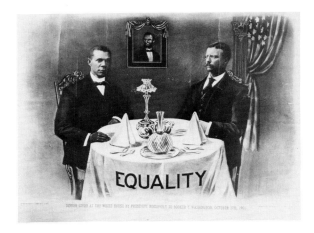

Theodore Roosevelt, the campaigner, c. 1903. *Roosevelt never stopped campaigning. He was known as a great speaker; surviving recordings indicate that he had a rather high-pitched voice that carried well.*

Even after the voters elected him, Theodore Roosevelt continued his campaigning. Following McKinley's death in 1901, "that damned cowboy," as Hanna had called Roosevelt, took charge, changing the rather bland governing style of McKinley into a series of dramatic, attention-getting public maneuvers. Roosevelt gave constant attention to cultivating the people. More than any of his predecessors he turned the conduct of the presidency into a perpetual campaign, always on display, dramatizing the office as never before. Observing that his strength for the campaign of 1904 would come from the people, Roosevelt wrote: "If my nomination is to come at all, it has to come at the initiative of the people." Effective support, however, would be from "my natural allies . . . the farmers, small businessmen and upper-class mechanics," voters who were "fundamentally sound, morally, mentally, and physically."

To insure that such voters would remain faithful, Roosevelt treated the presidency as a great stage, or as he put it, "a bully pulpit." Getting in the news, coining catchy phrases, mediating a bitter strike of coal miners, bringing together the belligerent powers Japan and Russia to settle their war, he became front-page copy for the national press. A careful historian, John Morton Blum, has described his technique: "Roosevelt was never merely a sounding board for the popular mind. He had, rather, in his halcyon days, an absolute sense of political pitch. He struck the notes that the chorus awaited." He impressed some observers as a superlative western actor: "Roosevelt . . . was the 'good guy' and the other fellows . . . the 'bad guys.'" As president, he "was a brilliant molder and interpreter of public opinion," who could work his way with the public, going just far enough but not far ahead of the people. With the people behind him, he could generally win his points with Congress, securing important legislation in several fields. Roosevelt practiced an activist approach to the highest office that made the president "a steward of the people." "My belief was that it was not only his right but his duty to do anything that the needs of the Nation demanded, unless such action was forbidden by the Constitution or by the laws." Employing such a concept of the office, Roosevelt took credit for "many things not previously done by the President." He used his office in a continuous personal quest for public attention.

Besides his aggressive executive behavior, Roosevelt modified presidential politics in other important ways, by personalizing the presidency as an office independent of the parties. The vivid force of his personality persisted after he retired from office. Leaving the presidency in 1909, Roosevelt took a big-game hunting trip to Africa that kept him in the public eye. After his return, in 1910, Roosevelt began to quarrel with his chosen successor, President William Howard Taft, and became involved with the Republican party's progressive faction. "The country was politically seething with the yeast of a progressive movement," remembered William Allen White, and Roosevelt moved to the insurgency's center. As the split among Republicans widened, an opportunity beckoned for the ex-president to lead again.

In 1911, the Rough Rider's battle with his successor could not be contained, and he determined to seek a third term. Early in 1912 the rivals began struggling for the Republican nomination, with Roosevelt leading in popularity but Taft ahead among the party leaders. Roosevelt hoped that by using the new mechanism of direct primary elections recently instituted in many states, he would have many delegates pledged to him for the Republican nomination. Some of the primaries were intensely competitive. In New Jersey, for example, an independent progressive group called the Roosevelt Republican League of the State of New Jersey had more than one hundred paid employees and two hundred automobiles available to carry campaign literature in a house-to-house canvass. A report of the campaign suggested its intensity: "Banners are swung across the streets in every city and town of importance, extolling the candidates. Billboards are plastered with huge posters eulogizing President Taft. Campaign pictures of 'Teddy' and Taft look out from windows everywhere. Every other man wears a campaign button."

Roosevelt's primary campaigns were the first of their kind, premonitions of crucial developments later in the century. Winning primaries in nine states, he secured 278 delegate votes in the Republican nominating convention, even capturing Taft's home state, Ohio. Conservatives in the party feared the Roosevelt boom, and despite his demonstrated popularity and plurality of primary votes, the party organization controlled the convention. By fair means and foul, the convention managers disqualified many Roosevelt delegates, and after bitter debates, amid accusations of a stolen nomination, President Taft became the Republican candidate.

Denied nomination by the Republicans, announcing, "We stand at Armageddon and battle for the Lord," Roosevelt bolted and formed a third party, the Progressives. Nicknamed the Bull Moose party, after one of Roosevelt's favorite sayings ("I am as strong as a bull moose"), the party took the great animal as its symbol – still another image for the ex-president.

Roosevelt ran a personal campaign against party regularity, drawing votes away from the candidates of both major parties, Republican incumbent William Howard Taft and Democratic challenger Woodrow Wilson. Wilson biographer Arthur S. Link represents the view of many historians that the campaign of 1912 was "largely a contest of personalities." Both Wilson and Roosevelt conducted campaigns that were more personal than partisan, independent of traditional party bosses. Roosevelt and his Bull Moose following campaigned to the theme song

Bull moose button, 1912. *The bull moose, supposedly an allusion to Teddy Roosevelt's insistence that he felt "as strong as a bull moose," became the trademark of the Progressive party, which splintered off from the Republicans to promote greater government activism.*

**Progressive
pennant, 1912.**
*Pennants emerged
as campaign
devices around the
turn of the century.
This one pairs a
profile of Theodore
Roosevelt, the
Progressive party's
first candidate,
with the party
emblem, a bull
moose.*

"Onward Christian Soldiers" and acted like crusaders in a national religious revival. By conducting a passionate yet doomed personal campaign in 1912, Roosevelt took millions of Republican votes away from Taft, enabling Wilson to succeed to the presidency. Their popularity contest resulted in a distinct shift away from partisanship in the presidential contest.

Through his constant cultivation of the people, Theodore Roosevelt altered public perceptions and expectations of presidents. He made showmanship in the nation's highest office a standard practice, creating the expectation that after his term, other presidents would be dramatic public figures, as he had been. His act was not an easy one to follow, however, as Taft quickly learned. During the two decades after Roosevelt's losing race in 1912, the nation did not see such a colorful personality as president.

Woodrow Wilson, the Rough Rider's victorious opponent in 1912, was a worthy successor in developing the perpetual campaign. Even before running for the highest office, Wilson had been a passionate campaigner. As a candidate for the governorship of New Jersey in 1910 he discovered the need to "maintain some electric identity" between his goals and the electorate's desires. In office, Governor Wilson battled some of the bosses who had supported him and operated as a reformer and "champion of the common people." By careful management and innovative leadership the governor turned the state Democratic party and the New Jersey government around. "This change, so rapidly effected," writes Blum, "brought Wilson a national reputation for courageous leadership."

To some extent Wilson, like Roosevelt, ran against his party in 1912. To gain the Democratic nomination he had to defeat the party favorite, Champ Clark, the House Speaker from Missouri whose campaign symbol was the folksy "hound dawg." Winning the party nomination in an uphill battle of compromise and intense maneuvering, his forces organized the Wilson Republican League with twenty thousand members, hoping to capture support from discontented Republicans. The governor also appealed to growing numbers of independent voters, who took the measure of individual candidates rather than their parties. Lacking Roosevelt's dramatic flair, Wilson campaigned for an attractive Progressive program that he called the New Freedom. It gave him an appealing image to Democrats, Republicans, and independents, helping him win in 1912. Traditional campaign devices probably played a minor role in his canvass.

President Wilson lacked Theodore Roosevelt's abilities at self-dramatization. A former professor of government, president of Princeton University, and a serious scholar of political leadership, Wilson often spoke eloquently and wrote thoughtfully about the chief executive's role. He cultivated a strong, rather professorial image. In his treatise on constitutional government (1908) he presented a grand conception of the presidency: "His is the only national voice in affairs. Let him once win the admiration and confidence of the country, and no other single force can withstand him, no combination of forces will easily overpower him. His position takes the imagination of the country. He is the representative of no constituency, but of the whole people. When he speaks in his true character, . . . he is irresistible; and the country never feels the zest for action so much as when its President is of such insight and calibre." Here Wilson

Debs whistle stop, 1908. *A spellbinding orator, Eugene Debs ran five times as the Socialist candidate for president. In 1908 his campaign included a whirlwind train tour on the Red Special, sometimes with twenty speeches a day near factories, coal mines, and railroad yards. Debs was himself a former railroad worker from Terre Haute, Indiana.*

articulated the definition of the president as leader of public opinion and perpetual campaigner. In his first years as president he caught the public imagination and achieved many of his and the public's purposes. Although his professorial manner and prim righteousness made him appear stiff and aloof in comparison with the aristocratic but folksy Roosevelt, Woodrow Wilson nevertheless carried out a "magnificent performance." His second administration, overshadowed by American participation in World War I, represented another kind of performance, of crisis management, that strengthened presidential authority. Unfortunately it exhausted the energies and patience of the American people and left Wilson a severely ill and broken man.

Wilson nutcracker, c. 1912. *This unusual, comic campaign novelty features the sculptured head of Democratic candidate Woodrow Wilson. Once the president of Princeton University, Wilson brought a reputation as an academic and a reformer to his first national campaign. The nutcracker was an attempt to soften that image with humor.*

The Last Front-Porch Campaign

It was nearly a generation after McKinley before the Republicans staged the next and final front-porch presidential campaign. In 1920 candidate Warren G. Harding spent most of the days between nomination and election on his front porch in Marion, Ohio. Here he met the people, mingled with party loyalists, celebrities, and Indian chiefs, and made pronouncements consisting of bland generalities and platitudes. Most important, he was on display to the thousands of Americans who arrived for a viewing of the next chief executive.

Symbolically, the porch was already an emblem of nostalgia for the simple, neighborly, small-town America, partly mythical, that had flourished briefly and was by the twenties rapidly passing from the national scene. Harding's porch was deliberately intended to resemble and recall the 1896 McKinley porch in another Ohio town, Canton. The revival of this symbol signified a return to pre-war business and patriotic values, thought to be so much in contrast to Wilson's moralistic preaching. Party operatives transported and erected the flagpole from

Harding photo opportunities, 1920. *The stream of cheerful visitors to Warren G. Harding's front porch in Marion, Ohio, was just the thing to feed the mass media's appetite for pictures. Left: Harding smokes a peace pipe with a group of Native Americans. Right: Broadway performers and a jazz band pose with the candidate. In front are Harding, an unidentified Broadway star, Mrs. Harding, and Al Jolson.*

McKinley's front yard to the Harding grounds. Each morning there was a ceremonial raising of the flag, reminding visitors of Ohio's loyalty to McKinley Republicanism.

On a practical level the front porch offered incontestable advantages. It avoided physical and nervous strain on the candidate. It enabled party officials to control the situation by carefully governing his speeches, with his writers and advisors always nearby. Thus he was less likely to make terrible mistakes while speechifying. As in the McKinley era, Harding's appearances were planned, delegations scheduled, and their messages cleared ahead of time so that the candidate might respond properly to his visitors. Little was left to chance.

One memorable visit brought show-business celebrities to Harding's front porch. Led by entertainer Al Jolson, the Harding and Coolidge Theatrical League with more than forty Broadway stars traveled to Marion. Parading from the station behind a hundred-piece band, the delegation greeted and performed for the enchanted candidate. Backed by a jazz band, Jolson sang his own campaign song, "Harding, You're the Man for Us," which included such immortal lines as "We need another Lincoln to do the nation's thinkin'." The candidate himself sat in for a few bars on the tuba. A brief skit and Harding's dignified reply testified to the mutual interests of performers and their candidate. A representative of the musician's union also declared his support for the man from Marion. In one of the first alliances between show business and presidential politics, two of America's favorite performance traditions were united. The practice has grown and become commonplace since Harding's and Jolson's time.

Overall, the results were generally favorable, entertaining, and wholesome. Harding appeared on his own terms, a simple yet appealing representative of middle America, expansive, performing his favorite rituals of greeting fellow citizens and shaking their hands. He entertained hundreds of delegations, including businessmen, civic and political clubs, religious societies, American Indians, interest groups of every sort.

Although they seemed spontaneous, Harding's front-porch efforts were skillfully organized. The routines and special events were overseen by one of the leading advertising executives of the period, Albert Lasker, the campaign's publicity director. Considered a genius of promotion, Lasker applied the principles of selling breakfast food, toothpaste, and cigarettes to the presidential contest. Lasker might have been inspired by the good feelings of the 1840 log-cabin

Coolidge phonograph record, c. 1920. *The invention of the phonograph gave candidates another way to communicate with the public. Massachusetts governor Calvin Coolidge, who had a reputation for being tight-lipped, used the medium to disseminate his speeches.*

campaign in "'humanizing' Harding as an old-fashioned, sage, honest-to-the-core Middle Westerner who could be trusted never to rock the boat." Harding made a few brief campaign trips away from Marion, but he was much safer at home.

The campaign seemed to appeal to a voting population weary of war and regimentation. As in so many postwar elections, the people wished to forget the strife and pressures of war. Harding and the Republicans spoke longingly, nostalgically of "normalcy," the virtues of "friendliness and neighborliness," "the social intercourse of friends and neighbors." Peace and prosperity, law and order: these were the apparent wants of the country. They seemed to emanate most fully from the porch in Marion and from the lips of the bland, handsome, affable man who looked like a president ought to look. When the votes were counted, Harding won in a landslide – more than sixteen million popular votes to just over nine million for Cox and Roosevelt. The electoral vote was 404 to 127.

Warren Harding, the last front-porch campaigner, was the first president to speak on radio. During the twenties radio, a new communication device, began a process that would alter political persuasion forever. In many respects the last front-porch campaign was a quaint antique, a throwback to the massive rallies and parades of the previous century. The army style of politics, with its mass involvement and enthusiasm, was disappearing. While they flourished the political parade and front-porch politics were effective methods of popular communication. They involved participants in symbolic actions, cemented loyalties, and reinforced partisan commitments. Accessories of the army style – campaign ribbons, banners, bandannas, badges, buttons, and torches – were all tangible elements of those participatory events. New styles of politics would diminish the significance of such political items.

In the context of rapid social and economic changes during the twenties and a pace of life that sped up each day, Harding's front porch in Marion, Ohio, seemed nostalgic and already out of

Smith and Hoover mugs, 1928. *These matching ceramic toby mugs contrast a smiling, personable Al Smith – the Democratic candidate who favored repeal of Prohibition – with the sober Republican Herbert Hoover.*

date. New forms of popular interests, from live entertainment such as vaudeville and professional athletic teams to mass media such as radio and motion pictures, were available in cities and towns across the country. To some extent, the new pastimes may have eroded popular political interests. Consumer goods and durables such as automobiles were available as never before during the twenties. These new products possibly served as substitutes for political involvement. New entertainment forms also fostered spectatorship rather than participation.

The Harding front-porch campaign reflected political change. One of its ingredients, mass participation, was on the wane. Two other facets of twentieth-century presidential electioneering showed up prominently in Harding's performance: personal campaigning by the candidate himself and cultivation of an appealing candidate image. They loomed large in the development of twentieth-century presidential politics.

After Harding's landslide victory, the normalcy of the twenties seemed to be reflected in his administration and those of Silent Cal Coolidge and the great engineer Herbert Hoover, leaving the presidency diminished in dynamism and prestige. Images told part of the story. Harding and Coolidge both associated themselves with Americanism of the small-town variety, looking backward to the nineteenth century. They also represented and advocated the values of business enterprise that reigned supreme during the twenties. Their campaigns were more subdued than those of the Roosevelt and Wilson eras, and campaign artifacts were relatively less important than they had been. Voter enthusiasm and participation fell far below the totals recorded around the turn of the century.

The most dramatic presidential campaign between 1916 and 1932 was that of 1928, matching up Republican Herbert Hoover, a cool efficiency expert, against Democrat Alfred E. Smith, a warm-hearted Irish American and the first Roman Catholic to run for the highest office. To a considerable extent the 1928 contest evolved into a personal contest emphasizing individual differences and contrasts between the two men. Hoover possessed the image of an engineer, a superb manager, a distinguished humanitarian for his services to refugees during World War I, a Protestant and supporter of prohibition. Smith's image was that of an ethnic Catholic son of New York City, a "wet" opposed to prohibition, loyal to the urban Democratic political machine of Tammany Hall, and a "Happy Warrior," as Franklin Roosevelt called him in a nominating speech. The campaign included direct attacks and vicious slanders against Smith's religious loyalties and resulted in a Hoover landslide. The candidates' clashing images were reflected in campaign devices such as banners, sheet music, and ceramic novelties.

As the twenties drew to a close, American politics was poised to confront momentous changes. Brought about by a combination of dramatic personal influences, profound economic disturbances, and technological innovations, these changes would transform presidential electioneering.

Rally 'Round the Candidate

Presidential campaign techniques and devices of the twentieth century must be understood in the context of a changing political environment that weakened party loyalties and diminished partisan power. New election procedures reduced party control over elections. New technologies of transportation and communication – railroads, automobiles, airplanes, film, radio, telephones, and television – enabled candidates to bypass partisan bodies and make appeals directly to the people. Innovations in campaigning derived from business advertising, and public relations provided models for new political styles. Finally, the presidency itself grew and changed from the time of the first Roosevelt to the time of his cousin Franklin.

Harding front-porch visitors, 1920. *An unidentified Marion, Ohio, photographer recorded this group of black dignitaries visiting with Warren G. Harding on the front porch of the president's home. The Republican party was still viewed as the party of Lincoln; African Americans did not shift their allegiance decisively to the Democrats until the New Deal.*

Overleaf:
Democratic banner, c. 1933. *In the depths of the Depression, one of the only reasons for celebration was the repeal of Prohibition. This banner, besides being displayed at political events, may have decorated bars and other establishments that sold alcoholic beverages.*

Even before 1910 electoral politics saw the introduction of several changes designed to clean up elections and enhance "direct democracy." Aimed at reducing the power of political bosses, these reforms included the secret ballot, the direct primary, the recall, and the referendum. Most of the new procedures aimed at purifying local more than national politics, but two – the secret ballot and the primary – had long-range effects on national politics and presidential elections. A side effect of the reformed procedures was to diminish party power and partisanship.

Through much of the nineteenth century American voters used printed ballots issued by political parties listing candidates of one party. The ballots were often identifiable by color or by other features, allowing observers at the polls to see the party choice of each voter. Unless prevented by law from having visible partisan identification, printed ballots might not be secret, and voters could be intimidated or observed by various means. Beginning in the 1880s the so-called Australian ballot system was introduced in the United States, permitting only official ballots to be used. With the Australian ballot the voter indicated by marks or another device a choice of candidates or a party preference. All ballots were identical, marked secretly, and submitted anonymously. Voters at primaries or using secret ballots at general elections tended to perform more independently or vote split tickets more often than they had when herded to the polls by party bosses.

In the early twentieth century numerous states held the first direct primaries as devices to reform nominating procedures. The parties had traditionally nominated candidates in conventions, in caucuses, or often behind closed doors and in secrecy. Commonly the real nominating power fell into the hands of political bosses, nominations were bought and sold, and varieties of corruption resulted. Reformers hoped that primaries would help purify the political process. For example, R. L. McCormick describes the situation in New York: "Those who advocated direct nominations . . . repeatedly urged them as a means of stopping the special interests from working through the bosses to dictate the choice of party candidates."

In another twentieth-century development, new nonpartisan interest groups gained increased electoral power at the expense of the parties. Specialized bodies of men and women

**Al Smith
license plate,
1928.** *Beginning
in the late twenties,
license plates and
other automotive
campaign devices
advertised candi-
dates.*

**Roosevelt
fireside chat,
c. 1936.** *More
than any other
political leader,
Franklin Roose-
velt understood the
possibilities of
radio communica-
tion and used it
effectively. In his
famous fireside
chats he spoke
directly but
informally to the
people, as if he
were in their living
rooms. His wife,
Eleanor, was an
effective broad-
caster in her own
right.*

enrolled in trade, professional, commercial, and labor associations, acting independently of and often at odds with party organizations. According to historian Samuel Hays, the new "function-ally organized" groups served economic and political interests more directly than political par-ties and, unlike parties, operated "at levels above that of the community, involving human relationships over broad geographical areas and often in impersonal rather than face-to-face contacts." In many respects the old party system with its hurrah campaigning was out of date, obsolescent.

Changing styles of campaigning also reduced the appeal of traditional political techniques. The spectacular or army style with its giant parades and vast rallies prevailed after the Civil War. Beginning in the 1870s upper- and middle-class reformers tried to eliminate unthinking partisan loyalties by replacing party spectacles with educational devices and publications to stimulate thoughtful consideration of issues. Another campaign style appeared around the turn of the century with the arrival of advertised or merchandised politics and its use of newspaper advertising and other devices of mass communication. Campaigning thus adopted some of the techniques of promotion gaining favor among businessmen in the late nineteenth century. To some extent, direct advertising of candidates replaced partisan agencies and techniques of per-suasion.

During the twentieth century, major changes took place in concepts of the presidential office itself, its functions and responsibilities. Two world wars, a major economic depression, and an era of cold war or quasi-war in the late forties laid a new range of duties at the president's door. Of the three branches of American government, the executive alone possessed the flexibility, initiative, authority, and "energy," in Alexander Hamilton's eighteenth-century phrase, to un-dertake a host of new activities in behalf of the national interest. Since roughly 1900 or 1933, the presidency has become, in the phrase of Clinton Rossiter and other students of the office, "the modern presidency."

Political scientist Theodore Lowi argues that these changes brought about a new kind of government, a Second American Republic centered on the presidency. "The new politics of the president-centered Second Republic can best be described as a plebiscitary republic with a personal presidency. Already we have a virtual cult of personality revolving around the White House. . . . This is the *personal presidency*: an office of tremendous personal power drawn from the people – directly and through Congress and the Supreme Court – and based on the new democratic theory that the presidency with all powers is the necessary condition for governing a large, democratic nation." The expansion of the presidential office and changed styles of national politics that accompanied it are largely products of the current century.

These long-term shifts affected the voting public and the material culture of politics. For reasons only partly understood, they reduced voter turnout. Roughly 80 percent of eligible voters went to the polls in the presidential election of 1896. No election in the twentieth century has drawn such a large turnout. Political circumstances and technical changes diminished the quantity and variety of political artifacts and paraphernalia of electioneering so prominent in late-nineteenth-century elections. Innovations in transportation, communication, and data processing rendered many traditional items such as banners, torches, even badges and buttons, obsolete.

The Roosevelt Revolution

A new national crisis in the thirties brought another Roosevelt to the highest office, revived the personal campaign, and enhanced the personal presidency. Franklin D. Roosevelt, inaugurated in 1933, faced the most serious economic depression in American history. Beginning with the stock market crash in 1929, the Great Depression brought the national economy to a standstill before Roosevelt's inauguration. Millions of people were unemployed and destitute, some of them on the edge of starvation.

Roosevelt campaigned in 1932 and 1936 with many paraphernalia of traditional electioneering. Yet increasingly the buttons, posters, sheet music, and novelties symbolized not old-fashioned hurrah contests but the new imagery of personal campaigning. Portraits of the candidate in the personal style on many traditional souvenirs depict some of the authority, charisma, and energy attributed to Roosevelt's personality. Some items featured one of the most popular planks in Roosevelt's program, repeal of prohibition, and others emphasized prosperity to come with the New Deal.

Campaign object collectors and students have shown that Franklin Roosevelt inspired an abundance of political buttons, ribbons, posters, paper devices, novelties, and many varieties of souvenirs. A portion of these objects were electioneering devices. A great many, perhaps the majority of Roosevelt objects were celebratory rather than persuasive. With his lengthy period in office and his cultivation of personal loyalty among his millions of followers, Roosevelt, like George Washington, inspired tremendous affection, even veneration. He also provoked much hostility and vituperation.

As a personal candidate Roosevelt dramatized himself in unprecedented ways, capturing the public imagination before he even began to campaign in 1932. For example, instead of waiting for weeks to accept notification of his presidential nomination, he flew immediately from New York to Chicago to speak to the Democratic convention with a ringing call to action, promising new programs to assist "men and women, forgotten in the political philosophy of the Government. . . . I pledge you, I pledge myself, to a new deal for the American people." That promise of a new deal was carried by radio to a national audience.

Franklin Roosevelt continued to expand the personal presidency as begun by Theodore Roosevelt and Woodrow Wilson. The "Roosevelt Revolution" is how some historians have described the array of federal programs initiated during the New Deal. In every way these new governmental services elevated the presidency above the legislative and the judicial branches. Despite resistance and bitter complaints from his opponents within and outside his Democratic party, Roosevelt prevailed, often going over the heads of his opponents to gain the admiring applause of a popular majority. During nearly eight years of New Deal activism, his programs stimulated both respect and contempt. Many New Deal agencies were represented in political devices and novelties, both pro and con.

President Roosevelt used national radio as a key instrument of his conduct in office, to project himself and his image. Although he made numerous national radio addresses, he was most renowned for the Fireside Chats – intimate, conversational speeches delivered to the nation by radio. Speaking simply, directly to "my friends," the American people, Roosevelt seemed to be a cordial visitor in the nation's living rooms, where families crowded around their radios to hear the president interpret the nation's needs and appeal for their support.

Besides his effective use of radio, Roosevelt campaigned personally and continuously through the press. Although opposed by most major newspaper publishers, he succeeded in gaining a sympathetic press by cultivating reporters. Correspondents found that he enjoyed their company, he held frequent press conferences, and he loved to provide juicy tidbits of information as well as longer expositions of his programs. As one New Deal era reporter described him: "He could be as rough and tough as a Third Avenue blackjack artist. And he could be utterly charming, disarming, and thoroughly likable." Through his intimacy with reporters, Roosevelt dramatized and personalized his administration.

Frankin Roosevelt's reelection in 1936 confirmed a new political alignment, replacing the Republicans with the Democrats as the majority party. A crucial segment of the Roosevelt Democratic coalition consisted of naturalized citizens, immigrants mainly from eastern and southern Europe, who had arrived in the United States by the millions between 1890 and 1920. This element of the new coalition demonstrated its power in 1928 when Roosevelt won election as governor of New York. Other voters from diverse and not always compatible interest groups included traditional white southern Democrats and black voters drawn to the Democratic party because of New Deal welfare and relief programs. Working-class northern whites, especially members of labor unions (inspired by pro-labor policies of the New Deal) and voters of Jewish

Roosevelt sheet music, c. 1934. *Sheet music has been a staple of American political culture from the days of the early Republic. The tradition continued in the thirties, when Democrats were encouraged to sing the praises of Franklin Roosevelt's New Deal.*

End of Prohibition, 1933. *Congress, at the request of President Franklin D. Roosevelt, repealed Prohibition in February 1933, and on April 7, beer was sold legally in the United States for the first time since 1919. These young women celebrated at a public bar. In St. Louis whistles and sirens sounded at midnight, and in Milwaukee mobs of revelers sang "Sweet Adeline."*

origin (attracted by Democratic tolerance and liberality), adhered to the Roosevelt coalition. Often volatile, some elements of the Roosevelt coalition outlived Franklin Roosevelt and his successor, Harry S Truman.

Following his landslide victory in 1936, in which he won all but two states ("as Maine goes, so goes Vermont"), Roosevelt determined to try reforming his party in accordance with the philosophy of the New Deal. Some leading Democrats in the more traditional and conservative wing of the party, especially those from the South, were targets of Roosevelt's attacks. In the congressional elections of 1938, he attempted to purge and campaign against many Democratic members of the Senate and House of Representatives who had opposed his programs. Except for a few victims, the purge failed, and it turned legislators he had opposed into bitter enemies.

One of Franklin Roosevelt's most audacious and precedent-breaking actions was his third-term campaign in 1940. Against the tradition of two-term presidents he laid his unmatched influence, popularity, and following. Unshaken by a Republican campaign accusing him of dictatorial aspirations or a wish to be president for life, the people retained confidence in his leadership. Roosevelt's third-term race was a bold antiparty movement. In that and other respects, the Franklin Roosevelt administration strengthened the personal presidency.

As his second term drew to a close the president began to consider a third-term race. Roosevelt employed a coy strategy of encouraging other Democrats to consider running in 1940, all the while keeping his own plans open. But the party had to be manipulated to suit his needs so that his nomination would not seem deliberate or forced. "Roosevelt's basic problem . . . was . . . how to be nominated in so striking a manner that it would amount to an emphatic and irresistible call to duty. This party call would be the prelude to a call from the whole country at election time." His performance alienated many leading Democrats, however, including Jim Farley, chairman of the Democratic National Committee. When Roosevelt decided to make a third-term race in 1940, Farley felt betrayed and ill-used and refused to manage the campaign.

Farley and others considered Roosevelt's third-term strategy detrimental to long-run Democratic party strength. A respected political pro, Farley observed that Roosevelt's purge and

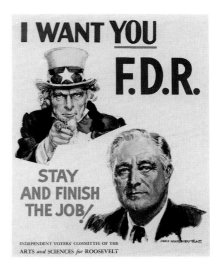

Roosevelt poster, 1940. *George Washington began the presidential tradition of stepping down after two terms, and it was accepted until the end of FDR's second term. In imitation of military recruitment posters, this poster implies that the extraordinary circumstances of economic depression and European war required the extraordinary measure of drafting Roosevelt for a third term.*

third-term ambitions violated party traditions: "The attempt to establish a personal party, the neglect of party leaders, the assumption of control over the judiciary and Congress, and the gratification of personal ambition in the third and fourth terms – all were the evil fruit of his breaking the rules of the game. Party leadership has its obligations as well as its privileges."

For both Democrats and Republicans the presidential campaign of 1940 was unusual. The Democratic party nominated its most successful leader in the twentieth century, even though many party loyalists had become disenchanted with Roosevelt's apparent violation of party customs. By harsh management at the Democratic convention, Roosevelt partisans obtained the party's nomination for their leader, manipulating the proceedings to give the appearance of a popular draft despite the president's feigned wish to retire.

The Republican party also rejected precedents in 1940, nominating Wendell L. Willkie, a public utilities executive. Rather than choosing among three party loyalists and front-runners, the Republican convention on the sixth ballot picked an ex-Democrat who had never held public office. Although surprising, the choice of Willkie was no accident. During the spring of 1940 an energetic publicity campaign stimulated outpourings of public support for the new man as a possible independent Republican candidate. Willkie, much like Roosevelt, had a colorful charismatic personality and campaigned personally for the nomination. Among other publicity devices leading up to his nomination, there suddenly appeared massive numbers of Willkie clubs, eventually amounting to many thousands of local branches. An amateur effort and a grass-roots nonparty movement, the Willkie clubs nevertheless represented an enthusiastic outlet for public opinion dissatisfied with Roosevelt and old-guard Republicanism. Largely in secret, Willkie supporters gained control of the Republican convention. Under the circumstances, and with an enormous independent popular following, the former Democrat became the party's candidate.

Both candidates had successfully challenged their parties' nominating traditions and both cultivated independent voters. The campaign that followed exhibited numerous instances of nonparty electioneering. Willkie's cause received additional support from thousands of new Willkie clubs that proliferated around the country. Another body, Democrats for Willkie, orga-

nized a significant movement among former Roosevelt enthusiasts against the president's third term. Roosevelt also gained support from non-Democratic political clubs: the Independent Voters for Roosevelt and the Committee of Regular Republicans for Roosevelt both appealed to Republicans who distrusted Willkie.

Consistent with the personal style of campaigning practiced by the candidates were the several hundred personal slogan buttons made especially to attack Roosevelt and delight button connoisseurs. Many of these negative buttons conveyed messages attacking the FDR third-term campaign. Others denounced First Lady Eleanor Roosevelt, who was hated by many conservatives, or other members of the president's family. Still others made fun of the president's apparent arrogance with messages such as "No more Fireside Chats," "There is no indispensable man," "Dictator? Not for us," "Franklin Deficit Roosevelt," "Worst Public Administration," "No royal family," and many others. Besides numerous buttons, other Willkie campaign items conveyed the challenger's personal magnetism, his energy, and his humor.

Willkie fought a strenuous, uphill, and somewhat amateurish campaign. He conveyed the image of an outsider, a decent, liberal man of simple small-town origins. It was an image that would reappear often in the decades that followed. Roosevelt played the role of commander-in-chief, above the battle, remaining at his post while World War II unfolded its tragic course in Europe. Toward the end of the contest the president made a few effective electioneering trips. But always, he was at his matchless best when broadcasting, responding with power and wit to Willkie's attacks, exploiting "his one great line of communication to the people – the radio." Finally the great personal campaigner had worked his magic once more, achieving the unprecedented, elusive third term. His biographer has observed: "In the last analysis Roosevelt himself was the issue. His campaign poses . . . had paid off; but his captaincy of a generation paid off too. His victory was largely a personal one."

Truman's Good-bye to an Era

Each personal presidential struggle is different, each campaign colorful in its own particular way. One of the memorable contests of the twentieth century took place in 1948 when incumbent underdog Harry Truman defeated challenger Thomas E. Dewey. People remember the campaign of 1948 for many reasons. One of the most vivid memories is Truman's victory in the face of overwhelming odds, almost entirely unexpected, except by the candidate himself. Vice President Truman succeeded Roosevelt upon the president's death in 1945. He oversaw the end of World War II and held office during a difficult, controversial postwar period. By 1948, his legislative program a failure, Truman had lost popularity. Leading Democrats hoped to replace him with another candidate – General Dwight Eisenhower was a favorite – but no other candidate emerged.

As the election of 1948 neared, most observers imagined that Truman was doomed. The explosive Democratic national convention in 1948 left the party in a shambles. The Republicans and their nominee, Governor Thomas E. Dewey of New York, were supremely confident as the campaign began. Dewey took a lofty stance in the contest, refusing to discuss specific issues and speaking in bland generalities. Most pollsters were so sure of Dewey's victory that they stopped taking serious polls as early as September.

In contrast to Dewey's blandness, Truman went directly to the people in a sensational, hard-hitting manner. On several cross-country whistle-stop train trips the president spoke again and

Truman campaign train, 1948.
The last great railroad campaign took place when Thomas E. Dewey and Harry Truman both rode the rails in 1948. Truman's whistle-stop tour of the nation became one of the legendary campaigns of all time. At hundreds of railroad stops Truman gave 'em hell, introduced his wife, Bess, as "the boss," and snatched the election from Dewey.

Dewey-Truman cartoon, 1948.
This satirical Ben Shahn lithograph parodies a photograph of President Truman playing for Hollywood star Lauren Bacall, replacing Bacall with Truman's Republican opponent, Thomas E. Dewey.

Truman ties, 1948. *In a merchandising version of political polling, Harvey's of Nashville, Tennessee, playfully reduced the price of Truman neckties shortly before election day, after an equal supply of Dewey ties had sold out at twice the price.*

again from the train's rear platform. Having been frustrated by the Republican Congress, Truman attacked the "do-nothing 80th Congress" and called Republicans "gluttons of privilege." Truman's folksy manner, plain speaking, and down-to-earth good humor contrasted with Dewey's empty platitudes. Many times, before his train pulled out of a whistle-stop, Truman would bring his wife, Bess, to the rear platform and introduce her as "the boss." Crowds roared at such antics, and as the campaign neared its conclusion, the president's audiences grew larger and larger. Newsmen, knowing the campaign was doomed, discounted the Missourian's unexpected popularity.

New Yorker magazine reporter Richard Rovere rode both the Truman and Dewey trains that year and found he was witness to the end of an era: "This turned out to be the last cross-country railroad tour of presidential candidates. It seemed to me then a supreme adventure." Rovere found the Truman train far more interesting and joyous than Dewey's traveling show. "The Truman campaign . . . was an old-fashioned and rather sloppy operation, with schedules often fouled up and plans often mislaid. There was a conviviality on the Truman train that was missing on Dewey's. We even had a theme song, with a refrain provided by the President." The reporter remembered vividly "the stops made, often in darkness, in the railroad yards of small cities and towns." Compared with the color and friendly folksiness of Truman's train, the Dewey train's businesslike efficiency seemed boring.

The election's results told the story. Whether the voters were impressed by Truman's feisty assertiveness or not, they reelected him with a popular majority of about two million votes and 304 electoral votes to Dewey's 189. The pollsters and the pundits had totally misunderstood the effect of Truman's fierce, solo crusade as a national underdog. H. L. Mencken, reporting the last political campaign of his long career, confessed to a colossal misjudgment. "How could so many wizards be so thumpingly wrong? How could the enlightenment play so scurvy a trick upon its agents?" Mencken tried to explain the "Missouri Wonder's" success: "Truman . . . assumed as a matter of course that the American people were just folks like himself. He thus wasted no high-falutin rhetoric upon them, but appealed directly to their self-interest. A politico trained in a harsh but realistic school, he naturally directed his most gaudy promises to the groups that seemed to be most numerous, and the event proved that he was a smart mathematician."

Between the election of 1948 and the contest four years later, a media revolution occurred. In 1948 fewer than half a million American families owned television sets. Four years later nearly nineteen million sets were in use. No national television networks yet functioned during the Truman campaign, but by the next presidential race the networks were in business and in fierce competition. Just four years after he upset Dewey, Truman's style was obsolete. No more did candidates need the transcontinental whistle-stop tours. Instead they were trying to learn to use the new medium effectively. It was the end of an era, the threshold of a new style of politics. The campaigns that followed would witness a further erosion of partisan loyalties and powers.

Be a Party Girl: Campaign Appeals to Women

BY EDITH P. MAYO

americans political parties have always produced and distributed campaign items with a special appeal for women, but it wasn't until the fifties that a political party launched the first deliberate campaign aimed at women voters. This effort – coming more than thirty years after women won the right to vote – generated a rich array of campaign artifacts that tell us much about attitudes toward women and their role in politics and society during the era of the Cold War.

Though excluded from voting until the passage of the Nineteenth Amendment in 1920, American women have participated in the nation's political culture in a variety of ways since the age of George Washington. Women in the Revolutionary era and in the early republic, for instance, developed an inclusive concept known as republican motherhood, which made their political awareness and participation a crucial part of American life. As the center of the home and family, women were to raise and educate good citizens for the republic, nurturing civic responsibility and love of country. By extension, women were to imbue their sons and daughters with partisan ideology and pride.

Centering women's political life within the home dictated that much of the material culture of politics would be directed there also. Early campaign objects from the era of Washington through the late nineteenth century carried a distinctly home appeal, calculated to reinforce the intensely personal, patriotic, and partisan attitudes of the family. Such items as clothing buttons bearing candidates' names and party slogans, ceramic tableware, and printed textiles were distributed. By the Jackson campaign of 1828, feminine items such as sewing boxes had been added, as well as lovely tortoiseshell combs with a likeness of Old Hickory to adorn a lady's hair. Women participated in a multitude of supportive, nonvoting activities such as rallies, parades, banquets, mass meetings, and barbecues. Women produced campaign materials themselves by sewing and decorating campaign banners.

The campaign of 1840, which pitted President Martin Van Buren against William Henry Harrison, generated an unprecedented explosion of political activity and a production of Harrison campaign items by the Whig party that went unequaled for another forty years. Women's campaign activities in 1840 included teas, speeches, torchlight parades, and letter-writing campaigns; they reportedly attended two- to three-day rallies by the thousands. To encourage and reinforce this political activity by women, the Whigs greatly expanded the range of ceramic wares available for the home, all with the Harrison log-cabin motif. Creamers and sugar bowls, as well as cups, plates, and glassware, abounded. Harrison's likeness appeared on the handles of tablespoons and women's hairbrushes. Lovely, colorful quilts, fashioned from campaign ribbons, were popular items made by women. Stationery, with Harrison's likeness and log-cabin motif, was plentiful. The Whigs' strong appeal to women undoubtedly increased female participation in Harrison's campaign.

Campaigns between 1844 and 1888 generally reveal a low production of women's items by either party. The campaign of 1888, however, marks a new trend in political campaigning: the use of the presidential hopeful's wife as a candidate for first lady. The young and beautiful Frances Folsom, who had married President Grover Cleveland in a White House ceremony, became an enormously popular figure. Earlier, in 1856, the Republicans produced a campaign medal for their first candidate, John C. Frémont, with the slogan "Jessie's Choice," referring to the candidate's wife and the daughter of Senator Thomas Hart Benton. Campaign posters were also produced for Mrs. Hayes in 1876 and for Mrs. Harrison and Mrs. Morton, wives of Cleveland's Republican opponents.

In 1888 and later, political materials reinforced the nineteenth-century ideal of womanhood (wife, mother, helpmate, queen of the domestic scene, in short, woman in the home) while technological progress increased the diversity of campaign artifacts. In addition to the time-

Overleaf:
Democratic convention program, 1956. *After the trauma of World War II, Americans turned their attention to their families and the comforts of home. Although this program cover implies a family focus for the Democratic national convention, Republicans exploited family images much more aggressively than the Democrats, who were hampered by Adlai Stevenson's status as a divorced man.*

honored plates, cups, spoons, and bandannas, new types of household objects were introduced: table napkins, cotton pillow cases with lithographs of the candidates, silk scarves and handkerchiefs with likenesses of the party hopefuls, metal trays, mirrors, tapestries, pin cushions, and jewelry such as rings and charm bracelets. Curiously, between 1900 and 1920 candidates' wives were not promoted for their first-lady appeal, and the production of campaign items for women declined dramatically. Wives did not appear on political buttons again until the thirties, and almost no campaign artifacts were made specifically for women. One might think that the women's suffrage movement would have presented the political parties with a golden opportunity to court a new constituency, but almost every suffrage item extant in political collections was produced by women's suffrage groups and not by the political parties. The absence of first-lady candidates and campaign appeals to women during this period suggests deep-seated ambivalence about the role of women in society and, particularly, in political life.

The passage of the Nineteenth Amendment in 1920, granting full voting rights to women (more than half the adult population), would also lead one to expect a concomitant party appeal to these new voters. Suffragists anticipated (and professional politicians and lobbyists feared) that women would constitute a powerful voting bloc. Their votes, it was thought, would command great political power for the enactment of social reforms that women had sought. An identifiable women's voting bloc in national elections did not materialize, however, and most women gradually affiliated with one of the two major parties.

Women, moreover, did not register or vote in numbers anywhere near those anticipated by either the suffragists or their opponents. Though eligible women voters were estimated at sixteen million in 1920, only 25 percent of them exercised their right to vote. The estimate of women voting in 1924 was only slightly higher. Like African Americans in the mid sixties, and eighteen-year-olds in the seventies, women were unaccustomed to their new right. It would take more than a generation for women to vote in the same numbers as men.

During the twenties, thirties, and forties, few campaign items were produced for women, including the traditional buttons, scarves, and plates. A variety of factors contributed to the lack of materials: women did not register or vote in the numbers expected, the Depression and World War II greatly reduced the production of campaign objects of any kind, and the general acceptance that there was no separate women's vote (a political axiom almost from the beginning of women's suffrage) generated the belief that no special appeal to women was necessary. If there was a women's vote it was a volatile unknown, and the parties preferred not to disturb the status quo.

Cleveland thread advertisement, 1886. *Pictures of first lady Frances Cleveland were used, without her consent, to advertise so many products that President Cleveland's supporters in Congress introduced a bill to prohibit the use of a person's image without the person's consent. The bill failed.*

Women as Political Consumers

The fifties marked a turning point in the relationship between women and political parties. By the postwar election of 1952, women had become accustomed to their role as voters and now constituted half of the voting electorate. Of the 61.2 million people casting ballots in 1952, 30.9 million were men and 30.3 million were women. The major political parties had to determine how to capture their ballots. The Republican party made a particularly concerted and effective effort. Led by Ivy Baker Priest, the assistant chair of the Republican National Committee and head of the party's women's division, the Republicans aimed a strong awareness campaign at women voters. Focusing on the fifties themes of women's return to the home and the solidarity of the family as a bulwark against communism, Republicans successfully translated their campaign issues into concepts that appealed to American women. Domestic images were potent because the American public craved stability after the economic chaos of the Depression and the devastation of World War II. The return to normal living was symbolized by an emphasis on the home, the traditional family, and traditional, feminine, supportive roles for women. In a political climate increasingly shaped by the emergence of the Cold War and anticommunist rhetoric, the American family became a symbol of the goodness of democracy and capitalism.

The Democratic party was less adept at using those themes to appeal to women. Despite the decision to sponsor a ladies' day at the convention in 1952, the party's women's division seems not to have undertaken a voting appeal to women comparable to the Republicans'. Indeed, the Democrats produced surprisingly little campaign material of any kind for the 1952 election when compared with the Republicans' tremendous output. Instead, the party stressed the integration of women into the political mainstream and, unlike the 1948 campaign, chose not to highlight women's issues as separate from those of interest to men.

In addition to their determination to capture women's votes, the Republicans had other advantages. In Eisenhower and Nixon they had the perfect candidates for the times. Ike and Dick, as they were often called, could be presented as the warrior hero, defender of the free world against its military foes, and the man who had built a reputation for defending the country against the subversion of communism. They also had the perfect presidential and vice presidential spouses, presented as the quintessentially supportive helpmates that the era extolled. Both families were active and highly visible during the campaign, allowing Republicans to exploit skillfully the themes of the campaign, making the opposition appear weak on issues central to the fight, while highlighting the family strength and solidarity of their own candidates. The Democratic nominee, Adlai Stevenson, was divorced, which in itself was a political liability in the fifties. Perhaps more significant, however, his marital status deprived the Democrats of the opportunity to capitalize on issues surrounding the family, a major social theme of the era.

True to their capitalist ideology and affiliations, the Republican advisors and analysts drew heavily from their market-research and advertising backgrounds to formulate the approach to

Republican comic book, 1956. *The years from 1935 to 1960 saw an explosion of interest in comic books. Comics were so popular that campaign managers found it advantageous to print campaign literature in comic form. This cartoon, from a booklet entitled "Forward with Eisenhower-Nixon, 1956," shows how one fictional woman considered the issues of the day and made up her mind to vote for Eisenhower.*

Eisenhower potholder, 1952. *Republican campaigns of the fifties strove to connect with the traditional values of hearth and home and also actively sought the votes of women, or at least of housewives.*

the campaign. They were able to translate the issues that the Women's Division wanted to emphasize into mass-produced and mass-marketed commodities for consumption. What better way to appeal to the housewife, who was being urged back into her role as consumer? In such a climate the issues of the fifties could be sold to the electorate in female terms. Republican pamphlets and leaflets, created by the Women's Division for women party workers, were widely circulated. One leaflet urged women to "be a Party Girl," a double entendre that urged them to work for the party while capturing the mindless, unthreatening, "fun-time girl" ideal of the fifties. Fit for kitchen and bedroom, and probably smart enough to stuff envelopes and dial phones, the Party Girl was certainly incapable of an independent thought. Properly reticent and unassertive, she had to be taught and urged to do everything. Republican literature always pictured women in supportive roles, in submissive postures, receiving explicitly detailed instructions from men or from the party on every subject. Pamphlets urged women party workers to conduct highly organized telephoning, radio, and television parties. And they responded. The strength of women's political organizations at the grass-roots level was startling.

The Republicans made effective use of these ardent amateurs, the local precinct workers, the largest group of women in political activity at the time. These women, who then outnumbered men in political volunteer work, staged political get-togethers, phone-calling parties, and television sessions. The Republicans knew their constituency. Campaign issues were presented as appeals to the little woman, picturing the American family as typically middle or upper-middle class, white, suburban, with a husband working outside the home for wages and a wife who remained at home with plenty of time for the PTA and volunteer work. Women's so-called

**"Ike girls,"
c. 1952.**
Often recruited from local Republican families at bandwagon stops, young women served as cheerleaders and ornamentation at Eisenhower rallies. Everything about them, including their parasols, said, "I Like Ike."

Eisenhower jewelry, 1952.
Republican women wore inexpensive costume jewelry like this set of earrings and pins at women's club meetings, during stints at the polls, and for telephone parties, where they would gather to drum up support for Ike and Dick.

"flexible domestic schedule" meant they had time for phoning, canvassing, meetings, tea parties, driving voters to the polls, and staffing the polls themselves.

The familiar buttons with the picture of the candidate's wife, Mamie, were again circulated, though to a degree previously undreamed of. The wife of the vice presidential candidate, Pat Nixon, appeared on campaign buttons for the first time in 1952 and was highly popularized. Mamie Eisenhower thoroughly enjoyed the role of political campaigner that she was thrust into in 1952 and left her personal stamp on her husband's campaign. Relatively unknown at the start of the campaign, Mamie had become a national celebrity by election time. In this first nationally televised campaign, she was an important image. A public that craved stability after World War II could not have asked for better symbols than Mamie and Pat to emphasize the traditional home and family. The candidates' devotion to their families was reflected in their wives' adoring regard, Mamie's admiring and supportive looks at Ike during televised interviews and Pat Nixon's appearances with her daughters and pet dog, Checkers. Photos of Ike and Mamie (with her in pajamas) on the back of the whistle-stop train became a campaign classic. Nixon wrapped himself in family sanctity and sympathy in a dramatic television speech by invoking Checkers as a ploy to refute charges that he had misused campaign funds.

The more visible presence of the candidates' wives in this campaign did not, however, signal a departure from traditional ideas about women's role. In both presidential elections in the fifties, campaign devices and images of women conveyed time-honored ideals of home and family. Objects with a feminine appeal were circulated in enormous quantities by Republicans in 1952. Many household items such as plates, cup and saucer sets, salt and pepper shakers, bud vases, pitchers, cream and sugar sets, and cast-iron trivets survive today, as does campaign jewelry in the form of necklaces, bracelets, earrings, and pins, all bearing the likeness of the candidate or "I Like Ike" in dangling rhinestones. There were Republican emery boards, nap-

Eisenhower stockings, 1952. *The "I Like Ike" slogan turned up everywhere, inspiring a merchandising bonanza. An unprecedented number of campaign novelties, like these rhinestone-studded stockings, were directed at women voters.*

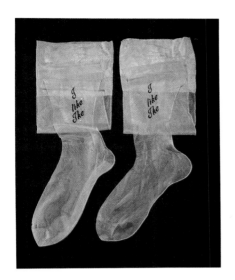

Republican buttons, 1952. *Mamie Eisenhower and Pat Nixon both were immensely popular with voters in the fifties, and the Republican party used the wives' images to promote their husbands as loyal and devoted family men.*

kins, mirrors, combs, thimbles, and fans. Though the silk scarves of 1888 foreshadowed an appeal to women through wearing apparel, they pale in comparison with the apparel appeal of the 1952 campaign. The well-dressed Party Girl would not leave home without wearing her "I Like Ike" blouse or dress (with full circle skirt, of course), her Republican umbrella, "Ike and Dick" sunglasses, complemented with the "I Like Ike" corsage and nylon stockings proclaiming to the world on both calves, "I Like Ike!" And what fashionable Republican woman would dare venture forth without her "I Like Ike" compact, in the configuration of a telephone dial, and her G.O.P. perfume, "For the Scent of Victory"?

The Republicans took political campaigning with a woman's slant a step beyond domestic objects and wearing apparel. Three major Republican themes were the Korean War, corruption (or "the mess in Washington," as it was called), and a balanced budget. The Republicans cleverly managed to find a particularly feminine angle for each of them. The Korean War was pictured as involving a son or husband. A campaign comic book published by the Republican National Committee graphically portrayed a woman whose son was being shot at in Korea and a sweetheart whose boyfriend would be unable to make it to their wedding because the war had intervened. Ike had promised to end the war and bring the boys home. Women were told that since Ike was a brilliant military hero and knew firsthand the horrors of war, he had not only the know-how but the incentive to make that a reality. Women obviously believed it. According to pollster Louis Harris, "Women . . . were more disturbed about the Korean War than men in 1952. In fact, there is evidence to indicate that women were among the real prime movers in making the Korean War a major and decisive influence in the final outcome of the election."

The problem of the balanced budget was also translated into the language of the average housewife – it was equated with her balancing of the family budget. The implication was clear: if she could do it, so could the government. A brochure displaying a housewife on the cover

Republican scrub pail, 1952. *This bucket held the water and sponge used to erase and update chalkboard tallies of election returns at a Republican victory celebration in Washington, D.C., on election night. Its slogan refers to the Republican promise to clean out the federal government and bring it under control again.*

asked women, "How much did your groceries cost you today?" It explained the rise in prices and the high cost of living by declaring that "waste, corruption, extravagance, blunders, bungling, bureaucrats, and taxes are hidden in your grocery bag." Following the theme to its logical conclusion, Republicans circulated extra-large "Ike and Dick" shopping bags – no doubt to show the housewife just how much she could buy if Ike were elected.

The mess in Washington was translated from an unintelligible bureaucratic problem into a simple matter that housewives could readily understand. Cleaning up the mess in Washington was portrayed in terms of a housewife cleaning up her home. Red, white, and blue scrub pails with the slogan "Let's clean up with Eisenhower and Nixon" and large "Ike and Dick" brooms, as well as broom pins, were widely distributed. Women were urged to help Ike, "a thrifty housekeeper," to "sweep out the mess."

Pollster Louis Harris pointed out that this appeal was not by any means lost on women voters. Pressures on the family budget to buy more than there was money for fell largely on women. "This was a crucial fact in the 1952 elections. Women lost faith in the Democratic Party to help them financially. Polls show . . . women thought there was more likelihood of the Republicans keeping prices in line than the Democrats. . . . Women more significantly than men felt the Republican Party would bring them economic security."

The Republican effort to capture the women's vote in 1952 was not without results at the polls. Earl Kruschke, after conducting polls in Michigan and studying polls of others in the 1952 election, concluded that women voted for Eisenhower in greater percentages than men (52 percent of men and 58 percent of women) and contributed significantly to his victory. Harris substantially agrees. In Kruschke's samplings, all the women interviewed who voted for Eisenhower mentioned one of the three "women's appeals" as their reason for voting Republican.

In many respects, the election of 1956 was a replay of the campaign of 1952. The Republicans again ran Eisenhower and Nixon, and the Democrats once more fielded Adlai Stevenson. The Democrats shifted their vice presidential candidate to Estes Kefauver, who had gained fame and popularity by conducting anticrime and racketeering hearings. As the menace of "godless communism" and the threat of nuclear war with the Soviet Union alarmed the public (recall the chilling "Duck and Cover" drills practiced in schools to "save" children from atomic attack), the social themes of family and religion were combined and emphasized. Religion – not a denominational variety – was the bland and amorphous "church of your choice." But family and religion continued as bulwarks against the communist threat. "The family that prays together, stays together" was a much-touted aphorism of the fifties.

The Republicans continued to capitalize on both themes: Ike and Dick were presented as religious, God-fearing men, while Adlai Stevenson was a Unitarian. (Wasn't that something like an atheist?) The Republicans circulated many of the items produced in 1952 but added campaign fliers entitled, "Ike and Dick, All American Partners," with prominent photos of Mamie and Pat; "This is the man, this is his family," a photo of Ike with Mamie looking at him adoringly; and a campaign advertisement urging, "For you, your family, your future – vote Republican." The Republican candidates and their wives seemed wholesome and traditional, appealing to the need for personal and national security.

The Democrats directed few items at women in 1956, but they did schedule Women's Day at the party's nominating convention. It featured Eleanor Roosevelt, Katie Loucheim (vice chair and director of the Women's Division), and seven Democratic congresswomen as speakers. The congresswomen, scheduled in the afternoon to attract housewives who watched television, were cut off by the networks.

Wives on the Campaign Trail

In many respects, the 1960 presidential campaign was a continuation of the fifties, emphasizing the Cold War, defense security, and the traditional role of family and women. When Richard Nixon launched his presidential bid, the selling of a candidate's wife to the voters had caught on. Voters knew Pat Nixon already as the vice president's wife. Campaigning was not new to her. In addition to campaign exposure in the 1952 and 1956 national campaigns, she had begun her career as a political wife in 1949, handing out plastic thimbles to win votes for Nixon's Senate campaign. The Pat and Dick team, as the Nixons were known, sometimes campaigned in 1960 from a station wagon: he stood on the back of the car giving speeches and Pat moved through the crowd handing out thimbles.

Nixon buttons, 1960. *When Vice President Richard Nixon ran for the presidency, the Republican party launched a concerted campaign for its first lady candidate as well. The Nixons were promoted as a team, and Pat appeared on her own at women's rallies and tea parties.*

Nixon favors, 1960.
Favors picturing the Nixon team – Dick, Pat, and their children Tricia and Julie – decorated tables at Republican women's luncheons. Such direct appeals to women and their sense of family continued a major Republican campaign theme of the fifties.

Coffee klatch accessories, 1960. *The locus of women's participation in politics during the fifties and sixties was the home. These items, including Republican "Party Girl" napkins and Democratic "Coffee with Kennedy" cups, were meant to be used at parties where women would discuss the virtues of the candidates over cake and coffee.*

Pat Nixon's visibility in 1960, however, was a central part of the campaign. The Republican National Committee and the Women's Division for the first time launched a campaign featuring a candidate's wife as a vote-getter in her own right. The "Pat for First Lady" campaign was directed by Clare Williams Shank, assistant chair of the Republican National Committee. The Republicans scheduled women's luncheons, teas, and coffees in her honor. Buttons proclaimed the "Winning Team: Pat and Dick" and "We Want Pat Too." Stamps and bumper stickers with "Pat for First Lady" were added to the usual feminine appeal items. The most amazing items from this campaign, however, are the favors given to women at a "Pat for First Lady" luncheon. They are cutout photo-figures of Pat, Tricia, and Julie Nixon mounted on sticks, used as table decorations.

The Republicans again produced a special promotional kit aimed at women entitled, "Politics Sunny Side Up." The kit was filled with brochures from the Women's Division on how to serve the party during the 1960 campaign. The logo on the kit's cover featured an elephant carrying a basket full of women on its back, no doubt riding to victory. Pencils were distributed with the kit, marked with the slogan "Ring for a Better America," urging women to have telephone parties for Republican candidates. "Party Girl" cocktail napkins, decorated with both elephants and donkeys, were suitable for use by women of either party.

Despite a strong emphasis on women's materials churned out by Republicans, the Democrats capitalized on Jack Kennedy's charm, youth, good looks, and self-confident performance in the televised debates. The usual campaign buttons presented images of Jacqueline and Jack; ceramic plates with their likenesses and Kennedy jewelry were abundant. Paper cups marked "Coffee with Kennedy," pencils and pads, and "Party Girl" napkins encouraged Democratic women in their traditional supportive campaign roles. Few other campaign objects directed toward women seem to have been produced by the Democrats.

To counter the strong G.O.P. images of the Pat and Dick team, Democratic candidate Jack Kennedy employed Jackie's pregnancy and the famous Kennedy clan to project an image of family solidarity. Although Mrs. Kennedy's pregnancy kept her from active campaigning, she was still projected as a loyal and supportive wife, doing her best to elect her husband. Having had experience as a roving photographer and sometime-columnist for a Washington, D.C., newspaper before her marriage, Jackie was photographed at her typewriter (in the latest, elegant, designer silk suit) writing her campaign column, "The Candidate's Wife." Developed and circulated by the Democratic National Committee, it was the first time a candidate's wife had her own column discussing campaign issues.

Despite the continued strength of the Republicans' special appeal to women, the Democrats' organized grass-roots efforts to utilize women as oilers of the party machinery were impressive as well. The candidate's charisma and his perceived win in the televised debates gave Jack Kennedy the presidency.

The 1964 electoral contest pitted Lyndon Johnson, heir to the presidency after Kennedy's assassination, against Republican Barry Goldwater. Johnson's backing of the Civil Rights Act of 1964 had turned much of the South into Goldwater country, solidly behind the conservative G.O.P. candidate. Clearly, Johnson needed a device to keep southerners in the Democratic camp, but Johnson himself was unwelcome in much of his home turf. Lady Bird Johnson decided to undertake a whistle-stop tour of the South, acting on her husband's behalf. Her four-day train trip through the South in October 1964 was the first independent whistle-stop tour by a candidate's wife. Mrs. Johnson knew that no southern gentleman would refuse to meet and welcome a southern lady, no matter what her husband's politics, and she used that knowledge deftly. The *Lady Bird Special*, as her campaign train was known, rolled south from Alexandria, Virginia, to New Orleans. Mrs. Johnson was presented in a nonchallenging light, as the supportive helping hand that good wives should be. She was to court votes in dulcet southern tones. Making speeches and courting local politicians, she actively campaigned in partisan politics, wielding the still-potent charm of southern womanhood. In four days of electioneering, she defined Lyndon Johnson's politics – and her own – for the nation. She made it clear that the Democratic party had not abandoned southern white voters.

Johnson button, 1964. *By reviving the whistle-stop campaign, Lady Bird Johnson engineered a public relations coup and courted the votes of the South for her husband's 1964 campaign. The tour was inspired by Harry Truman, who told LBJ, "There are still a hell of a lot of people in this country who don't know where the airport is. But they damn sure know where the depot is. And if you let 'em know you're coming, they'll be down to listen to you."*

Eisenhower compact, 1952. *This compact appealed to Republican women who had worked the telephones to get out the vote for Eisenhower. It also sums up the limited skills that political parties attributed to their female membership in the fifties: looking pretty and talking on the phone.*

The *Lady Bird Special* was the focus of many campaign items reminding women voters of this historic campaign by a first lady. There were toy trains, paper engineer hats, buttons, whistles, matchbooks, postcards, and ribbons – all with the toy-train logo of the *Lady Bird Special*. There were even invitations to breakfast aboard the train. Like the young women employed by car salesmen to sit on the hoods of the latest model automobiles, young Ladies for Lyndon sat aboard the rear platform of the train decked out in red, white, and blue. For Barry Goldwater, the Republicans circulated scarves (a western variety, to recall the candidate's home state of Arizona), jewelry, dolls imaginatively costumed as cowgirls, and perfume (Gold Water, of course). Still, in 1964 the production of campaign objects to court the women's vote had declined noticeably from the 1952 campaign. Lady Bird's whistle-stop tour was the last hurrah of a vanishing campaign style. By the time of the civil rights, antiwar, and nascent women's movements of the mid sixties, the use of such objects to appeal to women seemed a relic of the past. They no longer spoke to any political reality for women.

New Images for Women Voters

The 1952 campaign saw the first coordinated effort by a political party to win women's votes. Mainstream party politics have typically been unable to generate images of women in other than traditional, submissive roles, and the 1952 campaign was no different. Women have seen alternative political images at the height of the two waves of the women's movement, but those images originated within the movement itself, not from the political parties. Campaign artifacts have projected a traditional image of women throughout most of our history because political parties have had difficulty seeing women in alternative roles or in positions of power. Will parties finally devise effective political imagery appealing to the new realities of women's roles, lives, and voting power? Will party power be shared equally with women? Or will other interest groups be the force to organize the women's electorate around the social, economic, and family issues that vitally affect them? A distinct advantage will go to the group that can design vital, empowering appeals to energize the women's vote and engage women's newly emerged political influence.

TV and the Ike Age

BY WILLIAM L. BIRD, JR.

The fifties marked a transition in the history of American presidential campaigns. Buttons, banners, and other objects continued to play a part in the campaigns of Dwight D. Eisenhower and Adlai E. Stevenson, but these older campaign devices would soon be eclipsed by a new force, television. Television's effect on American political culture was decisive. In little more than a decade, the new medium transformed the nature of American campaigns, replacing the experience of a personal, hands-on engagement with a more sedentary, vicarious one. By 1952, television's power to project a candidate's personality had proven politically significant – and had sealed the fate of political Americana.

Television did not immediately displace the participatory remnants of the old hurrah campaigns. Until the sixties, old and new forms of campaigning enjoyed a symbiotic, if tenuous, relationship. Indeed, the participatory nature of old-style campaign objects helped to ease television's entry into the American home and into the heart of American political culture.

Though the system of electronic television that Americans know today was first introduced in 1939, it was not until the fifties that the medium began to boom. By late 1951 coaxial cables and microwave relays linked the rudimentary television networks of the East through Chicago to the West. In 1952 more than a third of all households in the United States owned a television receiver. By 1956 that percentage had nearly doubled to two thirds, reflecting a total of just under 35 million television homes.

The political potential of television was realized in the fifties by advertising and political specialists who employed a variety of highly controlled commercial broadcast formats to promote candidates, notably the spot and, later, the joint candidate appearance or debate. Where radio and material objects had once projected the images of candidates, Americans might now come to know presidential hopefuls by watching television.

Television specialists promoted the new medium as a democratic experience. Predictions for the future of television included the vitalization of social democracy via the instantaneous transmission of political rituals. That vision permeated the marketing of the television system in the late thirties and characterized the promotion of fledgling programs as a creative and potentially unifying national force. In this regard, the spectacle of the presidential campaign proved ideal. The earliest coverage of presidential campaigns dates to 1940, when the National Broadcasting Company telecast portions of the Republican National Convention live from Philadelphia to several hundred receivers within a fifty-mile radius of the network's transmitter atop the Empire State Building. That the new medium needed such events can be confirmed by the lengths to which its specialists went to telecast them. Lacking coaxial cable and other experimental relay equipment to telecast the Democratic National Convention live from Chicago, NBC arranged with Pathé News for filmed convention highlights to be televised in New York on a day-delay basis. Television receivers provided viewers with a vicarious convention experience. Viewer survey cards praised the telecasts. "Very good," wrote one enthusiastic set owner, "especially as we have never been to or seen a convention before." Another wrote, "This week alone was worth the cost of the machine."

The act of watching the convention spectacle symbolized, according to network specialists, television's revolutionary potential, for transmission of the convention offered not an actual experience but its instantaneous, democratic extension modeled on older (and idealized), real-life interactions of candidates and the electorate. If convention telecasts allowed viewers to experience the political process, albeit in a vicarious way, it took the development of another format to control and convey the image of an individual candidate.

Overleaf:
Eisenhower birthday scroll, 1956.
Retail Republicanism at its best, boxes like this were promoted as a way to wish the president happy birthday. They were placed in stores, where shoppers could sign a scroll promising that they would vote in November. Thousands of people signed, and piles of the scrolls were presented to Eisenhower at a televised birthday tribute two weeks before the election.

CBS election headquarters, c. 1952. *In the fifties, while political parties were learning to use the medium of television to promote candidates, the network news organizations were exploring new ways of reporting elections. This photograph shows a CBS studio on election eve.*

He stopped the war in Korea

He proved he could keep the peace

Under his administration we have...

PEACE... not war

Not a single American boy fighting anywhere in the world. A firm foundation for *lasting* peace. American defenses at their highest peace-time level. An "atoms for peace" program.

HONESTY... not corruption

Dignity and integrity in Washington. No Communist influence in high places. No mink coats, deep freezers, five percenters. Today — a President respected and honored all over the world.

JOBS... with PEACE

The harmony that is essential to progress. Goodwill between labor and management. Strike losses down 53% over 1952. Highest employment — best wages in history.

LET'S KEEP IT THAT WAY...

Republican pamphlet, 1956. *In Dwight Eisenhower's second campaign, the Republican party promised peace, progress, and prosperity and used a comfortable middle-class family gathered around a television set as the archetypal image of the good life under Ike.*

CBS vote projections, 1952. *CBS used this Univac computer to predict the vote on election night 1952 and as a promotional device to increase the television audience for the network's election coverage.*

The Spot Campaign Ad

Spot broadcasting had its roots in radio advertising. It began as an alternate form of radio networking, whereby an advertiser purchased time for an announcement on a large number of stations. Initially, the expression "spot announcement," or simply "spot," had less to do with the brevity of an announcement than with the geographical spread of the markets in which it aired. Advertisers spotted broadcasts according to the needs of specific markets, in place of or in addition to the radio coverage provided by conventional networks. Advertisers employed spots in regional promotions of seasonal goods, in saturation campaigns that accompanied product introductions, and in other special circumstances. During the Depression, for example, when crop reduction payments were distributed under the Agricultural Adjustment Act, automobile companies timed their spots to bring "special pressure to bear in the areas in which those payments were being made." The spot technique also saw extensive action in the wartime campaigns of the U.S. Office of War Information, whose Radio Bureau allocated appeals for the sale of war bonds, for car pools, rubber salvage, oil and gasoline conservation, and recruiting.

Television's growing popularity in the fifties opened new vistas for spot advertising in general and for political spots in particular. Commonly thought to be a Republican innovation, the execution of the first political television spot campaign was actually masterminded by a Democrat, William Benton. A former partner in the Madison Avenue agency of Benton and Bowles, and a successful Democratic candidate for the U.S. Senate from Connecticut in 1950, Benton grafted the possibilities of television to the traditional ways of the hurrah campaign. His experiment with one-minute televised films represents a pioneering attempt to invent a popular, politically successful small-screen grammar. That grammar featured a biographical focus, the candidate's accomplishments, and familiar domestic settings. Significantly, the spots also featured a campaign button that filled the final frame. In Benton's mind, television and ephemera walked hand in hand.

Benton television spot, 1950. *One of the first campaigns to use spot advertising on television was the successful Senate campaign of Democrat Bill Benton of Connecticut. Benton, who had been an advertising executive, produced the spots himself.*

Benton did not limit himself to living-room viewers. His spots also appeared on street corners and in storefronts throughout the state, where volunteers tended projectors that screened loops of the spots and twelve-minute films from Benton's weekly television series entitled *This Is Bill Benton*. Introducing five "quickie one-minute films" on the second of the series, Benton explained that though it was "customary for candidates to use billboards and handbills and newspaper advertisements and radio, . . . television and the motion picture are potentially a far more effective method of political communication – second only to a face-to-face meeting."

During the campaign Benton repeatedly tried to screen the spots for Democratic colleagues in Washington, and he told viewers that he planned to screen them for President Truman. "As an old campaigner who's been trying to advise me," Benton told viewers, "I think he'll get a great kick out of this modern way of telling a candidate's story." Whether Benton was successful or what reaction the president might have had is not known. In an earlier meeting, Truman had advised Benton to get out and shake hands with 25,000 people.

TV Likes Ike

Rosser Reeves, "Prince of the Hard Sell," also saw the potential of spot television and used the commercial format to purvey an image for Eisenhower in 1952. The Republican candidate's spot expert, Reeves sought to bring democratic and documentary qualities to the production. "I wanted to bring it down so that literally anybody that could talk could understand those spots," Reeves recalled. "So I went for the common denominator. You know, the guy says, 'Look, these groceries cost me three times as much.' And [Eisenhower] says, 'That's what my wife, Mamie, says.' Well, how documentary and plain and down to earth can you get?" Imparting spontaneity and straightforwardness to the spots required careful and knowing production. Reeves hired *March of Time* director Richard de Rochemont to supervise the shooting, believing that De Rochemont would "get the documentary feel" that the messages required. De Rochemont first filmed Eisenhower, then individual questioners who had been recruited from Radio City tourists because their "appearance and manner" made them seem like natural Eisenhower supporters. "The selection of these people," wrote a reviewer in the trade press after the campaign, "was meticulously accurate, honest and realistic. They looked the part mainly because most of them were actual people, not AFTRA members." As for Eisenhower's performance, Reeves marveled that the candidate "handled himself like a veteran actor. . . . We had [him] Thursday from quarter of eight in the morning till five o'clock. He cut 40 television spots – an all-time record. We went over to his office on Friday morning and he cut 25 radio spots! The man is very good."

Even before the campaign, television insiders had commented favorably on Eisenhower's telegenic appeal. In 1948, for example, *Broadcasting*'s Edwin H. James noted that "the Eisenhower grin is as infectious on video as it is in person or in films" and "probably would place

Republican pamphlet, 1952. *Printed on brown grocery-bag paper, this pamphlet focuses on problems familiar to women voters and uses their fears about inflation to cast doubt on Democratic economic policies. It also reflects the decade's emphasis on material comfort and consumption.*

among the top in the television sweepstakes." With Eisenhower's candidacy in 1952 came the opportunity to cultivate and project a television personality. *New York Times* television critic Jack Gould sounded a hopeful note, stating that Eisenhower had "the distinction, at least on television, of being a 'new act' as compared with his rivals and so enjoys a major advantage in front of the cameras."

The Eisenhower campaign's television advisors encouraged the telecast of events that would seem spontaneous, to dramatize their candidate's grass-roots appeal. Despite careful preparation, however, Eisenhower's announcement of his candidacy – telecast from the candidate's hometown of Abilene, Kansas – turned into a disaster. Instead of a dramatic campaign kick-off, recalled campaign manager Herbert Brownell, "everything went wrong, including the weather and the physical set-up, and Eisenhower made a poor appearance on TV. It was generally about as disappointing an opening campaign speech as I've ever experienced. . . . At that point, we were very discouraged . . . because we were afraid that meant that he was not going to project himself on the TV as a forceful personality." It turned out that misplaced microphones and other production errors, like "shots of people leaving and big stretches of empty seats," had contributed to the poor performance. Such lapses were not allowed to occur again, and after that, noted Brownell, "he did come over very well on TV."

Adlai Stevenson's television performance was as inept as Eisenhower's was successful at conveying a favorable impression. Stevenson never mastered his aversion to television and the constraints imposed by the half-hour speech. Democratic party regulars, used to the ways of Franklin D. Roosevelt, found themselves locked into an unrelieved schedule of television with Stevenson, a political essayist whose inability to complete a speech on time betrayed his contempt for the medium and its managers.

The election-eve telecasts of Eisenhower and Stevenson offered contrasts of style and substance that typified the two campaigns' approaches to the medium. The Citizens for Eisenhower presented an hour-long television spectacular entitled *Report to Eisenhower.* Produced by Arthur Pryor of Madison Avenue's Batten, Barton, Durstine and Osborn (BBDO), the Eisenhower show integrated fast-paced film clips and live television pickups, switching between Boston, San Francisco, Los Angeles, Seattle, Cleveland, Philadelphia, and New York over the recently completed coast-to-coast network transmission system. The program opened in Boston with Walter Williams, chairman of the Citizens, who invited the General and Mrs. Eisenhower to watch the show. "We've prepared a program to show you how the people have followed the beacon of your leadership," Williams explained. "We want you to sit just where you are relaxed – and watch as we report to you on this great crusade." According to a BBDO memorandum, street-corner interviews and demonstrations of affection for Ike sought to convey an impression of "a people dedicated to a cause" by using "a minimum of professional actors, high echelon people in political or private life, and staged acts." The program built to an extemporaneous speech delivered by Eisenhower at the telecast's conclusion.

In contrast, the Stevenson campaign's hour-long telecast delivered little comparable relaxa-

THE WASHINGTON EVENING STAR
April 18, 1956

PRESIDENTIAL PREFERENCE — President Eisenhower puts this Akron-made campaign gadget to good use as he tries on and peers through a cardboard slit eyeshade bearing the words "I Like Ike." The gadget on display in the lobby of a Washington hotel during the GOP national committee meeting is made by the Smith-Scherr & McDermott Co. of 41 S. Portage Path. It was designed by Austin Cox of Akron, an official of the firm. Ike tried it on after it was handed to him by one of the delegates. The visors are used for ball games and picnics and sun bathing.

AP- Photo

THE AKRON BEACON JOURNAL
April 18, 1956

SHE 'LIKES IKE.' TOO—Mrs. Eisenhower takes a "look see" through a cardboard slit eyeshade at the conference dinner last night. She must have seen more "I Like Ike" gadgets by the smile on her face.
—AP Photo.

Eisenhower sun shades, 1956. *Dwight and Mamie Eisenhower try on an unusual campaign novelty, sun shades emblazoned with the name "Ike." The photographs were taken at a Republican function in Washington and appeared in newspapers across the country.*

Stevenson bumper sticker, 1956. *Faced with the wildly popular slogan "I Like Ike," the Democrats struggled in vain to develop a competitive theme for their candidate Adlai Stevenson. "I Like Ike" so permeated the campaign that Stevenson's own managers used it as the background for this bumper sticker.*

tion or the vicarious mobility of the Eisenhower *Report*. The Democrats' broadcast featured speeches by President Truman, Vice President Alben Barkley, vice presidential candidate John Sparkman, and Stevenson, who characteristically failed to conclude his speech before the end of the broadcast at eleven. The Eisenhower spectacular, scheduled from eleven to midnight, thus began just as Stevenson was being cut from the air. So that Stevenson might finish his speech, the Democratic National Committee purchased additional time following *Report to Eisenhower*.

Stevenson's off-and-on performance amazed and amused the Eisenhower camp, including ad-man Rosser Reeves. In a letter congratulating BBDO head Ben Duffy on the "absolutely superb production" of *Report*, Reeves complimented "Eisenhower's little speech at the ending," noting that "it was made even more effective by Stevenson's abortive reappearance four or five minutes at the end, to conclude his earlier speech, that this show had 'interrupted.'" Reeves believed that the show's "psychological effect on the undecided voters was far, far more than anybody here will know." Eisenhower campaign officials shared that view and praised the program's popular appeal. Herbert Brownell, for example, who had once admonished Democrats for their embrace of popular entertainment in Roosevelt's 1944 election-eve broadcast, declared that *Report to Eisenhower* had delivered votes.

With Eisenhower's election, specialists whose campaign activities heretofore had centered on "figuring out new places to print the phrase 'I Like Ike'" now found themselves planning the "conduct of government." The legacy of the first presidential television campaign, particularly the belief that television could convey a sense of personality, proved decisive in the conception of the new administration's public relations. Evidence of Eisenhower's universal political appeal

Eisenhower decal, 1950s. *Although Dwight Eisenhower was famous as a military leader in World War II, his peacetime personality was so appealing to Americans in the fifties that Republican campaign literature tended to celebrate his likable nature; it seldom exhibited any martial overtones.*

Nixon postcard, 1952. *After Richard Nixon, the Republican vice presidential candidate, defended himself in the televised Checkers speech, thousands of letters of support flooded the party and the networks. Campaign managers responded to each letter with one of these postcards, styled as a personal thank-you from Nixon and his family.*

led opinion researchers to conclude that the issues of the campaign – communism, corruption, and Korea – "were of decidedly less importance than was the simple candidacy of Dwight D. Eisenhower." Students of the Eisenhower television personality suggested that viewers' preconceptions, expectations, and, most important, the carefully controlled context of a candidate's television performance weighed most heavily on viewers' perceptions of personality traits. Viewer reaction to the television events of the campaign seemed to corroborate the thesis.

Beyond the favorable preconceptions and expectations brought by the public to Eisenhower's candidacy, Richard M. Nixon's Checkers speech demonstrated that diligent preparation and mastery of production details could bathe a candidate in enough favorable light to overcome even unfavorable preconceptions. The speech was made in response to allegations in the press that Nixon had used campaign funds for personal expenses, a charge that posed a serious challenge to the Eisenhower-Nixon ticket. The broadcast's most memorable feature was Nixon's extemporaneous telling of the tale of Checkers, a black and white cocker spaniel sent to the Nixon children by "a man down in Texas who heard Pat on the radio mention the fact that our two youngsters would like to have a dog." The dramatic quality of Nixon's speech, his personal, extemporaneous delivery, and his insistence that the family would keep Checkers "no matter what" struck a chord among television viewers. A torrent of sympathetic cards and supportive letters rained down on the campaign, and relieved staffers responded to each one with a picture postcard of the candidate and his family, minus their new pet. "Dear friend," read the printed scrawl, "this is just a note to tell you how deeply Pat and I appreciated your expression of confidence after the broadcast last Tuesday. We want you to know we shall do our best never to let you down. Dick Nixon." Little doubt remained that the illusion of intimacy could be politically significant.

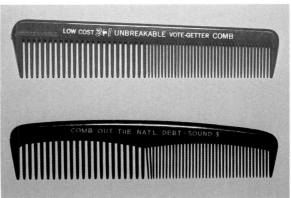

The Off-screen Campaign

By 1952 television had made its mark on the presidential campaign. Televised conventions, spot announcements, and speeches brought the campaign into American homes, giving viewers an intimate look at the candidates, upping the ante for personal campaigning and image-making. The new age of the televised campaign had begun. It would be wrong, however, to assume that television quickly displaced the older forms of campaign ephemera. Indeed, the Eisenhower years witnessed a resurgence of pinback buttons, bumper stickers, household gadgets, and other advertising specialties that helped ease the campaign to the forefront of attention in the home and, it was hoped, its viewers along the path of activism.

During the fifties, specialty manufacturers and small store owners continued to produce and market a variety of political objects that recalled the old hurrah campaigns. Among this constituency, as in no other, the popular appeal of Eisenhower met the retail economy of the fifties with a dynamic result: an outpouring of costume jewelry, pocket combs, comic books, matchbooks, cigarettes, swizzle sticks, sewing kits, statuettes, paper hats, pinback buttons, bow ties, sunglasses, shopping bags, nail files, and other specialty items. To be sure, manufacturers offered novelties for Democrats, too. Houston Williams of Murfreesboro, Tennessee, for instance, offered Crockett-style coonskin caps to all Estes Kefauver enthusiasts. Yet few items could match the "I Like Ike" triple flasher with its "dynamic, dazzling" design.

The Republican party used every device – including the massive Eisenhower bandwagon operation – to attract voters. Predicated on the dramatic use of all media, this Barnum-like extravaganza at its height in 1956 employed six 25-ton tractor trailer bandwagons outfitted with film projectors and public address systems, twelve station wagons, seven jeeps, a supply of "I Like Ike" buttons, Ike cotton dresses, and surplus forty-foot barrage balloons, organized in six touring units during the 1956 campaign. Each unit was "a versatile instrument of distribution for campaign materials and buttons, by extensive use of the Ike girls who rode the vehicles both during roving operations and formal parades." The brainchild of C. Langhorne Washburn, a Hiller Aircraft executive and cofounder of Young Industry for Eisenhower, the bandwagon operation had begun in 1952 with rallies and parades across the Midwest and East.

Eisenhower triple flasher, 1956. *This advertisement for the triple flasher – an electronic box that flashed the Republican slogan "I Like Ike" one word at a time – promises a miniature Times Square spectacle.*

Tethered in the sky above the crowd that assembled wherever the truck alighted, the barrage balloon in the glow of the searchlight cast what Washburn self-mockingly described as an "ethereal nocturnal spectacle."

Ubiquitous "I Like Ike" buttons and banners wreaked havoc on Robert H. Taft's bid for the 1952 Republican nomination. "If we could knock that phrase into a cocked hat and make it boomerang," wrote Taft advisor and National Association of Manufacturers publicist James P. Selvage, "we would have upset the entire campaign and they would have to start over again." Casting the problem as one of modern symbol management, Selvage proposed planting a counterslogan, "But What Does Ike Like?" with friendly columnists and newsmen and the available devices of the campaign. "At some of the hip, hip, hurrah Eisenhower meetings," Selvage explained, "we might put a couple of girls in front of the hall where they are carrying their 'I Like Ike' banners with similar banners saying, 'But What Does Ike Like?'" The plan included five thousand buttons, mainly for children. "Through every device we can think of," Selvage concluded, "we could begin to plow this phrase in and try to make them allergic to their own concoction." Failing to win the Republican nomination, the Taft forces ceded the problem to Democratic nominee Adlai E. Stevenson, whose campaign, like Taft's, labored under the slogan.

Stevenson shrine, c. 1956. *A fervent supporter of Adlai Stevenson made this object to commemorate the 1956 campaign. Reminiscent of a Fabergé egg, it is decorated with a variety of campaign ephemera, including buttons and pins. Its quasi-religious nature attests to the devotion that many Americans feel for candidates and the political process.*

Eisenhower measuring spoon, 1952. *Another object that connects the fifties focus on the home and consumerism with Republican politics is this functional plastic measuring spoon. The slogan on the handle reads "Ike measures up."*

Clearly, then, traditional ephemera such as banners and buttons continued to play a part in the campaigns of the fifties. What was new, however, was the way novel and time-honored devices would be integrated with the medium of television. The specialty items produced for the Republican National Committee's "Happy Birthday, Mr. President" campaign of 1956 provide a good example. The campaign featured cardboard counterstands decorated with a birthday-cake logo. Beneath the logo, a small box housing a scroll mechanism invited passersby to sign their names to this pledge: "You have asked that the coming election be 'the decision of America, not the decision of a minority.' Therefore, I pledge to vote, and to do all I can between now and Election Day to encourage my friends and neighbors to vote." The committee collected the devices and presented the signature scrolls to the president during a national birthday party telecast two weeks before the election. The program, "a musical birthday tribute" narrated by Jimmy Stewart, featured Howard Keel, Kathryn Grayson, Helen Hayes, Eddie Fisher, Nat King Cole, and James Cagney. The president and his family were televised as they followed the progress of the program on television from the White House. Fred Waring and the Pennsylvanians concluded the celebration leading a chorus of "Happy Birthday" atop an eight-thousand-pound rotating turntable in the likeness of a thirty-foot birthday cake cooked up for the occasion by C. Langhorne Washburn.

Eisenhower balloon, 1952. *At night rallies following band-wagon parades, an Ike balloon would be lit up by search-lights. The girls were often re-cruited from Re-publican families in each town the bandwagon campaign visited.*

Republican pamphlet, 1952. *The Republican party used the domestic image of house cleaning to encour-age voters to sweep the Democrats out of office in 1952. Some analysts of political Ameri-cana believe that the red color on the left margin is an indicator of the campaign's obsession with Communist infiltration of the federal govern-ment.*

These promotional strategies – one vicarious, the other merely ephemeral – were for a time quite complementary. In 1960, for example, the major parties' campaigns encouraged citizens to watch the television appearances of Richard M. Nixon and John F. Kennedy and emphasized the importance of wearing buttons and displaying car stickers every day until the election. The Women's Committee of the Democratic National Committee encouraged housewives to write for special "Coffee with Kennedy" paper cups to be used while watching the committee's new morning program, "Coffee with Senator and Mrs. Kennedy." Volunteers for Nixon-Lodge pro-moted the televised debate as "an exciting opportunity to participate in the very heart of a national campaign – *right in your own home!*" and suggested organizing television parties of ten or twelve friends, including some undecideds, who would then invite ten or twelve friends to their homes the following week, and so on. Each television party served as a distribution point for literature and buttons. The Democratic Women's Committee promoted a similar plan, not-ing, "Here is the perfect opportunity to bring everyone into the campaign. . . . *Anyone can join the Great Debate.*"

The participatory ideal represented by coffee cups and viewing parties made television the focus of domestic activism. This was understandable, for television, like specialty ephemera, brought politics into the home as another article of consumption, in keeping with the vision of more, new, and better living. The partisan claims of the Ike Age aspired to no less, envisioning homes in which the parallels of voting and consumption converged in a "shopping list ballot," and the iconography of diapers, grocery bags, buckets, and brooms symbolized change and the fight against waste and corruption.

Johnson television spot, 1964. *This ad, depicting a convention-hall floor strewn with Romney, Rockefeller, and Scranton placards, attempted to split liberal Republicans away from Barry Goldwater. The image itself, as well as the startling effectiveness of the Lyndon Johnson television campaign, suggests the waning of the age of traditional campaign devices.*

Jumping Off the Bandwagon

Was television the ultimate expression of political activism? Did the medium, as the focus of family attention in the home, stimulate participatory democracy or encourage voter complacency? Among some Eisenhower Citizens engaged in bandwagon operations, the vicarious thrill of the television campaign paled in comparison with the passing parade of bandwagons, barrage balloons, and roving operations. Enlarged to six times its original size for coast-to-coast coverage in 1956, the bandwagon spectacle collided with the highly focused interests of the campaign's television specialists, who disparaged the display as an anachronistic extravagance. Washburn countered that such spectacles were not only essential but also competitive in exerting "maximum influence on Democratic, Independent and lazy Republican voters." Future campaigns, he argued, would do well to consider such an approach. But that was not to be. Four years later, Vice President Nixon politely declined Washburn's offer to mount a Nixon bandwagon operation. Complacency in the Nielsen rating age would be combated with more television, not less.

The growing redundancy of political artifacts and the new centrality of television were symbolized in a spot produced by the Lyndon Johnson campaign in 1964. The camera shows the placards of the Republican party's unsuccessful nominees, governors William Scranton, George Romney, and Nelson Rockefeller, while a narrator recalls the disparaging remarks made by each about the party's presidential nominee, Barry M. Goldwater. The spot associates Republican political infighting and Goldwater's shortcomings as a candidate with convention-related debris on the floor, an impression reinforced by the echo of footsteps in an abandoned hall, an elevated camera angle, and a hand brushing confetti from each placard. The spot's creators littered the set to question the adequacy of the nominee, but the images of cast-away placards served to question the adequacy of the traditional forms of the American presidential campaign. Despite its promotion as a democratic force, television found little use for the participatory traditions of the presidential campaign. As the popularity of television surged into 1964, media specialists increasingly viewed campaign devices as bits and pieces of a parade gone by.

Tippecanoe and Tyler Too, No More, No More

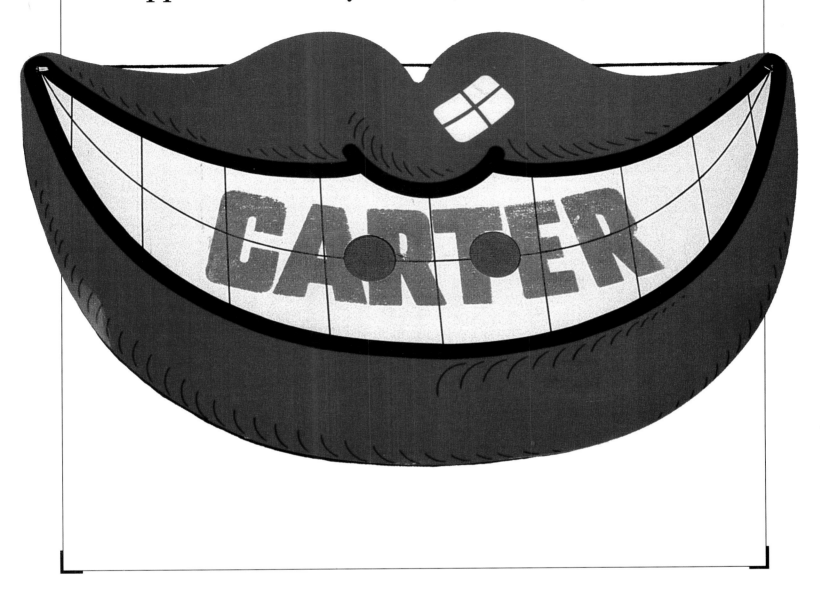

Where have all the buttons gone? Once the most common political devices of twentieth-century electioneering, tangible symbols of commitment to party programs and candidates and emblems of participation, campaign buttons are seen less often than they once were. During the election of 1988 in Washington, D.C., a party sympathizer had difficulty finding an ordinary official button to demonstrate interest in one of the candidates. When a button was finally located, it could only be obtained after a substantial donation to the local party organization. What a change from earlier campaigns!

Not even a generation ago, political buttons were widely available. During the 1964 campaign, there was great creativity in the button business. At the Republican and Democratic national conventions, button makers and salesmen peddled their devices and looked for ideas. For Republican standard-bearer Barry Goldwater, manufacturer Emmanuel Ress coined the button slogan "What's Wrong with Being Right?" "As he began to feel the mood of the convention, he explained, ideas and slogans would come to him and he would telephone orders to his factory for the speedy manufacture and shipment of timely buttons."

Bumper stickers too were popular in the Goldwater-Johnson race. Imagination and humor infused many of these items, which changed mundane automobiles into rolling political advertisements: "Bumper stickers that said Goldwater in a dozen different slogans, bumper stickers that said Goldwater in Spanish and French and Chinese, bumper stickers that said AuH_2O." In recent elections even bumper stickers have become relatively scarce. It is as though voters have lost the urge to display their political loyalties.

New Techniques

Over the past two decades, new varieties of devices, as well as new experts and specialists, have supplanted ribbons, buttons, banners, bumper stickers, and other traditional devices of political symbolism. For the most part, the new techniques encourage spectatorship rather then participation, software instead of hardware. They remove voters from hands-on contact with politics, from pressing the flesh. Television is at the center of a new universe of communication and advertising. From its emergence as a national medium in the fifties, television attracted the attention of political leaders, and by the sixties it dominated campaigning. The average voter, who might formerly have joined in rallies, parades, or visits from candidates, now receives images and information at home in the den or living room through the television screen. Political campaigning, once a participatory experience, has become largely a spectator activity.

Overleaf:
Carter mask, 1976. *This novelty was a hit at the Democratic national convention in New York. It is a throwback to the age of Teddy Roosevelt in that it emphasizes an easily recognizable physical characteristic, Jimmy Carter's toothy smile.*

One example of television's many effects is the change in national party conventions. Long ago devoted to decision-making about party platforms and candidates, and to raising party morale for the coming presidential contest, conventions have been transformed into prime-time entertainment spectacles starring network anchors, with a cast of politicians and hopeful candidates as supporting players. Governed by the personnel and the rules of entertainment news, the networks focus on convention episodes of sudden drama and confrontation. Convention schedules are organized to accommodate the networks so that their most exciting events appear on prime time. The atmosphere must be upbeat and reassuring, unity is stressed, and drama must be contrived and scripted in positive ways, to entertain and soothe the viewers. Of course national party conventions have been staged almost from their inception, but presenting these gatherings as public spectacles instead of party meetings has changed their character. A first-ballot nomination is almost guaranteed, for the selection must take place before the TV

IS YOUR CAMPAIGN READY FOR THE '90s?

CAMPAIGNS & ELECTIONS

Trade magazine cover, 1990. *This cover cartoon from* Campaigns & Elections, *a magazine for campaign specialists, depicts the transition from old-line party managers to media wizards and image consultants. It compares and discredits the old campaign methods, which relied on yard signs, envelopes, and other forms of direct democracy, with the new methods, which rely on computers, experts, charts, and models.*

AuH₂O·64→

viewers are lulled to sleep. The possibility looms that even the limited convention coverage of the eighties may be curtailed in the nineties. Despite the staging of conventions for television, some authenticity persists. Vendors peddle campaign buttons, and ordinary delegates participate, much as they did in bygone years, making real noise, joining in genuine excitement, wearing actual buttons, badges, and funny hats. National conventions still preserve a remnant of the mass enthusiasm of old-time political rallies.

Another device, the computer, has revolutionized campaigning. In the 1952 election, early computers were first united with television by the networks on election night to help report the outcome of presidential contests. Now, winners can be projected on a state-by-state basis or even at the county and local levels. Election results sometimes appear even before polls close in the West. As they became ubiquitous during the seventies and eighties, computers were programmed to perform all manner of political tasks that in the past had been done manually by campaign officials and volunteers. Sometimes eagerly, often with reluctance, political managers adopted computers and software programs designed to streamline the campaign process. An immense and rapidly growing technical literature, including trade journals such as *Campaigns & Elections,* deals with the wonders made possible by these devices. Computers assist in the preparation of demographic studies of voting populations, voting statistics, data about media markets, and results of opinion polling. They print literature, address mail, maintain lists, prepare financial reports, organize data. Machines can do what local political leaders had formerly done, serving as "today's functional equivalent of the ward and precinct leaders' personal knowledge of their neighborhoods."

The effects of these changes can only be suggested here. For example, the technique of direct-mail political fund-raising and advertising emerged during the sixties and seventies among supporters of both conservative and liberal causes. Richard Viguerie, a conservative, began assembling names from lists of supporters of Barry Goldwater's 1964 campaign and eventually accumulated twenty million names. Another successful direct-mail campaigner was liberal George McGovern, who acquired the names of thousands of Americans opposed to the war in Vietnam. Many of those war opponents later supported McGovern's 1972 presidential bid, contributing $12 million. Direct-mail fund-raising is frequently combined with secretive forms of advertising or persuasion mail that include the most negative distortions, even vicious, outright lies. Advertising by mail is difficult to answer because it often remains hidden. The mail process is also readily computerized. Mechanized mailings to specially targeted groups provide "a person-to-person approach to only that audience or audience segment which the candidate or cause wishes to reach."

Republican convention, 1976. *In 1952, when national television broadcasting first brought presidential campaigns into living rooms across the country, television coverage had to adjust to the rhythms and rituals of party conventions. By 1976, political parties were adjusting their conventions to accommodate the demands of television.*

Republican hat, 1980.

Funny hats and other flamboyant novelties have long been staples of American political culture. Today they are seldom seen outside a national party convention, which is where this version of the Republican elephant was found.

Reagan television ad, 1980. *When the Republican party ran Ronald Reagan for the presidency in the eighties, the campaign was based on the former Hollywood star's telegenic nature and on a mastery of the television medium. Because television time is so expensive, the financing provided by private groups, particularly political action committees, became a major influence in all campaigns.*

Paid for by
Americans for Reagan Congressional Club
And Not Authorized by Any Presidential Candidate

Another powerful fund-raising device is the political action committee (PAC). Formed largely in response to legislation of the seventies designed to regulate individual contributions to political campaigns, most PACs were established to raise money from trade associations, labor unions, and other interest groups for distribution to candidates. Growing in number from 113 to more than 4,100 in 1987, PACs have shown their influence by injecting many millions of dollars into campaign spending, especially for congressional races. PACs encourage interest groups to influence elections outside the party system and contribute to the further decline of the parties.

The revolution in modern campaigning includes the technique of opinion polling. Modern polling dates to the thirties, when it functioned mainly for commercial market research. News media first employed polling to find out who's ahead. Then campaigners began using polls to plan campaign strategies by identifying issues that seemed to move the voting public. A variant of the opinion poll is the focus group, a technique in which small representative groups of voters are assembled to discuss and test, in detail and in depth, a wide range of strategies and tactics, exploring how specific issues and political advertising will work.

New kinds of communication networks and machinery such as cable television and videocassette recorders can be used to distribute commercials to the public. These techniques allow much more precise targeting of audiovisual messages to specific "demographically homogeneous communities." Cable networks respond to particular audiences, reaching more than half of American homes. By choosing among the cable channels with their specialized audiences, candidates may air commercials aimed just at these groups, "based on where they live, how much they earn, and what interests them." Even more precise targeting is possible through distribution of videotaped commercials to be shown on home VCRs. With videotapes, candidates' organizations can create messages to reach narrow but motivated segments of the electorate. Video commercials are now employed in fund-raising and for showing in grass-roots household meetings. The possibility of candidates in every living room is too expensive to consider now, but as video costs come down, these devices will see greater use. "By combining the persuasive power of television with the pinpoint impact of a forceful, carefully-tailored message, A/V targeting may prove to be one of the most influential communication tools introduced to political campaigning since television itself."

New Participants

Besides the new techniques, new categories of people are participating in campaigns: women, minorities, young voters between 18 and 21. Perhaps the most influential new group, though, is political consultants. Campaign managers formerly came from the ranks of professional politicians. Men like Martin Van Buren, an organizer and manager of the Jacksonian Democratic party, or consummate manager Thurlow Weed, who helped found both the Whig and Republican parties, or Marcus A. Hanna, devoted and skilled campaign manager for William McKinley, represented nineteenth-century political professionals. In the twentieth century, James A. Farley, Franklin Roosevelt's manager, and Clark Clifford, architect of Harry Truman's victory in 1948, typify the old breed. Hundreds of other political professionals formerly helped to elect presidents. Now, to some extent, those old-timers are obsolete.

New participants, known as political consultants, reflect the application of new professions – advertising, public relations, media management, polling, communication – and new technologies to politics. Several writers trace the origins of modern campaign consulting to the first professional political consultants, the California firm of Clem Whitaker and Leone Baxter, who conducted more than seventy California state campaigns from 1933 to 1955. The firm avoided partisanship, managed each contest fully, developed issues, contrived themes and slogans, organized the media, and instructed the candidates. More specialized individuals and firms entered political consulting during the fifties. Ted Rogers, for example, produced Nixon's famous and effective 1952 Checkers television appeal to the American public. In Nixon's 1960 campaign Rogers coordinated television advertising. Joseph Napolitan, one of the founders of the profession, began in the fifties managing local elections at Springfield, Massachusetts. A specialist in effective use of television and radio, Napolitan has worked at all levels of campaigning. He

Rainbow coalition poster, 1984. *The Reverend Jesse Jackson attempted to expand his political image from its civil-rights base into a progressive multi-ethnic, cross-cultural political movement during the 1984 campaign, including women, Native American, Latin, African American, and white voters.*

gained renown during the presidential campaign of Hubert Humphrey when, after a poorly financed uphill struggle, he helped Humphrey come from behind to a near-victory over Richard Nixon.

Some consultants are generalists, able to tackle the whole range of campaign management tasks. But the majority are specialists who concentrate on certain fields of technical expertise: polling, media, direct mail. Candidates often employ several specialists, each one controlling a part of the campaign. In the new era, many candidates have become subordinate to political consultants in the planning of campaigns. Most leading consultants identify with one or the other of the major parties and at least half of them care about their clients' ideological stance. Although relatively new in politics, consultants have grown from being effective technicians into being darlings of the presidential race, media gurus, and wizards. But they are not universally admired. Given their far-ranging effect on campaigning, political consultants may deserve more criticism than they have received. A few analysts speculate that media experts, pollsters, and little-known managers have too much power.

Ferraro button, 1984. *The first woman to join a major party's national ticket, Geraldine Ferraro was the Democrats' vice presidential nominee in 1984. Her presence on the ballot reflected the growing number of women candidates and officeholders throughout the political system.*

New Challenges

The effects of all this new equipment and the new managers have been more than superficial. During the last few decades, according to leading observers of American politics, there have been changes of great magnitude in the process of electioneering. Summing up nearly thirty years of reporting on presidential campaigns from the fifties to the eighties, Theodore H. White argued that drastic shifts in political power, demographic changes, important transformations in political culture, and new communication media have modified presidential elections. As recently as 1988, a leading journalist, Elizabeth Drew, observed: "The process by which we choose our Presidential candidates more resembles a demolition derby

Babbit primary speech, 1988.

The New Hampshire primaries preserve the old-time quality of personal campaigning. Early in the 1988 primaries, Arizona governor Bruce Babbit, speaking here in Concord, braved the frigid New England air to garner support for his candidacy.

than a rational procedure." Numerous scholars agree with Arthur Schlesinger, Jr.: "Underlying the changes in the organization of presidential politics was the decay of the political party." Historically, parties were among the chief instigators of participation and political festivities, and along with the weakening of their influence there has been a corresponding decline in participatory activities and spectacles. The by-products of party decay include a loss of party control over nominations, the disappearance of party bosses, and fewer voters who identify with either major party.

Traditional participatory campaign styles and devices lost significance with the spread of presidential primaries. Promoted early in the twentieth century as a means of reforming the political process, the primary system has grown into a monster itself, consuming people and resources, emphasizing personal campaigns, and depleting party influence. With more than thirty state primaries designed to choose party candidates, the real contests for presidential nominations occur not at the nominating conventions but in the states months before the parties assemble. The New Hampshire primary, the earliest one in every presidential election, has emerged as the most newsworthy. In this small state with its critical test of the candidates, older campaign styles survive to some extent. There, face-to-face contacts between candidates and voters, campaign buttons, posters, bumper stickers, and novelties reappear every four years. Voters participate in campaigns, and would-be presidents cultivate support through the use of traditional campaign artifacts in somewhat the same way that loyalists promoted partisan candidates during the nineteenth century. But recently even the New Hampshire primaries have lost ground as instances of direct participation. They have been overshadowed by the Iowa party caucuses before the primaries. Most primaries that follow New Hampshire occur in larger states dominated by the mass media, and most primary campaign appeals appear on the television screen.

One of the notorious features of electioneering in the eighties is the spread of so-called negative campaigning. Although negative or attack-style campaigning has long been a technique of politics, modern negative strategies are conveyed almost entirely through the medium of television. Two early examples of negative television spots, used against Barry Goldwater in 1964, have become legendary. One, the daisy girl or bomb commercial, portrayed a little girl picking petals from a flower, transformed into the countdown for a nuclear bomb attack. Goldwater, the ad implied, was a madman ready to drop the bomb. The other spot showed two hands, supposed to be Goldwater's, ripping up a Social Security card. "I was depicted as a grotesque public monster," wrote Goldwater in his memoirs. Today, primary elections encourage a rash of negative attacks between candidates of the same party. For months preceding the general election, voters hear Democrats denouncing Democrats and observe Republicans abusing other Republicans. For instance, in 1983–84 John Glenn and Gary Hart, rival Democrats seeking the party nomination, accused front-runner Walter Mondale of being the tool of special interests. Mondale made sure that Glenn's record on the environment was stigmatized as "one of the worst." After a trashing from members of his own party, Mondale experienced similar attacks from Republicans when he ran in the general election. Again in the 1988 campaign, the primaries saw Republicans savaging rival Republicans and Democrats blasting Democrats. The Republican battle between George Bush and Robert Dole produced bitter attacks in which Bush tarred Dole with accusations of "meanness" and Dole lashed out at Bush: "Stop lying about my record." A damaging struggle among Democrats in the 1988 primaries produced dozens of negative television spots. Negative campaigning in the 1988 contest reached its lowest level with accusations by Republicans that Democratic candidate Michael Dukakis was soft on crime. A television spot made by a supposedly independent political action committee depicted the issue by showing the face of Willie Horton, a convicted murderer who had committed rape and robbery while out of prison on furlough. It accused Dukakis of being responsible for Horton's furlough and, by inference, for his crimes. There was more than a hint of racism in this effort to frighten the electorate by concentrating attention on Horton, a black man, and his white victims. Although they do not translate well into traditional campaign devices, such elusive television smears and distortions leave powerful impressions.

The high cost of getting elected became a concern of political analysts after 1960, when spending on television became a major factor in campaign costs. The leading expert on the subject, Herbert E. Alexander, has published a series of reports showing that election expenses have increased far more rapidly than the cost of living. Alexander estimates that $1.2 billion was spent at all levels of electioneering in 1980. Following the excesses of Richard Nixon's 1972 campaign and the Watergate scandal, reforms of campaign spending were instituted,

NBC candidate forum, 1988.
As the ability to purchase or manipulate television time becomes the deciding factor in more and more campaigns, TV networks struggle with issues of equal time and fair coverage in the news arena. With every election, *staging of televised debates seems to become more troublesome. Here, Tom Brokaw, news anchor for NBC, is flanked by presidential aspirants from both parties (Republicans to the left, Democrats to the right) during a preconvention television forum.*

including the public financing of presidential campaigns. The unexpected consequences of reform created new problems. Among the ways of evading new rules and regulations are so-called independent committees, which raise and spend private money without limit, as long as their efforts are not part of the official campaign. The Willie Horton ads in 1988 were sponsored by such an independent committee. Another way of avoiding the rules is through the use of "soft money," permitted in the reform legislation to support local expenses of electioneering, party-building activities, and grass-roots efforts. Although such money is used to supplement federal campaign subsidies, it need not be reported as part of the national costs. Finally there are the PACs, which have raised hundreds of millions of private dollars for election spending. Commenting on the loopholes in the reform laws and their abuses, Elizabeth Drew writes: "The point is that the intent of the public-financing law has been destroyed. And in a Presidential contest where other things are more nearly equal, a candidate's ability to generate private money could still make the difference. Given history, it is clear that attempts to affect the course of the Presidential campaign by private money will grow."

Another challenge to American political institutions is the continuing decline of voter turnout at elections, sliding downward from about 65 percent of those eligible to vote in 1960 to barely more than 50 percent in the 1988 presidential election. American voter participation is one of the lowest among democracies, ranking twenty-third among the top twenty-four nations. Reasons for nonparticipation are a subject of dispute. There are personal reasons: apathy, a lack of interest in politics, an impression that participation will make little difference, or a genuine cynicism and disgust about the whole process and outcome of government. Structural obstacles to voting are cited in a recent study by Frances Fox Piven and Richard A. Cloward, arguing that registration laws and procedures are inconvenient and disabling to voters, especially to poor and uneducated citizens and racial and ethnic minorities. Piven and Cloward maintain that elite groups managing American politics have deliberately sought to exclude disadvantaged voters by restrictive registration practices. It can also be argued that with diminished loyalties and resources at their command, political parties have lost the ability to get their supporters to go out and vote.

The Persistence of Campaign Imagery

Despite all the changes in presidential campaign devices and styles, one of the primary features of electioneering continues unabated: campaign imagery. Indeed, with party decline and the growth of visual media, it appears that images are more essential to campaigning than ever. During each presidential race, images help communicate candidates' appeals to the electorate by translating messages to the nation into visual devices that can be easily understood by the voters and that often resonate with fundamental American values and myths.

Reagan button, 1980. *Inflation, an oil crisis, and the failure to rescue hostages in Iran had sent the national morale into a nosedive in 1979. This button speaks to a nostalgia for the fifties, when the United States' economic and military dominance of the world had seemed unassailable.*

Reagan badge, 1980. *Combining the cowboy myth with patriotic images of the Statue of Liberty and the space program, this delegate badge from the Republican convention proclaims Reagan's knack for sending all the right signals through whatever medium was available.*

As Kathleen Hall Jamieson has shown, image creation flourishes in the age of television. Dwight Eisenhower, for example, appeared as a genial George Washington figure: the great military leader, above politics, savior of the nation, whose competence and patriotism were demonstrated through brilliant leadership in war. Other elements amplified the central image of a war hero, including the common-man symbolism associated with his modest upbringing in a small Kansas town and his nickname, "Ike." Also, later in his campaign, there arose the fatherly image of the general who healed the wounds of a divided nation by going to Korea to end an unpopular war and who reformed the nation's politics by ending the "mess in Washington." In sum, Eisenhower possessed one of the strongest images among twentieth-century candidates.

Ike's successor, John F. Kennedy, also exploited the war-hero image. Not a great leader in World War II but a brave young officer, Kennedy publicized his exploits as commander of PT-boat 109. Symbolized in numerous artifacts, the PT-boat image positioned the young hero as the leader of a new generation, replacing Eisenhower's venerable appeal. Kennedy combined heroism and dashing youth – he was the youngest candidate and only the second Catholic to run for president. As Jamieson suggests, Kennedy took advantage of his Catholicism by "dulling the edge of the religious issue among some and [turning] it to his use among others . . . and by creating the image of an heroic, family-oriented, good humored historian, and leader."

Kennedy T-shirt, 1960. *John F. Kennedy's World War II experiences as skipper of a PT-boat in the Pacific were an important element in his image as a young, heroic leader. This shirt recalls that war-hero image. Since the 1960 election, the T-shirt has become a medium of communication on a par with the bumper sticker.*

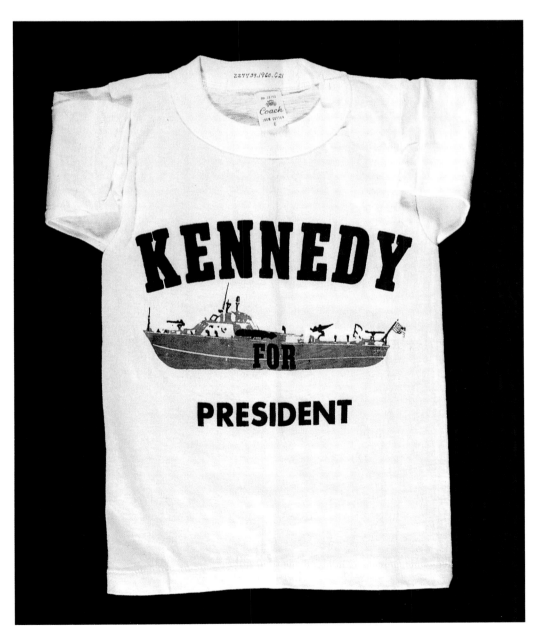

Kennedy-Nixon debate, 1960.

The presidential debate of 1960 recycled and reinvigorated an old idea from the age of Lincoln and Douglas. The first nationally televised debate in American history, it reached millions of citizens. Those who watched on TV declared John F. Kennedy, the telegenic young senator from Massachusetts (left), the winner. Those who listened on radio argued that Richard Nixon had won.

Richard Nixon's imagery in 1960 depended in part on his vice presidential service with Eisenhower from 1953 to 1960. Throughout the contest with Kennedy he emphasized his broad experience as Ike's protégé, his trips abroad, and effective handling of crises and confrontations overseas. Nixon thus ran as a tested leader, especially in international and national security affairs. There was also a strong element of the common-man image: Nixon as a poor boy raised in a small town by hard-working Quaker parents, the boy who had to fight for everything he had, compared with the wealthy Kennedy who had everything given to him, the humble cottage (or cabin) versus the gorgeous mansion.

Candidate images gained new dimensions in 1960 because of a dramatic campaign innovation, the television debates between Kennedy and Nixon. In format and presentation, the broadcasts were not debates at all in the classical sense of offering opposing systematic arguments. Instead, they were presented on the networks as contests featuring "the thrill of victory and the agony of defeat," with all the promotional excitement of an Academy Awards ceremony or sports playoff. Critics of the debates argued that style rather than substance predominated, that questions of who won the television event misled the audience, that the most trivial aspects of imagery emerged as principal results of the contests. In the debates of 1960, John Kennedy won by gaining the most in terms of visual impressions. He seemed "quick-witted, energetic, and poised." Nixon, because of his poor appearance and other blemishes in the first debate, projected a sinister and negative image, that of a loser in visual terms. By encouraging a direct comparison between the two candidates, the television debates had a powerful effect on their personal images.

Just as the military hero image served well for Eisenhower and Kennedy, another traditional pattern of candidate appeal has been even more useful to presidential contenders since the fifties: the small-town boy or log-cabin candidate. Although nobody believes in the literal log-cabin origins of modern politicians, the image of humble, rustic beginnings still recalls log-cabin symbolism. Nixon used the appeal of his modest background in 1960 and again in 1968. Another small-town boy, Hubert Humphrey, reminded voters of his origins and his father's simple pharmacy in 1968. In 1972, George McGovern could claim the beneficial effects of a rural upbringing. No recent candidate has asserted a more authentic small-town connection than Jimmy Carter, the peanut farmer of Plains, Georgia. Over and over in 1976, Carter seemed to trace his identity and moral strength to the rustic simplicity of down-home Plains. All sorts of novelties and advertising reminded voters of Carter's origins. Even Ronald Reagan recalled images of his beginnings in Tampico and Dixon, Illinois, despite the tinseled overlay of Hollywood. Old Tippecanoe might chuckle at the modern versions of his durable log-cabin image.

Another image somewhat congruent with the small town is that of the outsider, the advocate of change. In 1964 Barry Goldwater captured the Republican nomination with an outsider, antigovernment image that he projected bluntly and without shame. The candidate's slogan "Extremism in the defense of liberty is no vice; moderation in the pursuit of justice is no virtue" became the battle cry of a crusade calling for the dismantling of much of the federal

Carter coin bank, 1976.
This whimsical novelty spoofs President Carter's management of his family's peanut farm, while celebrating his rural roots and connection to the soil.

government. When Richard Nixon ran in 1968 he included several antigovernment and anti-Washington themes. Eight years later, Democrat Jimmy Carter presented himself as an outsider, appearing seemingly out of nowhere, a little-known but aggressive loner running for president. "It's time for someone like myself to make a drastic change in Washington," Carter declared. "The insiders have had their chance and they have not delivered." Ronald Reagan was surely the most successful outsider candidate of recent times. From his first prominence as a conservative supporter of Goldwater in 1964, through his two terms as governor of California, Reagan appeared to battle the establishment. Campaigning for the nomination in 1968 and 1976, he sharpened his outsider stance. As a candidate in 1980, Reagan said again and again that government was the problem, not the solution. Ironically, he accused Jimmy Carter, the

outsider candidate in 1976, of being a captive of Washington's bureaucrats and officeholders. And the voters seemed charmed by Reagan's outsider credentials; they let him perform for eight years.

"Hail to the Image" was the headline of a 1988 tribute to Reagan in the trade journal *Advertising Age*. The advertising industry's verdict signified a widespread view that no other recent political figure had used image-making techniques as effectively as President Reagan. Hedrick Smith, former *New York Times* Washington bureau chief, agreed with advertising's assessment: "No presidency has been more image conscious or image driven than that of Ronald Reagan." The Reagan White House staged the presidency with the aim of enhancing the president's image, making the actor-president the star of his own show. Reagan's reelection campaign in 1984 probably represented the peak of his image-driven career. After serving as president for nearly a full term, Ronald Reagan possessed a glamorous yet familiar identity that appealed to his party and the nation at large. White House staff members set out to engage the finest talent in the advertising trade to aid the campaign. Reagan's men approached several top advertising agencies but found them reluctant to take the job or unacceptable for the task of selling the president. Instead of hiring an agency, they chose to assemble a special group of the highest-powered talent among American advertising firms, including advertising executive Phil Dusenberry, who had spent many years producing ad campaigns for soft drinks and other products. Beginning with a tear-jerker film, *The Reagan Years*, the image makers produced a media campaign of warm-spirited, patriotic commercials reminiscent of spot advertisements for soft drinks.

The Reagan advertising group, named the Tuesday Team for its election-day assignment, traveled through the country to find authentic American settings as sources for appealing presidential images. The group gathered a video anthology of evocative, nostalgic vignettes, including a small-town barbershop and a little boy receiving a haircut. Other segments incorporated into thirty- and sixty-second commercial spots depicted the Statue of Liberty, wholesome families investing in homes and vehicles, sunny and welcoming communities, patriotic parades, Americans at work, scenes of rural tranquillity and urban bustle. The overall impression was that of "Morning in America." Reagan was made to seem the impresario of a national rebirth. Although he sometimes spoke, he seldom appeared in the spots, but he was always master of ceremonies. The images conveyed Reagan's world – "Morning in America" – an optimistic, happy, prosperous America as he imagined it. The message, reiterated implicitly or stated directly, was clear: reelect President Reagan to preserve the beautiful national spirit of harmony and prosperity. As Garry Wills has observed, "Reagan does not argue for American values; he embodies them." Journalist William H. Henry III summarizes the Reagan image: "In his most effective moments, Reagan appeared to have attained the ultimate goal of every national politician: to embody so thoroughly the myths and traits of the country's idealized image of itself that a vote for Ronald Reagan would be a vote for the real America."

The Reagan "Morning in America" campaign is only one recent example of successful presidential image-making. Although other elements of the electoral environment have been drastically altered, campaign images remain surprisingly familiar yet complex, often representing durable visual traditions. Images of festivity and celebration, humor and laughter, loyalty and commitment, remain alive, although they have diminished in importance compared with their nineteenth-century predecessors. Images promoting candidate personalities now overshadow other varieties of political imagery.

Images live on in American politics, perhaps because they are essential ingredients in our system of national leadership and elections. Image campaigning as practiced in the era of television, with thirty- and sixty-second spot advertising, has become one of the primary devices of contemporary political communication. Yet imagery is more than just a device. Campaign images seem to respond to fundamental myths, symbols, and beliefs in American culture.

This is not the place to discuss, in depth, the cultural values that give presidential campaign images their continuing vitality. Such a discussion would be largely speculative. Still, certain hints suggest where it might lead. The two most enduring campaign images are the hero candidate and the log-cabin candidate: the leader in battle and the self-made man. Often these two powerful appeals are combined in the same candidate personality. Part of the power of the self-made image lies in its apparent accessibility: according to the national myth, any American boy (but not yet girls or minorities) can aspire to rise from rags to riches, and in a citizens' army any virtuous soldier can succeed and become a hero. This image grew to embody one aspect of the national faith and was revised to confirm the achievements of supposedly self-made presidential candidates, from William Henry Harrison to Ronald Reagan. Historian Edward Pessen has analyzed self-made-man campaign imagery in his study *The Log Cabin Myth*. Although somewhat overstated, Pessen's examination of the log-cabin illusion reveals that even candidates depicted with log-cabin birthplaces, as Cincinnatus-like military heroes, outsiders, or underdogs, were more affluent than 90 to 95 percent of their countrymen. Still, the dream lives on among Americans who keep their faith in the possibility that every boy may become president. For the voters who bother to cast their ballots on election day, the old images endure.

But what of the others, the nearly 50 percent of eligible American voters who do not go to the polls? Have these people lost faith and interest in the images of opportunity still conveyed in presidential campaigns? Can it be that traditional images no longer reflect the belief of half our population in the American dream? Possibly the poor and alienated find few if any political images calculated to win their support. As one study of electoral turnout puts it, "Parties . . . do not put forward either the symbols that resonate with the culture of the worse off, or the policy options that reflect their life circumstances." Is it any wonder, then, that American voter turnout is one of the lowest among democratic nations?

Reagan voo-doo doll, c. 1980. *Poking straight pins into this doll was one more way for Democrats to poke fun at Ronald Reagan's campaign. It was inspired by the term "voo-doo economics," used by Republican rival George Bush to dismiss Reagan's tax and budget plans during the primaries. After serving as Reagan's vice president, Bush later inherited those economic policies.*

The Future of Campaign Participation

Where have all the buttons gone? The banners? The parades and rallies, the symbols and occasions of participation? Have they become obsolete or ineffective? Perhaps in some measure they have. But beyond their other failings, they have been devalued. New campaign consultants see little worth in traditional political celebrations and persuasive devices. Joe Napolitan, a leading advocate of electronic politics, dismisses billboards and "piddling little things such as newsletters and feathers and gimmmicks . . . sent around to people." To the consultant, such "unnecessary items" take valuable funds away from media budgets. Thus they deserve to be discarded.

In national politics, these traditional devices – buttons, hats, posters, placards, bumper stickers – have given way to videotapes, computers, mailing lists, television, and electronic communication.

There is less use now than in earlier campaigning for gadgets that encourage or depend on direct participation of the voters. To the media wizards voters are important not as participants but as members of the audience. Treated as spectators, voters are surveyed in polls, bombarded in telephone campaigns, and hit with direct-mail attacks. Seldom do they have opportunities to engage personally as actors in the campaign drama. Crowds, campaign devices, and festive environments are valued as props that cameras can capture to place candidates in colorful visual situations to appeal to television audiences.

Party managers in the nineteenth century mobilized the electorate by organizing their participation. Political action – great rallies and parades, vast and entertaining spectacles – captured the voters' attention and engaged their energies. Badges, buttons, and personal items

Anti-war buttons, c. 1968. *Over the last fifty years campaign buttons declined in number and variety, but buttons blossomed as a medium of protest. Specific issues inspired attractive and inventive buttons, such as these anti-war buttons from the late sixties and early seventies.*

were themselves central to the process of campaigning, symbolizing and representing participation. Mobilized by the political hoopla and campaign devices, voters came out in great numbers to vote. Since partisan loyalties and participatory campaigning began declining in the late nineteenth century, voter turnout slowly diminished. Campaign enthusiasm does not necessarily equate with numbers of voters going to the polls. Still, there may be connections between the two behaviors.

Direct political participation and artifacts representing personal commitment may be, as campaign consultants insist, ineffective in modern electioneering. Nevertheless, participation remains an important form of political commitment. As party festivities and symbolic artifacts diminished, other kinds of participation increased. Since 1900 scores of interest groups have promoted public rallies. In the early twentieth century groups such as the Ku Klux Klan, temperance groups, women's suffrage marchers, and labor organizations staged parades, festivities, and other events involving mass participation. After World War II several additional mass movements employed public participation for political purposes. Civil rights organizations carried out influential mass demonstrations during the sixties. Countless antiwar rallies took place around the country in the sixties and seventies, and more recently, environmental demonstrations engaged thousands of people as participants. Political enthusiasm and direct participation appeared in abundance during the eighties and early nineties during large-scale rallies for

Reagan television ad, c. 1984. *Although campaign managers are spending millions of dollars to address national audiences on television, the result has been a reduction in public participation in campaign rituals, including voting itself.*

movements engaged in social and economic reform. A few examples suggest how symbolic devices are used today. Important mass movements for peace generated thousands of banners, placards, and other parade devices, as well as buttons, T-shirts, and objects reflecting personal commitment. Movements for and against abortion employed a similar range of devices representing enthusiastic participation. The initiative for active involvement has shifted from broadly based political parties toward special interest groups with massive membership lists of people eager to join in direct action.

What about the revival of partisan rallies and the extensive use of campaign paraphernalia in the future? The rehabilitation of old techniques is possible but probably unlikely, unless there is a dramatic change in the condition of the political parties and a rebirth of enthusiasm for partisan participation.

What if electioneering remains a spectator activity? For those who collect and appreciate the lively spectacle and the colorful devices of traditional campaigning, the future is not especially appealing. As collector and Smithsonian Institution donor Ralph E. Becker has observed: "Past campaigns were the grand era of the button, badge, medal, lapel device, symbols of the election process, . . . a multi-assortment of paraphernalia known as political Americana. All played an emotional and essential role for almost two hundred years in broadcasting the image of the candidate and influencing the voter. Posterity is the loser in this new game of political campaigning. As the onset of a new technological era in American politics dawns, the age of 'Tippencanoe and Tyler Too' is truly no more."

American Presidential Candidates, 1789–1988

Winner's name heads the list of election-year candidates. Candidates are listed according to descending number of electoral college votes.

Election	Candidates	Parties
1789	George Washington	No party designations
	John Adams	
	John Jay	
	Robert H. Harrison	
	John Rutledge	
	John Hancock	
	George Clinton	
	Samuel Huntington	
	John Milton	
	James Armstrong	
	Edward Telfair	
	Benjamin Lincoln	
1792	George Washington	No party designations
	John Adams	
	George Clinton	
	Thomas Jefferson	
	Aaron Burr	
1796	John Adams	Federalist
	Thomas Jefferson	*Democratic-Republican*
	Thomas Pinckney	*Federalist*
	Aaron Burr	*Democratic Republican*
	Samuel Adams	*Democratic-Republican*
	Oliver Ellsworth	*Federalist*
	George Clinton	*Democratic-Republican*
	John Jay	*Federalist*
	James Iredell	*Federalist*
	Samuel Johnston	*Federalist*
	George Washington	*Federalist*
	John Henry	*Federalist*
	Charles C. Pinckney	*Federalist*
1800	Thomas Jefferson	Democratic-Republican
	Aaron Burr	*Democratic-Republican*
	John Adams	*Federalist*
	Charles C. Pinckney	*Federalist*
	John Jay	*Federalist*
1804	Thomas Jefferson	Democratic-Republican
	Charles C. Pinckney	*Federalist*
1808	James Madison	Democratic-Republican
	Charles C. Pinckney	*Federalist*
	George Clinton	*Democratic-Republican*
1812	James Madison	Democratic-Republican
	DeWitt Clinton	*Federalist*
1816	James Monroe	Democratic-Republican
	Rufus King	*Federalist*
1820	James Monroe	Democratic-Republican
	John Q. Adams	*Independent Republican*
1824	John Q. Adams	Democratic-Republican
	Andrew Jackson	*Democratic-Republican*
	William H. Crawford	*Democratic-Republican*
	Henry Clay	*Democratic-Republican*
1828	Andrew Jackson	Democratic
	John Q. Adams	*National Republican*
1832	Andrew Jackson	Democratic
	Henry Clay	*National Republican*
	John Floyd	*Independent Democrats*
	William Wirt	*Anti-Masonic*

Election	Candidates	Parties
1836	Martin Van Buren	Democratic
	William H. Harrison	*Anti-Masonic/Whig*
	Hugh L. White	*Whig*
	Daniel Webster	*Whig*
	W. P. Mangum	*Independent/Whig*
1840	William H. Harrison	Whig
	Martin Van Buren	*Democratic*
	James G. Birney	*Liberty (Prohibition)*
1844	James K. Polk	Democratic
	Henry Clay	*Whig*
	James G. Birney	*Liberty (Prohibition)*
1848	Zachary Taylor	Whig
	Lewis Cass	*Democratic*
	Martin Van Buren	*Free Soil (Democrat)*
	Gerrit Smith	*National Liberty/Liberty League*
1852	Franklin Pierce	Democratic
	Winfield Scott	*Whig*
	John P. Hale	*Free Soil (Democrat)*
	Daniel Webster	*Whig*
	George M. Troop	*Southern Rights*
	Gerrit Smith	*National Liberty*
1856	James Buchanan	Democratic
	John C. Fremont	*Republican*
	Millard Fillmore	*American (Know Nothing)/Whig*
	Gerrit Smith	*Land Reform*
1860	Abraham Lincoln	Republican
	John C. Breckinridge	*Southern Democratic*
	John Bell	*Constitutional Union*
	Stephen A. Douglas	*Democratic*
1864	Abraham Lincoln	Union
	George B. McClellan	*Democratic*
1868	Ulysses S. Grant	Republican
	Horatio Seymour	*Democratic*
1872	Ulysses S. Grant	Republican
	Horace Greeley	*Democratic/Liberal Republican*
	Thomas A. Hendricks	*Independent Democrat*
	B. Gratz Brown	*Democratic*
	Charles J. Jenkins	*Democratic*
	David Davis	*Democratic*
	Charles O'Conor	*"Straight-Out" Democrat*
	James Black	*National Prohibition*
	Victoria C. Woodhull	*People's/Equal Rights*
	William S. Groesbeck	*Independent Liberal Republican*
1876	Rutherford B. Hayes	Republican
	Samuel J. Tilden	*Democratic*
	Peter Cooper	*National Independent (Greenback)*
	Green C. Smith	*Prohibition*
	James B. Walker	*American National*
1880	James Garfield	Republican
	Winfield S. Hancock	*Democratic*
	James B. Weaver	*Greenback-Labor*
	Neal Dow	*Prohibition*
	John W. Phelps	*American/Anti-Masonic*

Election	Candidates	Parties
1884	Grover Cleveland	Democratic
	James G. Blaine	*Republican*
	Benjamin F. Butler	*Greenback-Labor*
	John P. St. John	*Prohibition*
	Belva Ann Lockwood	*Equal Rights*
	Peter D. Wigginton	*American*
	Samuel C. Pomeroy	*American Prohibition National*
1888	Benjamin Harrison	Republican
	Grover Cleveland	*Democratic*
	Clinton B. Fisk	*Prohibition*
	Anson J. Streeter	*Union Labor*
	Robert H. Cowdrey	*United Labor*
	James L. Curtis	*American*
	Belva Ann Lockwood	*Equal Rights*
	Albert Redstone	*Industrial Reform*
1892	Grover Cleveland	Democratic
	Benjamin Harrison	*Republican*
	James B. Weaver	*People's (Populist)*
	John Bidwell	*Prohibition*
	Simon Wing	*Socialist-Labor*
1896	William McKinley	Republican
	William J. Bryan	*Democratic*
	John Palmer	*National Democratic*
	Joshua Levering	*Prohibition*
	Charles H. Matchett	*Socialist-Labor*
	Charles E. Bentley	*Nationalist*
1900	William McKinley	Republican
	William J. Bryan	*Democratic*
	John G. Woolley	*Prohibition*
	Eugene V. Debs	*Social Democratic*
	Wharton Barker	*People's (Populist)*
	Joseph Maloney	*Socialist-Labor*
	Seth H. Ellis	*Union Reform*
	Jonah Leonard	*United Christian*
	Job Harriman	*Social Democrat of USA*
1904	Theodore Roosevelt	Republican
	Alton B. Parker	*Democratic*
	Eugene V. Debs	*Socialist*
	Silas C. Swallow	*Prohibition*
	Thomas E. Watson	*People's (Populist)*
	Charles H. Corregan	*Socialist-Labor*
	Austin Holcomb	*Continental*
	George E. Taylor	*National Liberty*
1908	William H. Taft	Republican
	William J. Bryan	*Democratic*
	Eugene V. Debs	*Socialist*
	Eugene W. Chafin	*Prohibition*
	Thomas L. Hisgen	*Independence*
	Thomas E. Watson	*People's (Populist)*
	August Gillhaus	*Socialist-Labor*
	Daniel B. Turney	*United Christian*
1912	Woodrow Wilson	Democratic
	Theodore Roosevelt	*Progressive*
	William H. Taft	*Republican*
	Eugene V. Debs	*Socialst*
	Eugene W. Chafin	*Prohibition*
	Arthur E. Reimer	*Socialist-Labor*

Election	Candidates	Parties
1916	Woodrow Wilson	Democratic
	Charles E. Hughes	*Republican*
	Allen L. Benson	*Socialist*
	James F. Hanly	*Prohibition*
	Theodore Roosevelt	*Progressive*
	Arthur E. Reimer	*Socialist-Labor*
	William Sulzer	*American*
1920	Warren G. Harding	Republican
	James M. Cox	*Democratic*
	Eugene V. Debs	*Socialst*
	Parley Christensen	*Farmer-Labor*
	Aaron S. Watkins	*Prohibition*
	James E. Ferguson	*American*
	W. W. Cox	*Socialist-Labor*
	Robert C. MacCauley	*Single Tax*
1924	Calvin Coolidge	Republican
	John W. Davis	*Democratic*
	Robert M. La Follette	*Progressive*
	Herman P. Faris	*Prohibition*
	Frank T. Johns	*Socialist-Labor*
	William Z. Foster	*Worker's (Communist)*
	Gilbert O. Nations	*American*
	William J. Wallace	*Commonwealth Land*
	John Zahnd	*National Independent (Greenback)*
	Jacob Coxey	*Farmer-Labor*
1928	Herbert C. Hoover	Republican
	Alfred E. Smith	*Democratic*
	Norman Thomas	*Socialist*
	William Z. Foster	*Worker's (Communist)*
	Verne L. Reynolds	*Socialist-Labor*
	William F. Varney	*Prohibition*
	Frank E. Webb	*Farmer-Labor*
	John Zahnd	*National Independent (Greenback)*
1932	Franklin D. Roosevelt	Democratic
	Herbert C. Hoover	*Republican*
	Norman Thomas	*Socialist*
	William Z. Foster	*Worker's (Communist)*
	William D. Upshaw	*Prohibition*
	William H. Harvey	*Liberty*
	Verne L. Reynolds	*Socialist-Labor*
	Jacob Coxey	*Farmer-Labor*
	John Zahnd	*National Independent (Greenback)*
	James R. Cox	*Jobless*
1936	Franklin D. Roosevelt	Democratic
	Alfred M. Landon	*Republican*
	William Lemke	*National Union*
	Norman Thomas	*Socialist*
	Earl R. Browder	*Communist*
	David L. Colvin	*Prohibition/National Prohibition/ Commonwealth*
	John W. Aiken	*Socialist-Labor*
	William D. Pelley	*Christian*
	John Zahnd	*National Independent (Greenback)*
1940	Franklin D. Roosevelt	Democratic
	Wendell L. Willkie	*Republican*
	Norman Thomas	*Socialist*
	Roger W. Babson	*Prohibition*
	Earl Browder	*Communist*
	John W. Aiken	*Socialist-Labor*
	Alfred Knutson	*Independent*
	John Zahnd	*National Independent (Greenback)*
	Anna Milburn	*National Greenback*

Election	Candidates	Parties
1944	Franklin D. Roosevelt	Democratic
	Thomas E. Dewey	*Republican*
	Norman Thomas	*Socialist*
	Claude Watson	*Prohibition*
	Edward Teichert	*Socialist-Labor*
	Harry F. Byrd	*Southern Democrats*
	Gerald L. K. Smith	*America First*
1948	Harry S. Truman	Democratic
	Thomas E. Dewey	*Republican*
	J. Strom Thurmond	*States' Rights Democratic*
	Henry A. Wallace	*Progressive*
	Norman Thomas	*Socialist*
	Claude A. Watson	*Prohibition*
	Edward Teichert	*Socialist-Labor*
	Farrell Dobbs	*Socialist Workers/Militant Workers*
	Gerald L. K. Smith	*Christian Nationalist Crusade*
	John G. Scott	*Greenback*
	John Maxwell	*Vegetarian*
1952	Dwight D. Eisenhower	Republican
	Adlai E. Stevenson	*Democratic*
	Vincent W. Halliman	*Progressive/American Labor*
	Stuart Hamblen	*Prohibition*
	Eric Hass	*Socialist-Labor*
	Darlington Hoopes	*Socialist*
	Douglas A. MacArthur	*America First*
	Farrell Dobbs	*Socialist Workers/Militant Workers*
	Henry B. Krajewski	*Poor Man's Party*
	Homer A. Tomlinson	*Church of God Bible Party*
	Frederick C. Proehl	*Greenback*
	Ellen L. Jensen	*Washington Peace*
	Daniel J. Murphy	*American Vegetarian*
1956	Dwight D. Eisenhower	Republican
	Adlai E. Stevenson	*Democratic*
	Walter B. Jones	*No party*
	T. Coleman Andrews	*Independent States' Rights*
	Harry F. Byrd	*Independent*
	Eric Hass	*Socialist-Labor*
	Enoch A. Holtwick	*Prohibition*
	William E. Jenner	*Texas Constitution*
	Farrell Dobbs	*Socialist Workers/Militant Workers*
	Darlington Hoopes	*Socialist*
	Henry B. Krajewski	*American Third Party*
	Gerald L. K. Smith	*Christian National*
	Homer A. Tomlinson	*Theocratic*
	Herbert M. Shelton	*American Vegetarian*
	Frederick C. Proehl	*Greenback*
	William Langer	*Pioneer*
1960	John F. Kennedy	Democratic
	Richard M. Nixon	*Republican*
	Harry F. Byrd	*Independent*
	Orval Faubus	*States' Rights*
	Eric Hass	*Socialist-Labor*
	Rutherford L. Decker	*Prohibition*
	Farrell Dobbs	*Socialist Workers*
	Charles L. Sullivan	*Texas Constitution*
	Joseph B. Lee	*Conservative Party of New Jersey*
	C. Benton Coiner	*Conservative Party of Virginia*
	Lar Daly	*Tax Cut*
	Clennon King	*Afro-American*
	Merritt B. Curtis	*Independent / Constitution*
	Symon Gould	*American Vegetarian*
	Whitney H. Slocum	*Greenback*
	Homer A. Tomlinson	*Theocratic*

Election	Candidates	Parties
1964	Lyndon B. Johnson	Democratic
	Barry M. Goldwater	*Republican*
	Eric Hass	*Socialist-Labor*
	Clifton DeBerry	*Socialist Workers*
	Earle H. Munn	*Prohibition*
	John Kaspar	*National States' Rights*
	Joseph B. Lightburn	*Constitution*
	Kirby J. Hensley	*Universal*
	Homer A. Tomlinson	*Theocratic*
	T. Coleman Andrews	*Independent States' Rights*
	Yette Bronstein	*Best Party*
	D.X.B. Schwartz	*National Tax Savers*
	Louis E. Jaeckel	*American*
1968	Richard M. Nixon	Republican
	Hubert H. Humphrey	*Democratic*
	George C. Wallace	*American Independent*
	Henning A. Blomen	*Socialist-Labor*
	Dick Gregory	*Various parties*
	Fred Halstead	*Socialist Workers*
	Eldridge Cleaver	*Peace and Freedom*
	Eugene McCarthy	*New Party*
	Earle H. Munn	*Prohibition*
	Charlene Mitchell	*Communist*
1972	Richard M. Nixon	Republican
	George S. McGovern	*Democratic*
	John G. Schmitz	*American*
	Linda Jenness	*Socialist Workers*
	Louis Fisher	*Socialist-Labor*
	Gus Hall	*Communist*
	Earle H. Munn	*Prohibition*
	Joseph Hospers	*Libertarian*
1976	Jimmy Carter	Democratic
	Gerald Ford	*Republican*
	Eugene McCarthy	*Independent*
	Roger L. MacBride	*Libertarian*
	Lester G. Maddox	*American Independent*
	Thomas J. Anderson	*American*
	Peter Camejo	*Socialist Workers*
	Gus Hall	*Communist*
	Margaret Wright	*People's*
	Lyndon H. LaRouche	*U.S. Labor*
	Benjamin Bubar	*Prohibition*
	Jules Levin	*Socialist-Labor*
	Frank P. Zeidler	*Socialist*
1980	Ronald Reagan	Republican
	Jimmy Carter	*Democratic*
	John B. Anderson	*Independent*
	Ed Clark	*Libertarian*
	Barry Commoner	*Citizens*
	Clifton DeBerry	*Socialist Workers*
	Gus Hall	*Communist*
	John R. Rarick	*American Independent*
	Ellen McCormack	*Independent*
	Maureen Smith	*Peace and Freedom*
	Percy L. Greaves	*American*
	Deidre Griswold	*Workers World*
	Benjamin Bubar	*National Statesman*
	David McReynolds	*Socialist*
	Kurt Lynen	*Middle Class*
	Bill Gahres	*Down With Lawyers*
	Martin Wendelken	*Independent*
	Harley McLain	*Natural People's League*

Election	Candidates	Parties
1984	Ronald Reagan	Republican
	Walter F. Mondale	*Democratic*
	David Bergland	*Libertarian*
	Lyndon H. LaRouche	*Independent Democrat*
	Sonia Johnson	*Citizens*
	Bob Richards	*Populist*
	Dennis Serrette	*Independent Alliance*
	Gus Hall	*Communist*
	Mel Mason	*Socialist Workers*
	Larry Holmes	*Workers World*
	Delmar Davis	*American*
	Ed Winn	*Workers League*
	Earl F. Dodge	*National Statesman*
	John D. Anderson	*National Unity Party of Kentucky*

Election	Candidates	Parties
1988	George Bush	Republican
	Michael S. Dukakis	*Democratic*
	Ron Paul	*Libertarian*
	Lenora B. Fulani	*New Alliance*
	David E. Duke	*Independent Populist*
	Eugene J. McCarthy	*Consumer*
	Warren Griffin	*American Independent*
	Lyndon H. LaRouche	*Independent*
	William Marra	*Right to Life*
	Ed Winn	*Workers League*
	James Mac Warren	*Socialist Workers*
	Herbert Lewin	*Peace and Freedom*
	Earl F. Dodge	*National Statesman*
	Larry Holmes	*Workers World*
	Willa Kenoyer	*Socialist*
	Delmar Dennis	*American*
	Jack Herer	*Grassroots*
	Louie G. Youngkeit	*Independent*
	John G. Martin	*Third World Assembly*

Reference Notes and Illustration Sources

Notes and sources are located by page number, followed by key words or opening words of the relevant paragraph from the text. The illustrations in this book are from the collection of the Smithsonian Institution's Division of Political History, except for those noted below.

Abbreviations

DPH
Division of Political History, Department of Social and Cultural History, National Museum of American History

NMAH
National Museum of American History, Smithsonian Institution

NPG
National Portrait Gallery, Smithsonian Institution

Introduction: Hurrah for the Campaign!

p. 7 NORTON REMINISCENCES: A. B. Norton, *The Great Revolution of 1840: Reminiscences of the Log Cabin and Hard Cider Campaign*, Mount Vernon, Ohio: A. B. Norton and Co., 1888, p. 215.

8 A PARTISAN WROTE: John Van Fossen to Thurlow Weed, July 20, 1840, Thurlow Weed Papers, Library of Congress Manuscript Division; New York *Log Cabin*, July 25, 1840. PREPARING INSTRUCTIONS TO WHIG PARTISANS: Albert J. Beveridge, *Abraham Lincoln, 1809–1858*, Boston: Houghton Mifflin, 1928, vol. 1, pp. 270–75. CHARLES MCDOWELL, JR.: *Campaign Fever*, New York: William Morrow, 1965, pp. 1, 58. THE NEW STYLE APPEARED: David M. Potter, *The Impending Crisis, 1848–1861*, ed. Don E. Fehrenbacher, New York: Harper and Row, 1976, pp. 433–36.

9 *The County Election*, 1852, George Caleb Bingham, oil on canvas, 38 × 52 inches; Art Collection of the Boatmen's National Bank of St. Louis.

14 A COMPANY OFFICIAL WROTE: C. H. Coster to Spencer F. Baird, Dec. 6, 1884, Smithsonian Institution accession records.

19 IN 1961: Becker's remarks were carried in the *Congressional Record*, 87th Congress, First Session, Vol. 107, No. 52, March 24, 1961.

21 IMAGE MAKING: Compare this approach to the concept of image with Merrill Peterson's in *The Jefferson Image in the American Mind*, New York: Oxford University Press, 1960, p. vii, and Daniel J. Boorstin's in *The Image: or, What Happened to the American Dream*, New York: Atheneum, 1962, pp. 185–94. THEODORE H. WHITE: *The Making of the President 1960*, New York: Pocket Books, 1961, p. vii.

22 ELIZABETH DREW: "Letter from Washington," *New Yorker* Dec. 12, 1988, p. 120. LARRY J. SABATO: *The Rise of Political Consultants: New Ways of Winning Elections*, New York: Basic Books, 1981, p. 16.

1: The Imagery of Campaigning and Campaign Devices

23 CLINTON ROSSITER: *The American Presidency*, rev. ed., New York: New American Library, 1962, pp. 175, 178. On the issues of meaning and functions of popular campaigning, see Michael McGerr's *Decline of Popular Politics: The American North, 1865–1928*, New York: Oxford University Press, 1986, pp. 37–41, and Jean H. Baker's *Affairs of Party: The Political Culture of Northern Democrats in the Mid-Nineteenth Century*, Ithaca: Cornell University Press, 1983, ch. 7.

30 RICHARD M. DORSON: "Material Components in Celebration," in *Celebration: Studies in Festivity and Ritual*, ed. Victor Turner, Washington: Smithsonian Institution Press, 1982, p. 33. JOHN J. MACALOON: "Sociation and Sociability in Political Celebrations," ibid., pp. 264–65. ELECTIONS ALSO CELEBRATE: Barbara Myerhoff, "Rites of Passage: Process and Paradox," ibid., pp. 109–35. "POLITICAL AND CIVIC CELEBRA-

TIONS": MacAloon, "Sociation and Sociability," p. 255. A MODERN STUDENT OF CAMPAIGNING: Bruce E. Gronbeck, "Functional and Dramaturgical Theories of Presidential Campaigning," *Presidential Studies Quarterly* 14 (Fall 1984): 496.

31 BANNERS TRADITIONALLY REPRESENT: Norton, *Great Revolution of 1840*, pp. 95–137, 60–64. The description of the Henry Clay celebration is from "Young Men's Whig National Convention of Ratification," *Baltimore Patriot* May 3 (?), 1844. Some studies of American political banners: Herbert R. Collins, *Threads of History: Americana Recorded on Cloth, 1775 to the Present*, Washington: Smithsonian Institution Press, 1979, pp. 89–96, 109–16; Edmund B. Sullivan, *Collecting Political Americana*, New York: Crown Publishers, 1980, pp. 124–32; see also Susan G. Davis, *Parades and Power: Street Theatre in Nineteenth-Century Philadelphia*, Philadelphia: Temple University Press, 1986.

32 CAMPAIGN TORCH: See Herbert R. Collins, "Political Campaign Torches," Contributions from the Museum of History and Technology, Paper 45, *U.S. National Museum Bulletin* 241 (1964); McGerr, *Decline of Popular Politics*, ch. 1. HUMOR AND LAUGHTER: Political humor deserves closer study than it has received. Several masters of political humor have themselves been candidates or officeholders: Abraham Lincoln, both Roosevelts, John F. Kennedy, Barry Goldwater, Ronald Reagan, and Morris Udall. See Leonard C. Lewin, ed., *A Treasury of American Political Humor*, New York: Dial Press, Delacorte Press, 1964; Morris Udall, *Too Funny to Be President*, New York: Henry Holt, 1988 (quotations, pp. xiii–xv). Today's leading comedians, such as Mark Russell and Johnny Carson, find a gold mine of comic material in politics. Many terms in William Safire's delightful and useful book *The New Language of Politics* refer to the humorous side of political life and campaigning, from "gaffes" and "bloopers" to "invective" and "self-deprecating humor" (2nd ed., New York: Collier Books, 1972, pp. 60–61, 307–308, 287–88). The entertaining volume *Presidential Anecdotes* (by Paul F. Boller, Jr., New York: Penguin Books, 1981) provides countless stories of the windy side of the nation's successful presidential candidates, from Lincoln, the greatest humorist to occupy the White House, to Harding, who confessed that he loved to "bloviate" and was frequently laughable by mistake (see especially pp. 122–29, 229–31). LINDA K. KERBER: *Federalists in Dissent: Imagery and Ideology in Jeffersonian America*, Ithaca: Cornell University Press, 1980, p. 23.

34 STEPHEN LEACOCK: *Humor and Humanity*, New York: Holt, 1938, p. 15. Charles E. Schutz, *Political Humor: From Aristophanes to Sam Ervin*, Rutherford, N.J.: Fairleigh Dickinson University Press, 1977, pp. 8, 38.

35 THE LATE NINETEENTH: Sullivan, *Collecting Political Americana*, p. 33; see Roger A. Fischer's *Tippecanoe and Trinkets Too: The Material Culture of American Presidential Campaigns, 1828–1984* (Urbana: University of Illinois Press, 1988, pp. 108–89) for a detailed description of political material culture of this period.

37 CARTOONS: Ralph E. Shikes, *The Indignant Eye: The Artist as Social Critic in Prints and Drawings from the Fifteenth Century to Picasso*, Boston: Beacon Press, 1969, p. 308. THOMAS NAST: Morton Keller, *The Art and Politics of Thomas Nast*, New York: Oxford University Press, 1968, pp. 7–9; Thomas C. Leonard, *The Power of the Press: The Birth of American Political Reporting*, New York: Oxford University Press, 1986, pp. 97–131. ILLUSTRATED MAGAZINES: On Keppler see Richard Samuel West's *Satire on Stone: The Political Cartoons of Joseph Keppler*, Urbana: University of Illinois Press, 1988; Stephen Hess and Milton Kaplan give a more general account in *The Ungentlemanly Art: A History of American Political Cartoons*, New York: Macmillan, 1968.

38 MCGERR: *Decline of Popular Politics*, pp. 13–14, 22–41; see also Baker, *Affairs of Party*, ch. 1. THE EARLIEST SUCH DEVICES: Edmund B. Sullivan, *American Political Badges and Medalets, 1789–1892*, Lawrence, Mass.: Quarterman Publications, 1981, pp. 1–117. AFTER 1896: The history of campaign buttons has been told by Ted Hake and Russ King in *Price Guide to Collectible Pin-Back Buttons, 1896–1986*, York, Pa.: Hake's Americana and Collectible Press, 1986, pp. 273–308; Fischer, *Tippecanoe and Trinkets Too*, pp. 144–48, ch. 5. Sullivan, *Collecting Political Americana*, ch. 3.

39 JACKSONIAN DEMOCRATS LED: Robert V. Remini, *The Election of Andrew Jackson*, Philadelphia: J. B. Lippincott, 1963, pp. 76–87. AT ITS MOST EXTREME: Baker, *Affairs of Party*, pp. 38–42, 48–50, ch. 7.

40 "DURING THE 1874 CAMPAIGN": Keller, *Art and Politics of Thomas Nast*, p. 281.

43 GENERAL OR MILITARY HERO: Christine Scriabine gives a convincing account of war heroes as presidential candidates, especially in post–Civil War America, in "American Attitudes Towards a Martial Presidency: Some Insights from Material Culture," *Military Affairs* Dec. 1983: 165–72.

46 HEROIC IMAGES EMERGED: William Burlie Brown, in *The People's Choice: The Presidential Image in the Campaign Biography* (Baton Rouge: Louisiana State University Press, 1960), comments on the history of campaign images. DEVICES OF ATTACK: A general survey of attack-style campaigning is found in Bruce L. Felknor's *Dirty Politics*, New York: W. W. Norton, 1966. SMEARS AGAINST THE PRESIDENT: Ibid., pp. 17–21.

47 A TYPICAL ANTI-JEFFERSON PAMPHLET: "A Short Address to the Voters of Delaware," n.p., n.d.; courtesy of the Library of Congress. A GENERATION LATER: Remini, *Election of Andrew Jackson*, pp. 151–63. SULLIVAN: *American Political Badges*, pp. 37–41.

48 SERIOUS ATTACKS: On the accusations of Van Buren extravagance see "Election of 1840," by William Nisbet Chambers, in *History of American Presidential Elections, 1789–1968*, ed. Arthur M. Schlesinger, Jr., New York: Chelsea House, 1971, pp. 677–78. ABRAHAM LINCOLN: See Rufus Rockwell Wilson's *Lincoln in Caricature*, New York: Horizon Press, 1953.

49 HORACE GREELEY: Hess and Kaplan, *Ungentlemanly Art*, pp. 100–102; Keller, *Art and Politics of Thomas Nast*, ch. 4. WARREN G. HARDING: See Francis Russell's *Shadow of Blooming Grove: Warren G. Harding in His Times*, New York: McGraw-Hill, 1968. FRANKLIN D. ROOSEVELT: Robert Rouse, "100 Million Buttons Can Be Wrong: 1940 Willkie Slogan Buttons," *APIC Keynoter* Spring 1986: 15–22.

51 MCGERR: *Decline of Popular Politics*, pp. 39–40. WILCOMB E. WASHBURN: "Symbols and Images," *Every Four Years*, ed. Robert C. Post, Washington: Smithsonian Exposition Books, 1980, p. 173.

2: Emblems of Honor and Glory

53 WHEN A RELUCTANT: Donald Jackson and Dorothy Twohig, eds., *The Diaries of George Washington*, vol. 5, Charlottesville: University Press of Virginia, 1979, pp. 445–48.

54 WASHINGTON COMMEMORATIVE BUTTONS: Sullivan, *Collecting Political Americana*, pp. 24–25, and *American Political Badges*, pp. 1–7. EZRA STILES: Quoted by Barry Schwartz in *George Washington: The Making of an American Symbol*, New York: Free Press, 1987, p. 41. See also pp. 34–103, and Garry Wills, *Cincinnatus: George Washington and the Enlightenment*, Garden City, N.Y.: Doubleday, 1984. PAUL K. LONGMORE: *The Invention of George Washington*, Berkeley and Los Angeles: University of California Press, 1988. JOHN ADAMS EXPRESSED CONCERN: Marcus Cunliffe, *George Washington, Man and Monument*, Boston: Little, Brown, 1958, p. 197.

55 *Salute to General Washington in New York Harbor*, L. M. Cooke (active

c. 1875), oil on canvas, 27 × 40¼ inches; National Gallery of Art, Washington; gift of Edgar William and Bernice Chrysler Garbisch. A PHILADELPHIAN: Carl Van Doren, *The Great Rehearsal: The Story of the Making and Ratifying of the Constitution of the United States*, New York: Penguin Books, 1986, p. 22. CUNLIFFE: *George Washington*, pp. 7–20 (quotation p. 18). HIGHLY SELF-CONSCIOUS: Margaret B. Klapthor and Howard A. Morrison, in *G. Washington, a Figure upon the Stage* (Washington: Smithsonian Institution Press, 1982), interpret Washington's role-playing in life as the behavior of an actor on a stage. BARRY SCHWARTZ: *George Washington*, pp. 132–34.

56 *George Washington*, 1780, Charles Willson Peale (1741–1827), mezzotint, 9⅞ × 11⅞ inches; NPG; gift of the Barra Foundation.

57 ON HIS ARRIVAL: Douglas S. Freeman, in *George Washington, Patriot and President* (New York: Charles Scribner's Sons, 1954, vol. 6, ch. 7), gives the most detailed account of Washington's procession to his inauguration. See also James Thomas Flexner, *George Washington and the New Nation, 1783–1793*, Boston: Little, Brown, 1970, pp. 174–88; Michael P. Riccards, *A Republic If You Can Keep It: The Foundations of the American Presidency, 1700–1800*, Westport, Conn.: Greenwood Press, 1987, pp. 65–75.

58 THE TWO SIDES NEVER ORGANIZED: Quotation from Austin Ranney and Willmoore Kendall, *Democracy and the American Party System*, New York: Harcourt, Brace, 1956, p. 96. The present interpretation of the party system owes much to Ralph E. Becker and Harry Grundy, formerly of the Congressional Research Service. FIRST AMERICAN PARTY SYSTEM: Richard P. McCormick, *The Second American Party System: Party Formation in the Jacksonian Era*, Chapel Hill: University of North Carolina Press, 1966, pp. 19–31. On the founders' opposition to parties see Richard Hofstadter's *Idea of a Party System: The Rise of Legitimate Opposition in the United States, 1780–1840*, Berkeley and Los Angeles: University of California Press, 1969. RANNEY AND KENDALL: *Democracy and the American Party System*, p. 85. THE FIRST TWO PARTIES: Hugh A. Bone, *American Politics and the Party System*, 4th ed., New York: McGraw-Hill, 1971, p. 29. AN ADMINISTRATION OR FEDERALIST PAPER: Noble E. Cunningham, "Election of 1800," in *History of American Presidential Elections*, ed. Schlesinger, pp. 13–27.

59 *Alexander Hamilton*, 1804, William Rollinson (1762–1842), after Archibald Robertson, stipple engraving, 17⅝ × 13¾ inches; NPG. IN 1793: Philip S. Foner, ed., *The Democratic-Republican Societies, 1790–1800*, Westport, Conn.: Greenwood Press, 1976, pp. 3–40. FAREWELL ADDRESS: *The Writings of George Washington, from the Original Manuscript Sources, 1745–1799*, ed. John C. Fitzpatrick, Washington: U.S. Government Printing Office, 1940, vol. 35, pp. 226–27. See also Michael Wallace, "Changing Concepts of Party in the United States: New York, 1815–1828," *American Historical Review* 77 (Dec. 1968): 473. VIGOROUS NAME-CALLING: William Nisbet Chambers, *Political Parties in a New Nation: The American Experience, 1776–1809*, New York: Oxford University Press, 1963, p. 116.

60 *New Orleans*, 1803, Boqueto de Woieseri, oil on canvas; Chicago Historical Society. THE REPUBLICAN PARTY WON: Chambers, *Political Parties*, pp. 150–69; Cunningham, "Election of 1800," pp. 101–34.

61 *Thomas Jefferson*, 1798–99, Michel Sokolnicki (1760–1816), after Thaddeus Kosciusko, hand-colored aquatint, 9¾ × 8⅛ inches; NPG.

62 WE KNOW THAT "REPUBLICANS": Cunningham, "Election of 1800," pp. 133–34. ANOTHER SCHOLAR: Portrait information from accession records, NMAH.

63 MERRILL PETERSON: "The Election of 1800," in *American Critical Elections: Memoirs of the American Philosophical Society* 99 (1973): 1. HIS DEATH IN 1799: On Washington's death tributes, see Schwartz's *George Washington* (pp. 91–103) and "The Character of Washington: A Study in Republican Culture," *American Quarterly* 38 (Summer 1986): 202–22.

65 DANIEL BOORSTIN AND OTHERS: Wills, *Cincinnatus*, pp. 35–53; Daniel J. Boorstin, *The Americans: The National Experience*, New York: Vintage Books, 1965, pp. 339–49; Cunliffe, *George Washington*, pp. 8–12; Karal Ann Marling, *George Washington Slept Here: Colonial Revivals and American Culture, 1876–1986*, Cambridge: Harvard University Press, 1988; Dixon Wecter, *The Hero in America: A Chronicle of Hero-Worship*, New York: Scribner's, 1941, pp. 132–36 (Weems quotation p. 134). MOST UNITS: David Hackett Fischer, *The Revolution of American Conservatism: The Federalist Party in the Era of Jeffersonian Democracy*, New York: Harper and Row, 1965, pp. 113–28. FRED SOMKIN: *Unquiet Eagle: Memory and Desire in the Idea of American Freedom, 1815–1860*, Ithaca: Cornell University Press, 1967, pp. 133, 167, ch. 4.

66 *Le General Lafayette*, c. 1825, Achille Moreau (active 1825–1842), after Jean Auguste Dubouloz, aquatint and etching, 16 ⅜ × 21 9/16 inches; NPG. SUCH PROMOTIONAL ARTIFACTS: See Marling, *George Washington Slept Here*.

67 ELECTIONS AFTER 1800: Ralph Ketcham, *Presidents Above Party: The First American Presidency, 1789–1829*, Chapel Hill: University of North Carolina Press, 1984, pp. 220–21; M. J. Heale, *The Presidential Quest: Candidates and Images in American Political Culture, 1789–1852*, London: Longman, 1982, pp. 1–22.

68 NEW RIVALRIES: Richard P. McCormick, in *The Presidential Game: The Origins of American Presidential Politics* (New York: Oxford University Press, 1982), treats the general changes in presidential contests from the time of the Constitution until the 1840s; see especially pp. 76–163 for the period between 1800 and 1830.

3: Mobilizing the Multitudes

69 *The Verdict of the People*, 1854–55, George Caleb Bingham, oil on canvas, 46 × 65 inches; Art Collection of the Boatmen's National Bank of St. Louis. SECOND AMERICAN PARTY SYSTEM: See *The American Party Systems: Stages of Political Development*, ed. William Nisbet Chambers and Walter Dean Burnham (2nd ed., New York: Oxford University Press, 1975), including "Political Development and the Second Party System," by Richard P. McCormick, pp. 90–116; also by McCormick, *Second American Party System* and *Presidential Game*.

70 MARTIN VAN BUREN: Van Buren's contributions are assessed by Robert V. Remini in *Martin Van Buren and the Making of the Democratic Party*, New York: Columbia University Press, 1959. STATE NEWSPAPERS: On the partisan press and political organizing of this period, see Gerald J. Baldasty's "The Press and Politics in the Age of Jackson," *Journalism Monographs* 89 (August 1984): 1–29; Remini, *Election of Andrew Jackson*, pp. 53–86. POTTER: *Impending Crisis*. CHEVALIER: Quoted by McCormick in "Political Development," pp. 108–109; Davis, *Parades and Power*.

71 "NEW WASHINGTON": John William Ward, *Andrew Jackson: Symbol of an Age*, New York: Oxford University Press, Galaxy Book, 1962, pp. 42–44.

72 ARTIFACTS CELEBRATING JACKSON: Collins, *Threads of History*, pp. 65–69.

74 "THE BEER-BARRELS": *New York Spectator* Nov. 4, 1828, courtesy of the *Smithsonian Magazine*. POLITICAL PROPAGANDA ISSUED FORTH: Ward, *Andrew Jackson*. JACKSONIAN STRATEGY: Robert V. Remini, "Election of 1828," in *History of American Presidential Elections*, ed. Schlesinger, pp. 413–36.

75 THROUGH THE 1830s: McCormick, *Second American Party System*. THE CONTEST FEATURED: The campaign of 1840 has received extensive and varied treatment in the historical literature. The most modern, comprehensive interpretation is that of Chambers ("Election of 1840," in *History of American Presidential Elections*, ed. Schlesinger, pp. 643–90). A sample of studies and sources includes: Fischer, *Tippecanoe and Trinkets Too*, pp. 29–49; Horace Greeley, *Recollections of a Busy Life*, New York: J. B. Ford and Co., 1868; Gronbeck, "Functional and Dramaturgical Theories," pp. 486–99; Robert Gray Gunderson, *The Log-Cabin Campaign*, Lexington: University of Kentucky Press, 1957; Heale, *Presidential Quest*, ch. 6; McCormick, "Political Development," in *American Party Systems*, ed. Chambers and Burnham; Norton, *Great Revolution of 1840;* William H. Seward Manuscripts, microfilm edition, Library of Congress; Martin Van Buren Manuscripts, Library of Congress; *The Log Cabin* newspaper, published in New York and Albany by H. Greeley and Co., May 2–Nov. 20, 1840. BEVERIDGE: *Abraham Lincoln*, vol. 1, pp. 270–75; see Wilcomb E. Washburn, "The Great Autumnal Madness: Political Symbolism in Mid-Nineteenth-Century America," *Quarterly Journal of Speech* 49 (Dec. 1963): 417–31.

77 JOKE FROM A DEMOCRATIC NEWSPAPER: Gunderson, *Log-Cabin Campaign*, pp. 74–75.

78 "CABIN RAISINGS": *Albany Evening Journal* July 9 and 14, 1840. "GRAND PROCESSION": Norton, *Great Revolution of 1840*, pp. 44–53. SIMILAR SCENES: See Richard Smith Elliott's *Notes Taken in Sixty Years*, St. Louis: R. P. Studley, 1883, pp. 120–22; also Gunderson's *Log-Cabin Campaign* and Norton's *Great Revolution of 1840*.

79 NEW YORK STATE RALLY: *Log Cabin* Aug. 22, 1840.

81 FOR COLLECTORS: Quotation from Fischer, *Tippecanoe and Trinkets Too*, p. 33. Estimate of ribbon types from Edmund B. Sullivan

and Roger A. Fischer, *American Political Ribbons and Ribbon Badges, 1825–1986*, Lincoln, Mass.: Quarterman Publications, 1985, pp. 27–45.

82 TWENTY DISTINCT EXAMPLES: Sullivan, *American Political Badges*, pp. 58–72.

83 GLASSWARE WITH IMAGES: See Sullivan's *Collecting Political Americana*, pp. 88–89, 104–105. VALENTINE'S ENGRAVERS: *Log Cabin* July 25, 1840.

85 ANIMATED PAPER DEVICES: Sullivan, *Collecting Political Americana*, pp. 51, 62–63. A YOUNG POLITICIAN: George Washington Julian, *Political Recollections, 1840–1872*, Chicago: Jansen, McClurg, and Co., 1884, p.17.

87 "WHAT HAS CAUSED THIS GREAT COMMOTION?": Irwin Silber, *Songs America Voted By*, Harrisburg, Pa.: Stackpole Books, 1971, pp. 33–45.

88 DEMOCRATS WERE BAFFLED: This is clear from numerous letters among the Martin Van Buren papers at the Library of Congress, for example, letters to Van Buren from William L. Marcy (May 9 and Oct. 25, 1840), Thomas Richie (June 1, 1840), and John Hunter (June 2 and July 4, 1840) and Van Buren's letter to Andrew Jackson dated Sept. 5, 1840. ANOTHER SIGNIFICANT INNOVATION: Chambers, "Election of 1840," p. 678, also pp. 682–84; Gunderson, *Log-Cabin Campaign*, pp. 164–72. DANIEL WALKER HOWE: *The Political Culture of the American Whigs*, Chicago: University of Chicago Press, 1979, p. 15. POLITICS FILLED A YEARNING: Chambers and Burnham, *American Party Systems*, p. 11; McCormick, "Political Development," pp. 107–109.

89 LOG-CABIN CAMPAIGN: See Heale, *Presidential Quest*, ch. 6, especially pp. 106–107 and 129–32. A MORE SEVERE VIEW: Arthur M. Schlesinger, *The Age of Jackson*, Boston: Little, Brown, 1953, p. 304. ITS SEVEREST CRITICS ADMIT: Gunderson, *Log-Cabin Campaign*, pp. 10, 231, 256; Schlesinger, *Age of Jackson*.

90 *Henry Clay*, 1844, Nathaniel Currier (1813–1888), hand-colored lithograph, 12 11/16 × 9 ⅜ inches; NPG.

91 A SYMPATHETIC WRITER: "Young Men's Whig National Convention of Ratification," edition of the *Baltimore Patriot* May 3 (?), 1844. LINCOLN: *Lincoln Day by Day: A Chronology, 1809–1865*, Washington, D.C.: Lincoln Sesquicentennial Commission, 1960, vol. 1, pp. 231–38. NILES' REGISTER: Quoted by Charles G. Sellers in *James K. Polk, Continentalist, 1843–1846*, Princeton: Princeton University Press, 1966, vol. 2, p. 143.

93 NINETY DIFFERENT STYLES: Sullivan and Fischer, *American Political Ribbons*, pp. 69–89. IN 1844: Sellers, *James K. Polk*, pp. 138–61; see also Sellers, "Election of 1844," in *History of American Presidential Elections*, ed. Schlesinger, pp. 747–96.

94 *The Bay and Harbor of New York*, 1855, Samuel B. Waugh (1814–1885), oil on canvas, 97 × 198 inches; Museum of the City of New York; gift of Mrs. Robert M. Littlejohn. FEWER EXAMPLES: Sullivan and Fischer, *American Political Ribbons*, pp. 92–99.

95 AS THE CONTEST EVOLVED: On the 1848 contest see Holman Hamilton's "Election of 1848," in *History of American Presidential Elections*, ed. Schlesinger, pp. 865–96.

96 REVIVED THE LOG-CABIN SYMBOL: *New York Times* July 8 and 10, Aug. 2 and 19, 1856. MASS MEETINGS: *New York Times* July 21, Sept. 20, Oct. 31, 1856; *Albany Evening Journal* Sept. 22 and 27, 1856.

98 "FLAGS WERE STREAMING": *Springfield Republican* (Massachusetts) Sept. 19, 1856. "JESSIE PIC-NIC": *Springfield Republican* Aug. 2, 4, 7, 1856. THE REPUBLICAN STRUGGLE: *Albany Evening Journal* July 12 and Aug. 19, 1856; *New York Times* Sept. 10, 1856; see also Allan Nevins, *Frémont, Pathmarker of the West*, New York: F. Ungar Publishing, 1961, vol. 2, pp. 440–55. EYEWITNESS DESCRIBED THE FIRST DEBATE: Horace White, in *The Lincoln Reader*, ed. Paul M. Angle, New Brunswick: Rutgers University Press, 1947, pp. 234–35. See also Don E. Fehrenbacher's *Prelude to Greatness: Lincoln in the 1850's*, Stanford: Stanford University Press, 1962, pp. 96–112.

99 *Senator Stephen A. Douglas*, c. 1859, James Earle McClees (1821–1887) and Julian Vannerson (c. 1827–?), photograph, salt print, 7¼ × 5¼ inches; NPG.

100 ROY F. NICHOLS: *The Disruption of American Democracy*, New York: Macmillan, Free Press Paperback, 1967, p. 20.

4: Partisan Campaigning, 1860–1896

101 Republican banner, 1860; private collection of Kendall Mattern.

102 HARTFORD CLUB: Quotation from papers and clippings of E. S. Yerga-

son, 1860–1909, Nannos accession, DPH. Osborn H. Oldroyd, in *Lincoln's Campaign: or, The Political Revolution of 1860* (Chicago: Laird and Lee, 1896, pp. 104–109), details the rise of the Wide-Awakes. LINCOLN SPOKE AT HARTFORD: *Lincoln Day by Day*, vol. 2, p. 275. BEFORE THE SUMMER: Collins, "Political Campaign Torches," pp. 4, 20. HERBERT R. COLLINS: Ibid., pp. 18–22.

104 LINCOLN BANNERS: Collins, *Threads of History*, pp. 150–63. AT SPRINGFIELD: *Springfield Republican* May 31, 1860. FORMATION OF A YOUNG WOMEN'S: Ibid., Oct. 15, 1860. ONE ACCOUNT REPORTED: *New York Times* Oct. 3, 1860. AT JACKSONVILLE: *Illinois State Journal* Sept. 10, 1860; see also Don Harrison Doyle's *Social Order of a Frontier Community: Jacksonville, Illinois, 1825–70*, Urbana: University of Illinois Press, 1978, pp. 173–75.

106 PRINCETON: *Bureau County Republican* Oct. 4, 1860. IN OCTOBER: *New York Herald* Sept. 19 and Oct. 4, 1860; *New York Times* Oct. 1–4, 1860. On marchers besides the Wide-Awakes, see Emerson David Fite's *Presidential Campaign of 1860*, New York: Kennikat Press, 1967, pp. 225–30, and Reinhard Henry Luthin's *First Lincoln Campaign*, Gloucester, Mass.: P. Smith, 1964, pp. 173–75. RICHARD JENSEN: "Armies, Admen, and Crusaders: Types of Presidential Campaigns," *History Teacher* 2 (1969): 33–59. RAIL CANDIDATE: Luthin, *First Lincoln Campaign*, pp. 90, 169.

108 RAIL-SPLITTER IMAGE: Harold Holzer, Gabor S. Boritt, and Mark E. Neely, Jr., *The Lincoln Image: Abraham Lincoln and the Popular Print*, New York: Scribner Press, 1985, pp. 6, 15–16. PUBLISHERS LIKE CURRIER AND IVES: Ibid., p. 30. IN LINCOLN'S HOMETOWN: Oldroyd, *Lincoln's Campaign*, pp. 110–12. FOLLOWING THE TRADITION: *Lincoln Day by Day*, vol. 2, p. 288; Heale, *Presidential Quest*, ch. 1.

109 IN A FORLORN EFFORT: The fusion parade is reported in *New York Times* Oct. 24, 1860. Lincoln's 1860 campaign is described by Fite in *Presidential Campaign of 1860* (pp. 225–29), by Melvin Hayes in *Mr. Lincoln Runs for President* (New York: Citadel Press, 1960, pp. 124–63), and by Luthin in *First Lincoln Campaign* (pp. 173–219). DOUGLAS HIMSELF: Elting Morison, "Election of 1860," *History of American Presidential Elections*, ed. Schlesinger, p. 1116. IN 1868: Parade descriptions from *New York Times* Sept. 5 and 6, Aug. 26, and Sept. 11, 1868.

110 PARADES: Descriptions from *New York Times* Aug. 19 and 30, 1868; Aug. 9 and 11, 1872; Sept. 1, 6, 11, Oct. 4, 8, 10, 23, 1876; July 4, 15, 16, 20, 23, 24, 1868.

111 WHEN CLEVELAND RETURNED: *Harper's Weekly* Oct. 11, 1884, quoted by Collins in "Political Campaign Torches," p. 11. UNEXCELLED FIREWORKS: Ibid., pp. 13–15. IN 1884: Quotations from the DPH collections of dealers' advertising: *Harper's Weekly* July 3, 1880, p. 431; "The Nation's Choice" circular, Mount Nebo Printing Co., S. Manchester, Conn., 1884; catalogue of C. M. Linington, Chicago, 1888.

112 BANDANNAS: Collins, *Threads of History*, p. 7.

113 RICHARD J. JENSEN: *The Winning of the Midwest: Social and Political Conflict, 1888–1896*, Chicago: University of Chicago Press, 1971, p. 165 (quotation), pp. 6–18. GRANT'S IMAGE: Wecter, *Hero in America*, pp. 307–30.

114 *Grant and His Generals*, 1865, Ole Peter Hansen Balling (1823–1906), oil on canvas, 120 × 192 inches; NPG; gift of Mrs. Harry Newton Blue. AFTER GRANT: See Scriabine, "American Attitudes Towards a Martial Presidency."

115 THE IMAGE OF PROTECTION: On the role of protection in Republican campaigning, see H. Wayne Morgan, "The Republican Party 1876–1893," in *History of U.S. Political Parties II*, ed. Arthur Schlesinger, Jr., New York: Chelsea House, 1973, pp. 1415–17.

118 POPULISM: Lawrence Goodwyn, *Democratic Promise: The Populist Movement in America*, New York: Oxford University Press, 1976, pp. 521–43. On the silver issue, see Stanley L. Jones, *The Presidential Election of 1896*, Madison: University of Wisconsin Press, 1964, ch. 2.

120 OTHER EXAMPLES: Fischer, *Tippecanoe and Trinkets Too*, pp. 145–63.

121 HISTORY OF BUTTON MANUFACTURING: See Hake and King's *Price Guide to Collectible Pin-Back Buttons*, pp. 273–308; Fischer, *Tippecanoe and Trinkets Too*, pp. 144–48.

5: Personal Campaigning

123 HEALE: *Presidential Quest*, ch. 1.

124 ONE OF THE LEADING FEATURES: Leonard Dinnerstein, "Election of 1880," *History of American Presidential Elections*, ed. Schlesinger, pp.

1506–507. IN RESPONSE TO THESE SCANDALS: Mark D. Hirsch, "Election of 1884," ibid., p. 1575.

125 JENSEN: *Winning of the Midwest*, pp. 12–15 (quotation p. 14). WILLIAM JENNINGS BRYAN: The candidate's *First Battle* (Chicago: W. B. Conkey Co., 1896) is the best description of his tours in 1896; see also McGerr, *Decline of Popular Politics;* Jensen, *Winning of the Midwest;* Keith Melder, "Bryan the Campaigner," Contributions from the Museum of History and Technology, paper 46, *U.S. National Museum Bulletin* 241 (1965).

126 IN CHICAGO: McGerr, *Decline of Popular Politics*, pp. 138–45; Jensen, *Winning of the Midwest*, pp. 283–91. THE RESULT: Ibid., pp. 292–306.

127 MCGERR: *Decline of Popular Politics*, p. 145. POPULAR MAGAZINE WRITER: Oliver Shedd, "A Transient Industry—Millions Spent for Campaign Paraphernalia," *Leslie's Weekly* Oct. 13, 1904.

128 AN OBSERVER: Quoted by Edmund Morris in *The Rise of Theodore Roosevelt*, New York: Coward, McMann and Geoghegan, 1979, pp. 683–84.

129 HE OUT-CAMPAIGNED EVEN BRYAN: Ibid., p. 730. Roosevelt quotations from *New York Times* Sept. 4, 1900, p. 3; see also Theodore Roosevelt's *Works* (ed. Hermann Hagedorn, New York: Charles Scribner's Sons, 1926, vol. 14, pp. 342–400), and *New York Times* Sept.–Oct. 1900.

130 CAMPAIGN BUTTONS: See Ted Hake's *Encyclopedia of Political Buttons, United States, 1896–1972*, New York: Dafran House, 1974, pp. 55–69. TEDDY BEAR: Peggy and Alan Bialosky, *The Teddy Bear Catalog*, New York: Workman Publishing, 1980. A PROGRESSIVE FOLLOWER: William Allen White, *Autobiography*, New York: Macmillan, 1946, p. 436. ROOSEVELT-WASHINGTON BUTTONS: See Fischer, *Tippecanoe and Trinkets Too*, pp. 172–75. DESPITE SOME EVIDENCE: For differing views on the changing nature of campaigning and its effect on campaign paraphernalia, see McGerr's *Decline of Popular Politics*, pp. 145–51, and Fischer's *Tippecanoe and Trinkets Too*, pp. 163–72.

132 ROOSEVELT WROTE: Quoted by John Morton Blum in *The Republican Roosevelt*, New York: Atheneum, 1962, p.55. A CAREFUL HISTORIAN: Ibid., pp. 55–56. HE IMPRESSED SOME: Rossiter, *American Presidency*, p. 97; see Blum's *Republican Roosevelt*, pp. 55–92, for a concise, thoughtful summary of Roosevelt's dramatic yet pragmatic public profile. "MY BELIEF WAS": Theodore Roosevelt, *Theodore Roosevelt: An Autobiography*, New York: Macmillan, 1919, p. 389.

133 WHITE: *Autobiography*, p. 436; pp. 444–60 describe how Roosevelt became more and more involved in the Progressive insurgency. A REPORT OF THE CAMPAIGN: *New York Times* May 26, 1912. ROOSEVELT'S PRIMARY CAMPAIGNS: See George Mowry's "Election of 1912," in *History of American Presidential Elections*, ed. Schlesinger, pp. 2140–47; Blum, *Republican Roosevelt*, pp. 146–49. ARTHUR S. LINK: *Wilson*, Princeton: Princeton University Press, 1947, vol. 1, pp. 467–523 (quotation p. 476).

134 JOHN MORTON BLUM: *Woodrow Wilson and the Politics of Morality*, Boston: Little, Brown, 1956, pp. 39–52. TRADITIONAL CAMPAIGN DEVICES: Fischer, *Tippecanoe and Trinkets Too*, pp. 180–84. IN HIS TREATISE: Quoted by Rossiter in *American Presidency*, pp. 29–30.

135 Debs whistle stop, 1908, campaign photograph; Brown Brothers. ALTHOUGH HIS PROFESSORIAL MANNER: Blum, *Wilson*, ch. 4.

136 ONE MEMORABLE VISIT: *Ohio State Journal* (Columbus) and *New York Times* Aug. 25, 1920. ALBERT LASKER: John Gunther, *Taken at the Flood: The Story of Albert D. Lasker*, New York: Harper, 1960, p. 112. The most detailed account of the Harding front-porch technique is Russell's in *Shadow of Blooming Grove*, pp. 398–418. Other accounts are by Samuel Hopkins Adams (*Incredible Era: The Life and Times of Warren Gamaliel Harding*, Boston: Houghton Mifflin, 1939, pp. 170–78) and Donald R. McCoy ("Election of 1920," in *History of American Presidential Elections*, ed. Schlesinger, pp. 2370–85).

137 HARDING AND THE REPUBLICANS SPOKE: Ibid., p. 2379.

6: Rally 'Round the Candidate

140 PRINTED BALLOTS: On ballots and balloting, see Baker's *Affairs of Party*, pp. 306–309. RICHARD L. MCCORMICK: *From Realignment to Reform: Political Change in New York State, 1893–1910*, Ithaca: Cornell University Press, 1981, p. 243.

141 SAMUEL HAYS: "Political Parties and the Community-Society Continuum," in *American Party Systems*, ed. Chambers and Burnham, p. 166, also pp. 157–78; see, also by Hays, *American Political Systems as Social Analysis*, Knoxville: University of Tennessee Press, 1980, pp. 250–55. CHANGING STYLES: McGerr, *Decline of Popular Poli-*

tics, pp. 22–41, 65–106, 144–47, 159–83; Jensen, *Winning of the Midwest*, pp. 11–17, 164–77; Melvyn H. Bloom, *Public Relations and Presidential Campaigns: A Crisis in Democracy*, New York: Crowell, 1973, pp. 8–42; Kathleen Hall Jamieson, *Packaging the Presidency: A History and Criticism of Presidential Campaign Advertising*, New York: Oxford University Press, 1984, pp. 3–37. ROSSITER: *American Presidency*, ch. 4; see also *Power of the Presidency: Concepts and Controversy*, ed. Robert S. Hirschfield, Chicago: Aldine Publishing, 1973, pp. 82–100. THEODORE J. LOWI: *The Personal President: Power Invested, Promise Unfulfilled*, Ithaca: Cornell University Press, 1985, pp. xi–20.

142 THESE LONG-TERM SHIFTS: McGerr, *Decline of Popular Politics*, pp. 184–210. CAMPAIGN OBJECT COLLECTORS: See the *APIC Keynoter* special issue "Franklin D. Roosevelt and the Age of the New Deal" (Spring-Summer 1983) for lengthy surveys of Roosevelt political material.

143 AS A PERSONAL CANDIDATE: *History of American Presidential Elections*, ed. Schlesinger, pp. 2729–30, 2791. "ROOSEVELT REVOLUTION": See Lowi's *Personal President*, pp. 48–66. ROOSEVELT USED NATIONAL RADIO: Arthur P. Molella, *FDR, the Intimate Presidency: Franklin Delano Roosevelt, Communication, and the Mass Media in the 1930s*, Washington: Smithsonian Institution, 1982, pp. 47–54. ONE NEW DEAL ERA REPORTER: A. Merriman Smith, quoted by Molella in *FDR*, p. 56. THE NEW COALITION: Samuel Lubell, *The Future of American Politics*, New York: Harper, 1952, pp. 30–36, ch. 3, pp. 196–97, 210–12. Also Everett Carll Ladd, Jr., with Charles D. Hadley, *Transformations of the American Party System*, New York: Norton, 1975, chs. 1–2, pp. 42–87.

144 End of Prohibition, 1933, photograph; the Bettmann Archive. ROOSEVELT'S ATTACKS: James M. Burns, *Roosevelt: The Lion and the Fox*, New York: Harcourt, Brace, 1956, pp. 375–80. "ROOSEVELT'S BASIC PROBLEM": Ibid., p. 412. JIM FARLEY: James A. Farley, *Jim Farley's Story: The Roosevelt Years*, New York: Whittlesey House, 1948, pp. 223–98 (quotation p. 147); Burns, *Roosevelt*, pp. 411–15, 422–32.

145 "I Want You, FDR," 1940, James Montgomery Flagg (1877–1960), color halftone poster, 21¼ × 16⅝ inches; NPG. WILLKIE CLUBS: Robert Rouse, "Willkie Clubs," *APIC Keynoter* Spring 1986: 30–31; see also *New York Times* May 19, 1940: 2, July 15: 7, August 5: 7. DEMOCRATS FOR WILLKIE: *New York Times* July 28, 1940: 3, Aug. 13: 12; Robert Rouse, "Democrats for Willkie," *APIC Keynoter* Spring 1986: 32–34.

146 NON-DEMOCRATIC POLITICAL CLUBS: *New York Times* Sept. 29, 1940: 38, Oct. 20: 12. STILL OTHERS MADE FUN: *Life* Sept. 30, 1940: 82, Oct. 7: 97; *New York Times Magazine* Oct. 13, 1940: 2; Robert Rouse, "100 Million Buttons Can Be Wrong," *APIC Keynoter* Spring 1986: 15–21. HIS BIOGRAPHER: Burns, *Roosevelt*, pp. 446–47, 455.

147 Dewey-Truman cartoon, 1948; © 1991 by Estate of Ben Shahn/VAGA, New York.

148 RICHARD ROVERE: *Final Reports: Personal Reflections on Politics and History in Our Time*, Garden City: Doubleday, 1984, pp. 107–109. H. L. MENCKEN: *Mencken's Last Campaign: H. L. Mencken on the 1948 Election*, Washington: New Republic Book, 1976, pp. 133–34. On Truman's campaign, Irwin Ross gives the fullest treatment in *The Loneliest Campaign: The Truman Victory of 1948*, New York: New American Library, 1968.

7: Be a Party Girl:
Campaign Appeals to Women

149 WOMEN IN THE REVOLUTIONARY ERA: Linda K. Kerber, *Women of the Republic: Intellect and Ideology in Revolutionary America*, Chapel Hill: University of North Carolina, 1980.

150 CENTERING WOMEN'S POLITICAL LIFE: Louise M. Young, "Women's Place in American Politics: The Historical Perspective," *Journal of Politics* 38 (August 1976): 309; Michael McGerr, "Political Style and Women's Power, 1830–1930," *Journal of American History* 77 (Dec. 1990): 867–68; Mary P. Ryan, *Women in Public: From Banners to Ballots, 1825–1880*, Baltimore: Johns Hopkins University Press, 1990; Paula Baker, "The Domestication of Politics: Women and American Political Society, 1780–1920," *American Historical Review* 89 (June 1984): 620–47. THE CAMPAIGN OF 1840: Washburn, "Great Autumnal Madness"; Fischer, *Tippecanoe and Trinkets Too*. No Van Buren items appealing to women have been found. WOMEN'S CAMPAIGN ACTIVITIES: Young, *Women's Place*, p. 311. Whether the Whig appeal to women paid off in women's

influence over the choices men made at the polls is impossible to determine, but it is an interesting point for speculation in view of Harrison's victory. CAMPAIGNS BETWEEN 1844 AND 1888: For the development of first ladies as campaign symbols and women's political button iconography see Edith Mayo's "Ladies and Liberation: Icon and Iconoclast in the Women's Movement," in *Icons of America*, ed. Ray B. Browne and Marshall Fishwick, Bowling Green, Ohio: Popular Press, 1978, pp. 209–27.

151 THE ESTIMATE OF WOMEN VOTING: Sophonisba Breckinridge, *Women in the Twentieth Century: A Study of Their Political, Social and Economic Activities*, New York: McGraw-Hill, 1933, pp. 245–56. S. A. Rice and M. M. Willey note in "American Women's Ineffective Use of the Vote" that most states did not separate ballots by sex, and it was, therefore, impossible to determine whether the women's vote was effective; *Current History* 20 (1924): 645. A host of experts and studies into the eighties likewise conclude that there were no gender-related differences in voting behavior or party affiliation; Frank R. Kent, *The Great Game of Politics*, Garden City: Doubleday, Doran, 1928, pp. 172–73; Paul Felix Lazarsfeld, Bernard Berelson, and Hazel Gaudet, *The People's Choice: How the Voter Makes Up His Mind in a Presidential Campaign*, New York: Columbia University Press, 1948, pp. 16–43; Edward M. Bennett and Harriet M. Goodwin, "Emotional Aspects of Political Behavior: The Woman Voter," *Genetic Psychology Monographs* 58: 3–53; Martin Gruberg, *Women in American Politics*, Oshkosh, Wis.: Academia Press, 1968, ch. 1; Maurice Duverger, *The Political Role of Women*, Paris: Unesco, 1955, ch.1; Gabriel Almond and Sidney Verba, *The Civic Culture*, Boston: Little, Brown, 1965; Fred Greenstein, "Sex-Related Political Differences in Childhood," *Journal of Politics* 23 (1961): 353–71; Kenneth Langton and M. Kent Jennings, "Mothers Versus Fathers in the Formation of Political Attitudes," in *Political Socialization*, ed. Kenneth Langton, New York: Oxford Press, 1969; William Chafe, *The American Woman: Her Changing Social, Economic, and Political Role, 1920–1970*, New York: Oxford University Press, 1972, p. 45.

152 THE FIFTIES MARKED A TURNING: Earl Roger Kruschke, *The Woman Voter*, Washington: Public Affairs Press, 1955, p. 4. The Republican party established a women's division in 1919, under the directorship of Ruth Hanna McCormick Simms, daughter of party boss Mark Hanna; *Republican Women Are Wonderful: A History of Women at Republican National Conventions*, Washington: National Women's Political Caucus, 1980. The Democratic party's Women's Bureau, as it was first called, was founded by Mrs. George Bass, from Illinois, in 1916 to organize Democratic women to work for the party. After the 1916, 1920, and 1924 elections, however, the women's files were destroyed, their organizations disbanded, and their offices closed. In 1928 the renamed Women's Division continued, but its status was uncertain. Not until the 1932 election did the division, then under Nellie Tayloe Ross, become a strong force within the party. See handout, "A History of Democratic Women's Move to Leadership," prepared by Women's Division, Democratic National Committee, Washington, D.C., 1980; also *Democratic Women Are Wonderful: A History of Women at the Democratic National Conventions*, Washington: National Women's Political Caucus, 1980. Brought in by the Roosevelts in 1933, Molly Dewson built the grassroots strength of the Democratic women's division into an even more potent force. See Susan Ware, *Partner and I: Molly Dewson, Feminism, and New Deal Politics*, New Haven: Yale University Press, 1987.

153 FIT FOR KITCHEN AND BEDROOM: *Playboy* magazine, which was founded and flourished in the fifties, was based on the same rampant sexism, viewing women as playthings who were not to be taken seriously. GRASS-ROOTS LEVEL: *Ladies' Home Journal* outlined political campaign activity conducted by both Republican and Democratic women's organizations and gave a glimpse of just how vast this network had become in the fifties; "Political Pilgrim's Progress – Women Organize for Action," *Ladies' Home Journal* 69 (Sept. 1952): 25, 162. POLITICAL VOLUNTEER WORK: Marion K. Sanders, *The Lady and the Vote*, Boston: Houghton Mifflin, 1956.

154 TELEVISED CAMPAIGN: The Republicans exploited this new campaign medium. They produced a pamphlet entitled "Your Television Image," which showed insight into the problems presented by a largely unknown campaign technique. Suggestions to the candidate include how to dress to advantage for television, what colors to wear, what makeup to employ, how to stand and sit, when to walk around, and how to illustrate a speech to hold the attention of a television audience. Nixon

would have done well to reread it before the 1960 debates with Kennedy.

155 LOUIS HARRIS: *Is There a Republican Majority?: Political Trends, 1952–1956*, New York: Harper and Brothers, 1954, p. 111 (quotation) and ch. 7. Also, Sandra Baxter and Marjorie Lansing, in *Women and Politics: The Visible Majority* (Ann Arbor: University of Michigan Press, 1983), discuss the voting patterns of women historically, including the 1952 election, and examine the growing gender gap in electoral politics in the last decade and its potential effects. BROCHURE DISPLAYING A HOUSEWIFE: *How Much Did Your Groceries Cost Today?* Washington: Republican National Committee, 1952, p. 1; DPH.

156 WOMEN WERE URGED TO HELP: Ibid., p. 2. HARRIS: *Is There a Republican Majority?* p. 110. KRUSCHKE: *Woman Voter*, pp. 4, 6–14. Also Harris, *Is There a Republican Majority?* ch. 7.

157 WOMEN'S DAY: *Democratic Women Are Wonderful*, p. 17.

158 "PAT FOR FIRST LADY": *Republican Women Are Wonderful*. "Pat for First Lady," *Washington Post* 1960, DPH.

160 MAINSTREAM PARTY POLITICS: The mainstream suffrage movement produced images of social motherhood – often termed social housekeeping – and civic service, which generally skirted the issues of women's self-promotion or equality with men; the second wave of the women's movement generated demands for equality and countercultural images of feminist rage and separation in the mid-sixties to mid-seventies. Those images were perceived by large segments of the public as destructive, too contrary to mainstream concepts of women's role to be acceptable. See *Rights of Passage*, ed. Joan Hoff-Wilson, Bloomington: Indiana University Press, 1986; Mary Frances Berry, *Why ERA Failed: Politics, Women's Rights, and the Amending Process of the Constitution*, Bloomington: Indiana University Press, 1986.

8: Campaigns, TV, and the Ike Age

162 THOUGH THE SYSTEM: Christopher H. Sterling and John M. Kittross, *Stay Tuned: A Concise History of American Broadcasting*, Belmont, Calif.: Wadsworth, 1978, p. 535; on networks, pp. 263–64. THE POLITICAL POTENTIAL: Robert B. Westbrook, "Politics as Consumption: Managing the Modern Election," in *The Culture of Consumption: Critical Essays in American History, 1880–1980*, ed. Richard Wightman Fox and T. J. Jackson Lears, New York: Pantheon, 1983, pp. 143–73; Stanley Kelley, *Professional Public Relations and Political Power*, Baltimore: Johns Hopkins, 1956; John E. Hollitz, "Eisenhower and the Admen: The 'Spot' Campaign of 1952," *Wisconsin Magazine of History* 66 (Autumn 1982): 25–39; Jamieson, *Packaging the Presidency*; Edwin Diamond and Stephen Bates, *The Spot: The Rise of Political Advertising on Television*, Cambridge, Mass.: MIT Press, 1984. TELEVISION SPECIALISTS PROMOTED: "Dedication of RCA Seen on Television," *New York Times* April 21, 1939: 16; David Sarnoff, "Possible Social Effects of Television," *Annals of the American Academy of Political and Social Science* 213 (Jan. 1941): 145–52. VIEWER SURVEY CARDS: "The Eyes Have It . . ." and cover letter, Alfred H. Morton to E. P. H. James, Oct. 2, 1940, box 9, folder 3, NBC Research, television promotional literature, James Papers, State Historical Society of Wisconsin. In its coverage of the Democratic National Convention NBC incorporated President Roosevelt's acceptance speech filmed at the White House. See letter from Robert Eichberg to Roosevelt, July 24, 1940, official file 136, miscellaneous, television folder, Roosevelt Library.

164 CROP REDUCTION PAYMENTS: Herman S. Hettinger and Walter J. Neff, *Practical Radio Advertising*, New York: Prentice-Hall, 1938, pp. 45, 59–67, 82–83; Hettinger, *A Decade of Radio Advertising*, Chicago: University of Chicago Press, 1933, pp. 137–72; Preston H. Pumphrey, "Spot Versus Chain Broadcasting," in *The Advertising Agency Looks at Radio*, ed. Neville O'Neill, New York: D. Appleton and Co., 1932, pp. 122–30; Erik Barnouw, *The Sponsor: Notes on a Modern Potentate*, New York: Oxford University Press, 1978, pp. 14–27. OFFICE OF WAR INFORMATION: "A Proposal for a National Allocation Plan for Spot Radio," RG 208, E-103, general correspondence (of the Allocation Division), 1942–46, box 644, National Spot Allocation Plan folder, records of the Office of War Information, National Archives and Records Administration, Suitland, Maryland. Additional detail may be found in the author's "Order, Efficiency and Control: The Evolution of the Political Spot Advertisement, 1936–1956," Ph.D. dissertation, Georgetown University, 1985, pp. 46–55.

165 BENTON DID NOT LIMIT: Benton to Philip Coombe, Oct. 13, 1950, box 318, folder 11, publicity, films; Leonard A. Schine to Benton, Oct. 23, 1950, box 318, folder 11; script, "Benton TV Program #2," Oct. 16, 1950, and script draft, "This is the first of my television programs," box 493, folder 11, speech files; script, "Senator Benton TV Program #3," box 318, folder 11, William Benton papers, Regenstein Library, University of Chicago; Bird, "Order, Efficiency and Control," pp. 107–10. Benton won election in 1950, defeating Republican Prescott Bush (George Bush's father). Sidney Hyman, *The Lives of William Benton*, Chicago: University of Chicago Press, 1969, p. 442. The Benton spots are in the Victoria Schuck Collection, John F. Kennedy Library, Boston, Mass. ROSSER REEVES: interview with author, New York, Oct. 10, 1983. Reeves to Bernard C. Duffy, Sept. 10, 1952, box 19, folder 1, Rosser Reeves papers, State Historical Society of Wisconsin. On the casting of questioners see memorandum from Miss Erikson, Mrs. Omrod, and Mrs. Somerville to Mr. Taranton, Oct. 2, 1952. Bob Foreman, "Commercial Reviews," *Sponsor* (1952): 52, 54, box 19, folder 13, Reeves papers. On Eisenhower's performance, see letter from Reeves to William S. Cuthins, Sept. 15, 1952, box 19, folder 1, Reeves papers; Bird, "Order, Efficiency and Control," pp. 131–32. EDWIN H. JAMES: "Is Your Candidate Telegenic?" *Broadcasting* 34 (April 12, 1948): 27, 38.

166 JACK GOULD: "The X of the Campaign-TV 'Personality,'" *New York Times Magazine* June 22, 1952: 14, 40–41. HERBERT BROWNELL: oral history interview transcript, Columbia University Oral History Office, New York, 1972, p. 75. DEMOCRATIC PARTY REGULARS: Memoranda, Lou Frankel to Hyman Raskin, Sept. 22, 1952, and Ken Fry to Wilson Wyatt, Sept. 28, 1952, box 372, misc. TV and radio folder, Records of the Democratic National Committee Television and Radio Division, Kennedy Library, Boston. On Stevenson's television performance, see Jamieson's *Packaging the Presidency*, pp. 58–68, and Kelley's *Professional Public Relations*, p. 172. THE ELECTION-EVE TELECASTS: Ibid., pp. 193–95; "Huckster's Last Gasp for Ike," *New York Post* Nov. 3, 1952: 2, 27.

167 REEVES: To Benjamin Duffy, Nov. 13, 1952, box 19, folder 3, Reeves papers. HERBERT BROWNELL: Gabriel Bayz interview with the author, New York, Oct. 15, 1983. Bayz worked for BBDO during the period. WITH EISENHOWER'S ELECTION: William Lee Miller, "Can Government Be Merchandised?" *Reporter* 9 (Oct. 7, 1953): 11–16.

168 OPINION RESEARCHERS: Herbert H. Hyman and Paul B. Sheatsley, "The Political Appeal of President Eisenhower," *Public Opinion Quarterly* 17 (Winter 1953–54): 443–60. NIXON'S CHECKERS SPEECH: Kurt Lang and Gladys Engel Lang, "The Television Personality in Politics: Some Political Considerations," *Public Opinion Quarterly* 20 (Spring 1956): 103–12; the Langs conclude, "The viewer cannot apprehend the personal qualities of the familiar face with which he is confronted, but he may believe he can. And that belief has its political consequences which are well worthy of investigation." Richard M. Nixon, *Six Crises*, Garden City: Doubleday and Co., 1962, pp. 73–129; Garry Wills, *Nixon Agonistes: The Crisis of the Self-Made Man*, Boston: Houghton Mifflin, 1970, pp. 93–114; David Culbert, "Television's Nixon: The Politician and His Image," in *American History / American Television: Interpreting the Video Past*, ed. John E. O'Connor, New York: Frederick Unger, 1983, pp. 184–207; "Nixon Tells How to Win TV Friends," *New York Times* Sept. 15, 1955, sec. 1, p. 22.

169 MANUFACTURERS CAPITALIZED: J. Richard Gruber, with Dennis Medina, offers a glimpse of the range of items in *We Like Ike: The Eisenhower Presidency and 1950s America*, Wichita, Kans.: Wichita Art Museum, 1990. C. LANGHORNE WASHBURN: "Campaign Activities and Bandwagon Operation Summary Report, 1956," *Summary Report*, National Citizens for Eisenhower-Nixon, box 6, proposals 1956 campaign, Young and Rubicam papers, Eisenhower Library, Abilene, Kans.

170 JAMES P. SELVAGE: To L. Richard Guylay, February 2, 1952, box 38, Sen. Robert H. Taft folder, 1951–53, John W. Hill papers, State Historical Society of Wisconsin, Madison.

171 BIRTHDAY PARTY TELECAST: Kinescope, National Ike Day Committee, Oct. 23, 1956; National Ike Day Committee of the Republican State Committees and the District of Columbia present a musical birthday tribute to President Eisenhower (EL-MP16-98A); Washburn, "Campaign Activities and Bandwagon Operation."

172 VOLUNTEERS FOR NIXON-LODGE: "Action Memo"; Democratic National Committee, "1960 TV Listening Party Program" and memorandum "TV Listening Parties," Sept. 23, 1960, pamphlet files, DPH.

173 TELEVISION SPECIALISTS: David Levy to S. S. Larmon, March 8, 1957. WASHBURN: "Campaign Activities and Bandwagon Operation." THE GROWING REDUNDANCY: David Beiler, *The Classics of Political Television Advertising: A Viewer's Guide*, Washington: Campaigns and Elections, 1987, p. 37; Jamieson, *Packaging the Presidency*, pp. 188–90.

9: Tippecanoe and Tyler Too, No More, No More

176 "AS HE BEGAN TO FEEL THE MOOD": McDowell, *Campaign Fever*, pp. 81, 152. "BUMPER STICKERS": Ibid., p. 48. TELEVISION IS AT THE CENTER: A small sample of works interpreting television and politics includes L. John Martin, ed., "The Role of the Mass Media in American Politics," *Annals of the American Academy of Political and Social Science* 427 (Sept. 1976); Doris A. Graber, *Mass Media and American Politics*, Washington: Congressional Quarterly Press, 1984; and Martin Schram, *The Great American Video Game: Presidential Politics in the Television Age*, New York: Morrow, 1987. ONE EXAMPLE: Theodore H. White, *America in Search of Itself: The Making of the President, 1956–1980*, New York: Harper and Row, 1982, ch. 11, especially pp. 316–17, 332, 335–36; Dan Nimmo, "Media Watch: Unconventional Coverage," *Campaigns and Elections* May–June 1986: 52–55.

178 MACHINES CAN DO: Robert Agranoff, ed., *The New Style in Election Campaigns*, Boston: Holbrook Press, 1972, pp. 118–19. See also Agranoff's *Management of Election Campaigns*, Boston: Holbrook Press, 1976; Robert G. Meadow, ed., *New Communication Technologies in Politics*, Washington: Annenberg School of Communications, 1985; S. J. Guzzetta, *The Campaign Manual*, 3rd ed., Alexandria, Va.: S. J. Guzzetta and Associates, 1989. DIRECT-MAIL FUND-RAISING: Richard Armstrong, *The Next Hurrah: The Communications Revolution in American Politics*, New York: Morrow, 1988, pp. 42–63. "A PERSON-TO-PERSON APPROACH": Roger M. Craver, "Direct Mail and the Political Process," in *New Communication Technologies*, ed. Meadow, p. 75.

180 POLITICAL ACTION COMMITTEE: See Larry Sabato's *PAC Power: Inside the World of Political Action Committees*, New York: W. W. Norton, 1984; Larry Boyle, "PACs and Pluralism: Dynamics of Interest-Group Politics," *Campaigns and Elections* Spring 1985: 6–16. OPINION POLLING: Sabato, *Rise of Political Consultants*, ch. 2, on focus groups p. 77; Larry Sabato and David Beiler, *Magic . . . or Blue Smoke and Mirrors?* Washington: Annenberg Washington Program in Communication Policy Studies, 1988, pp. 15–17; Murray Fishel, "Group Process Techniques and Campaign Planning, Part I: Four Basic Sessions," *Campaigns and Elections* Spring 1985: 17–22. NEW KINDS OF COMMUNICATION: Armstrong, *Next Hurrah*, p. 175; Sabato and Beiler, *Magic*, pp. 10–12.

181 NEW PARTICIPANTS: The standard work on political consultants is Sabato's *Rise of Political Consultants;* see also Frank I. Luntz's *Candidates, Consultants, and Campaigns*, New York: Basil Blackwell, 1988. See *Campaigns and Elections* May–June 1986: 70–73 for comments about the gender gap and women's growing political involvement. On women candidates in 1990 see the *Washington Post* June 10, 1990: A1–A16. SEVERAL WRITERS TRACE: Bloom, *Public Relations and Presidential Campaigns*, pp. 25–27; White, *America in Search of Itself*, pp. 67–69. TED ROGERS: Jamieson, *Packaging the Presidency*, pp. 71, 78, 150–53. JOSEPH NAPOLITAN: *The Election Game and How to Win It*, Garden City: Doubleday and Co., 1972.

183 SOME CONSULTANTS: The names of some of these men and their firms are well known: Walter DeVries, a generalist Democrat; Matt Reese, a generalist Democrat; and Stuart Spencer, a generalist Republican active in several Ronald Reagan campaigns. Polling specialists include Democrats Pat Caddell and Peter D. Hart, Republicans Robert Teeter and Richard Wirthlin. Among the media specialists are the Republican firm of Douglas Bailey and John Deardourff, Republican Robert Goodman, Independent David Garth, Democrats Charles Guggenheim, Gerald Rafshoon, Tony Schwartz, and Robert Squier. Direct-mail companies include the liberal Craver, Mathews, Smith, and Co., and Richard A. Viguerie Co., the leading conservative firm. See profiles of many consultants in David Chagall's *New Kingmakers: An Inside Look at the Powerful Men Behind America's Political Campaigns*, New York: Harcourt Brace Jovanovich, 1981; Sabato, *Rise of Political Consultants*, pp. 347–55; Luntz, *Candidates*, pp. 240–44, 26–27, 50–51, 56–58. Kiky Adatto, "The Incredible Shrinking Sound Bite," *New Republic* May 28, 1990: 22. Sabato, in *Rise of Political Consultants* (ch. 6), provides one of the most searching critiques of political consultants. WHITE: *America*

in Search of Itself. ELIZABETH DREW: *Election Journal: Political Events of 1987–1988*, New York: William Morrow, 1989, p. 86.

184 SCHLESINGER: *History of American Presidential Elections*, supplemental volume, 1986, p. xi (quotation). The causes and consequences of party decay have been analyzed at length by Schlesinger (ibid., pp. xi–xv), Frank J. Sorauf, (*Party Politics in America*, 4th ed., Boston: Little, Brown, 1980, pp. 397–409), David S. Broder, (*The Party's Over*, New York: Harper and Row, 1971), Kay Lawson, ("Party Renewal and American Democracy," *Essays in Honor of James MacGregor Burns*, ed. Michael R. Beschloss and Thomas E. Cronin, Englewood Cliffs, N.J.: Prentice-Hall, 1989, pp. 144–64), and in many other studies. See also Xandra Kayden and Eddie Mahe, Jr., *The Party Goes On: The Persistence of the Two-Party System in the United States*, New York: Basic Books, 1985; and the review by Everett Carll Ladd, *Campaigns and Elections* Winter 1986: 73–74. NEW HAMPSHIRE PRIMARY: Jules Witcover, *Marathon: The Pursuit of the Presidency, 1972–1976*, New York: New American Library, 1978, pp. 235–54; Jack W. Germond and Jules Witcover, *Whose Broad Stripes and Bright Stars?* New York: Warner Books, 1989, pp. 132–34, 273; Dayton Duncan, *Grass Roots: One Year in the Life of the New Hampshire Presidential Primary*, New York: Viking, 1990.

185 BARRY M. GOLDWATER: With Jack Casserly, *Goldwater*, New York: Doubleday, 1988, p. 198. FOR INSTANCE, IN 1983–84: Peter Goldman, Tony Fuller, et al., *The Quest for the Presidency, 1984*, New York: Bantam Books, 1985, pp. 129–30, 241; Elizabeth Drew, *Campaign Journal: The Political Events of 1983–1984*, New York: Macmillan, 1985, pp. 267–68, 337–39. AGAIN IN THE 1988 CAMPAIGN: Ibid., pp. 107–13, 128–29, 252–53, 304–305, 323–46; Martin Schram, "The Making of Willie Horton," *New Republic* May 28, 1990, pp. 17–19. HERBERT E. ALEXANDER: *Financing Politics: Money, Elections, and Political Reform*, 3rd ed., Washington: Congressional Quarterly, 1984, especially pp. 8–13, ch. 5.

187 THE UNEXPECTED CONSEQUENCES: See Fred Wertheimer, "Campaign Finance Reform: The Unfinished Agenda," *Annals of the American Academy of Political and Social Science* 486 (July 1986): 86–102. ELIZABETH DREW: *Politics and Money: The New Road to Corruption*, New York: Macmillan, 1983, p. 142 (quotation); on the myth of public financing of presidential campaigning, see pp. 99–145. On PACs, see Alexander's *Financing Politics*, pp. 90–110, and Sabato's *PAC Power*. DECLINE OF VOTER TURNOUT: Sorauf, *Party Politics*, pp. 174–97. Frances Fox Piven and Richard A. Cloward, *Why Americans Don't Vote*, New York: Pantheon, 1988.

188 JAMIESON: *Packaging the Presidency*, chs. 2–3; also Fred I. Greenstein, *The Hidden-Hand Presidency: Eisenhower as Leader*, New York: Basic Books, 1982, pp. 11–54.

189 JAMIESON: *Packaging the Presidency*, p. 162, ch. 4.

191 TELEVISION DEBATES: See Herbert A. Seltz and Richard D. Yoakam's "Production Diary of the Debates," in *The Great Debates: Kennedy Vs. Nixon, 1960: A Reissue*, ed. Sidney Kraus, Bloomington: Indiana University Press, 1977, p. 123. This interpretation is based on an unpublished paper by Jerry K. Frye, "Televised Presidential Debates," 1985. The descriptions of Kennedy and Nixon are from Jamieson's *Packaging the Presidency*, pp. 158–61 (Philip E. Converse quotation, p. 158).

192 DEMOCRAT JIMMY CARTER: Quoted by Betty Glad in *Jimmy Carter: In Search of the Great White House*, New York: W. W. Norton, 1980, pp. 250–51. For an alternative view of political imagery see Victor Gold's "Image Stratagems: Pick One for the '80s," *Campaigns and Elections* Summer 1980: 43–48.

193 HEDRICK SMITH: *The Power Game: How Washington Works*, New York: Random House, 1988, p. 397. THE REAGAN WHITE HOUSE STAGED: Steven W. Colford, "Hail to the Image," *Advertising Age* June 27, 1988, pp. 3, 32. REAGAN'S REELECTION CAMPAIGN: Tom Shales, "Stars, Stripes and Reagan," *Washington Post* August 23, 1984, pp. D1, 11. An excellent summary of the modern mediated campaign is Robert B. Westbrook's "Politics as Consumption: Managing the Modern American Election," in *The Culture of Consumption: Critical Essays in American History, 1880–1980*, ed. Richard Wrightman Fox and T. J. Jackson Lears, New York: Pantheon Books, 1983, pp. 145–73. "MORNING IN AMERICA": This campaign is treated in a feature story in *Life* Nov. 1984; also Goldman et al., *Quest for the Presidency*, pp. 264–69. GARRY WILLS: *Reagan's America: Innocents at Home*, New York: Penguin, 1988, p. 5. WILLIAM H. HENRY III: *Visions of America*, Boston and New York: Atlantic Monthly Press, 1985, p. 3.

194 EDWARD PESSEN: *The Log Cabin Myth: The Social Backgrounds of the*

Presidents, New Haven: Yale University Press, 1984; see also *Campaigns and Elections* Summer 1985: 70–71. ONE STUDY OF ELECTORAL TURNOUT: Piven and Cloward, *Why Americans Don't Vote,* p. 20.
196 NAPOLITAN: *The Election Game,* pp. 68–69.

American Presidential Candidates, 1789–1988

Sources: Bernard Bailyn, David Brion Davis, David Herbert Donald, John L. Thomas, Robert H. Wiebe, and Gordon S. Wood, *The Great Republic: A History of the American People,* Boston: Little, Brown, 1977; *The World Almanac and Book of Facts, 1991,* New York: Pharos Books, 1990; National Portrait Gallery, *"If Elected . . . ": Unsuccessful Candidates for the Presidency, 1796–1968,* Washington: Smithsonian Institution Press, 1972; Joseph Nathan Kane, *Facts About Presidents,* New York: H. W. Wilson, 1989.

Index